Chicken Soup for the Soul®

Our **101** BEST STORIES

Loving Our Dogs

Chicken Soup for the Soul® Our 101 Best Stories:
Loving Our Dogs; Heartwarming and Humorous Stories about Our Companions
and Best Friends by Jack Canfield, Mark Victor Hansen & Amy Newmark

Published by Chicken Soup for the Soul Publishing, LLC   www.chickensoup.com

The publisher gratefully acknowledges the many publishers and individuals who
granted Chicken Soup for the Soul permission to reprint the cited material.

Cover photos courtesy of iStockPhoto.com/Fotosmurf03, GlobalP, Mike Panic, and
stray_cat; and Photos.com/Jupiter Images

Cover and Interior Design & Layout by Pneuma Books, LLC
For more info on Pneuma Books, visit www.pneumabooks.com

Distributed to the booktrade by Simon & Schuster. SAN: 200-2442

Publisher's Cataloging-In-Publication Data
(*Prepared by The Donohue Group, Inc.*)

Chicken soup for the soul. Selections.
    Chicken soup for the soul® : loving our dogs : heartwarming and humorous
stories about our companions and best friends / [compiled by] Jack Canfield
[and] Mark Victor Hansen ; [edited by] Amy Newmark.

    p. ; cm. -- (Our 101 best stories)

    ISBN-13: 978-1-935096-05-4
    ISBN-10: 1-935096-05-2

1. Dogs--Literary collections. 2. Dogs--Anecdotes. 3. Dog owners--Anecdotes. 4.
Human-animal relationships--Anecdotes. I. Canfield, Jack, 1944- II. Hansen, Mark
Victor. III. Newmark, Amy. IV. Title.

PS509.D6 C483 2008
810.8/03629772   2008929325

Chicken Soup for the Soul®
Loving Our Dogs

Our 101 BEST STORIES

Heartwarming and Humorous
Stories about Our Companions
and Best Friends

Jack Canfield
Mark Victor Hansen
Amy Newmark

CSS

Chicken Soup for the Soul Publishing, LLC
Cos Cob, CT

Chicken Soup for the Soul

Contents

❸
~Bringing Out the Best in Us~

❹
~Pets Have Pets Too~

❺
~Man's Best Friend~

❻
~Support Dogs~

❼
~It's My Family Too! ~

❽
~ Dogs and Their Soldiers~

❾
~Great Dog Moments~

⑩
~Canine Matchmakers~

⑪
~Letting Go~

Chicken Soup for the Soul

A Special Foreword

by Jack and Mark

For us, 101 has always been a magical number. It was the number of stories in the first *Chicken Soup for the Soul* book, and it is the number of stories and poems we have always aimed for in our books. We love the number 101 because it signifies a beginning, not an end. After 100, we start anew with 101.

We hope that when you finish reading one of our books, it is only a beginning for you too—a new outlook on life, a renewed sense of purpose, a strengthened resolve to deal with an issue that has been bothering you. Perhaps you will pick up the phone and share one of the stories with a friend or a loved one. Perhaps you will turn to your keyboard and express yourself by writing a Chicken Soup story of your own, to share with other readers who are just like you.

This volume contains our 101 best stories and poems about our best friends and faithful companions—our dogs. We share this with you at a very special time for us, the fifteenth anniversary of our *Chicken Soup for the Soul* series. When we published our first book in 1993, we never dreamed we had started what has become a publishing phenomenon, one of the best-selling lines of books in history.

We did not set out to sell more than one hundred million books, or to publish more than 150 titles. We set out to touch the heart of one person at a time, hoping that person would in turn touch another person, and so on down the line. Fifteen years later, we know that it has worked. Your letters and stories have poured in by the hundreds of thousands, affirming our life's work, and inspiring us to continue to make a difference in your lives.

On our fifteenth anniversary, we have new energy, new resolve, and new dreams. We have recommitted to our goal of 101 stories or poems per book, we have refreshed our cover designs and our interior layout, and we have grown the Chicken Soup for the Soul team, with new friends and partners across the country in New England.

For this volume, we selected our 101 best dog stories and poems for you from our rich 15 year history. These heartwarming stories will make you appreciate your own dogs more deeply and see them with a new eye. Some of these stories describe amazing contributions made by dogs and highlight their intelligence and intuitive abilities. Many of these stories made us laugh or cry. They all renewed our admiration for our canine companions.

We hope that you will enjoy reading these stories as much as we enjoyed selecting them for you, and that you will share them with your families and friends. We have identified the 25 *Chicken Soup for the Soul* books in which the stories originally appeared, in case you would like to explore our other books about pets. We hope you will also enjoy the additional books about cats, families, faith, and life in general in "Our 101 Best Stories" series.

With our love, our thanks, and our respect,
~*Jack Canfield and Mark Victor Hansen*

Loving Our Dogs

Chapter 1

On Mutual Love and Admiration

I hope to be the kind of person my dog thinks I am.
~Unknown Author

Patience Rewarded

Love is something eternal.
~Vincent van Gogh

Albert Payson Terhune, the famed dog writer of the 1920s and 1930s who authored the Lassie books, often told this story about his friend Wilson to illustrate the deep love that people and dogs share. It also shows how sometimes what seems to be in the best interest of all concerned may not apply when one of those concerned is a dog.

Wilson's dog, Jack, was an energetic, six-year-old collie that would meet him every day at the trolley station when Wilson returned from work. This was a ritual that had begun when Jack was a pup. The dog knew the route to and from the station like the back of his paw—and following that route was the highlight of his day. So when Wilson changed jobs and had to move to California, he thought it best to leave Jack on his home turf in Philadelphia with a relative. He explained all this to the dog upon leaving and told him that they both would have to adjust to new homes.

But Jack didn't want a new home. He would not stay with the family he'd been left with. He returned to Wilson's old house, even though it was boarded up, and there he passed his solitary days beside an abandoned chair beneath the portico. But every evening, tail wagging, he trotted off to the trolley station. For as long as Jack had been in the world, Wilson had always taken the same trolley home from work, and Jack had been there to greet him. But evening after evening, there was no sign of the devoted dog's master. Confused and sad, he would return alone to the deserted house.

The dog's depression grew. He refused the food left for him, and as the days passed, he became thinner and thinner, his ribs noticeable even through his thick blond coat. But every evening, ever hopeful, he'd go to the station to meet the trolley. And every evening, he'd return to the porch more despondent than before.

No one knows why Jack's new family didn't contact Wilson, but Jack's deteriorating condition did not go unnoticed. A friend who lived nearby was so upset by it that he took it upon himself to send a telegram to Wilson in California, informing him of the dog's situation.

That was all it took.

Wilson bought a return train ticket immediately; he knew what he had to do. Upon arriving in Philadelphia, he waited several hours just so that he could take the same trolley that he always did when coming home. When it arrived at the station, sure enough, there was Jack, waiting and watching as the passengers got off. Looking and hoping. And then suddenly there he was, his beloved owner. His master had returned at last! Jack's world was whole once more—and so was Wilson's.

Wilson later told Terhune, "Jack was sobbing almost like a child might sob. He was shivering all over as if he had a chill. And I? Well, I blew my nose and did a lot of fast winking."

Wilson took his devoted dog, Jack, back to California with him. They were never separated again.

~Hester Mundis
Chicken Soup for the Dog Lover's Soul

Love Makes Us Whole

Where there is great love there are always miracles.
~Willa Cather

We got him with the other animals when we purchased the farm. Not that we wanted the black, shaggy mongrel. We had our hearts set on a collie—a pup we could train for the farm and as a companion for five-year-old Tim. But when the former owners informed us he was part of the deal, we resigned ourselves to keeping him. Temporarily, we thought, just until we can find him another home.

But the big dog apparently considered the farm his permanent responsibility. Each dawn, he inspected the animals and the farm buildings. Then he made a complete circuit of the entire eighty acres. That finished, he bounded across the sloping fields to slip beneath the fence for a visit with old Mr. Jolliff, who lived near a brook at the farm's edge.

The dog—we learned from Mr. Jolliff that his name was Inky—was pensive and aloof those first weeks. Grieving for his former masters, Inky asked no affection; busy settling in, we offered none. Except Tim, who sat by the hour on the back steps, talking softly to the unresponsive animal. Then, one morning, Inky crept close and laid his head in the boy's lap. And before we knew it, he had become Tim's second shadow.

All that summer the boy and the dog romped through fields and roamed the woods, discovering fox dens and groundhog burrows. Each day, they brought back treasures to share.

"Mom, we're home!" Tim would shout, holding the screen door wide for Inky. "Come see what we've got!" He'd dig deep in his jeans and spread the contents on the kitchen table: a pheasant's feather; wilted buttercups with petals like wet paint; stones from the brook that magically regained their colors when he licked them.

September arrived all too soon, bringing with it school for Tim and Carl, my schoolteacher husband, and lonely days for Inky and me. Previously, I'd paid little attention to the dog. Now he went with me to the mailbox, to the chicken coop, and down the lane when I visited Mr. Jolliff.

"Why didn't they want to take Inky?" I asked Mr. Jolliff one afternoon.

"And shut him up in a city apartment?" Mr. Jolliff replied. "Inky's a farm dog; he'd die in the city. Besides, you're lucky to have him."

Lucky? I thought ruefully of holes dug in the lawn, of freshly washed sheets ripped from the clothesline. I thought, too, of litter dumped on the back porch: old bones, discarded boots, long-dead rodents.

Still, I had to admit that Inky was a good farm dog. We learned this in early spring when his insistent barking alerted us to a ewe, about to lamb, lying on her broad back in a furrow, unable to rise. Without Inky's warning, she'd have died. And he had an uncanny way of knowing when roving dogs threatened the flock, or when sheep went astray.

Inky's deepest affection was reserved for Tim. Each afternoon when the school bus lumbered down the road, Inky ran joyously to meet it. For Inky—and for Tim—this was the high point of the day.

One mid-October day when I had been in town, Tim rode home with me after school. He was instantly alarmed when Inky wasn't waiting for us by the driveway.

"Don't worry, Tim," I said. "Inky always expects you on the bus, and we're early. Maybe he's back by the woods."

Tim ran down the lane, calling and calling. While I waited for him to return, I looked around the yard. Its emptiness was eerie.

Suddenly I, too, was alarmed. With Tim close behind me, I ran down to the barn. We pushed the heavy doors apart and searched the dim coolness. Nothing. Then, as we were about to leave, a faint whimper came from the far corner of a horse stall. There we found him, swaying slightly on three legs, his pain-dulled eyes pleading for help. Even in the half-light I saw that one back leg hung limp, the bone partially severed. With a little moan, Tim ran to Inky and buried his face in the dog's neck.

By the time the vet arrived, Carl was home. We placed the dog on his blanket and gently lifted him into the pet ambulance. Inky whimpered, and Tim started to cry.

"Don't worry, son," the vet said. "He's got a good chance." But his eyes told a different story.

At Tim's bedtime, I took him upstairs and heard his prayers. He finished and looked up. "Will Inky be home tomorrow?"

"Not tomorrow, Tim. He's hurt pretty bad."

"You tell me that doctors make people well. Doesn't that mean dogs, too?"

I looked out across the fields flooded with amber light. How do you tell a little boy that his dog must either die or be crippled? "Yes, Tim," I said at last. "I guess that means dogs, too." I tucked in his blanket and went downstairs.

I tossed a sweater over my shoulders and told Carl, "I'm going down to Mr. Jolliff's. Maybe he'll know what happened."

I found the old man sitting at his kitchen table in the fading light. He drew up another chair and poured coffee.

Somehow I couldn't talk about the dog. Instead, I asked, "Do you know if anyone was cutting weeds around here today?"

"Seems to me I heard a tractor down along the brook this morning," Mr. Jolliff replied. "Why?" He looked at me. "Did something happen?"

"Yes," I said, and the words were tight in my throat. "Inky's back leg's nearly cut off. The vet came for him...." I wanted to say more, but couldn't. "It's growing dark," I finally murmured. "I'd better head home."

Mr. Jolliff followed me into the yard. "About Inky," he said hesitantly, "if he lives, I'd give him a chance. He'll still have you folks and Tim, the farm and the animals. Everything he loves. Life's pretty precious... especially where there's love."

"Yes," I said, "but if he loses a leg, will love make up for being crippled?"

He said something I didn't catch. But when I turned to him, he'd removed his glasses and was rubbing the back of his stiff old hand across his eyes.

By the time I reached our yard, the sun was gone. I walked down by the barn and stood with my arms on the top fence rail. Then I dropped my head to my arms and let the tears come.

I cried because Inky had been so gentle with the animals, and because he loved Tim so much, and Tim loved him. But mostly I cried because I hadn't really wanted him; not until now, when this terrible thing had happened.

Inky's paw couldn't be saved. Too vividly, I recalled how Inky had raced across fields and meadows, swift and free as a cloud shadow. I listened skeptically as the vet tried to reassure us: "He's young and strong. He'll get along on three legs."

Tim took the news with surprising calmness. "It's all right," he said. "Just so Inky comes home."

"But those long jaunts the two of you take may tire him now," I cautioned.

"He's always waited for me. I'll wait for him. Besides, we're never in much of a hurry."

The vet called a few days later. "You'd better come for your dog. He's homesick." I went immediately and was shocked at the change in Inky. The light was gone from his eyes. His tail hung limp and tattered, and the stump of his leg was swathed in a stained bandage. He hobbled over and pressed wearily against my leg. A shudder went through the hot, thin body and he sighed—a long, deep sigh filled with all the misery and loneliness of the past few days.

At the farm, I helped Inky from the car. He looked first to the sheep, grazing in the pasture; then, beyond the fields of green winter wheat, to the autumn woods where the horses, dappled with sunlight, moved among the trees. My heart ached as I realized how great must have been his longing for this place. At last, he limped to the barn and slipped between the heavy doors.

While his wound healed, Inky stayed in the barn, coming out only in the evenings. Throughout those days a sick feeling never left me. You are a coward to let him live in this condition, I told myself. But in my heart I wasn't sure.

About a week after bringing Inky home, I was in the yard raking leaves. When I'd finished under the maple, I sat on the steps to rest. It was a perfect Indian summer day; our country road was a tunnel of gold, and sumac ran like a low flame along the south pasture.

Then, with a flurry of leaves, Inky was beside me. I knelt and stroked the fur so smooth and shiny again. He moved, and I was achingly aware of the useless limb. "I'm so sorry, Inky," I said, putting my arm around his neck and pressing my head against his.

Sitting awkwardly, he placed his paw on my knee and looked up at me with soft, intelligent eyes. Then he pricked his ears and turned to listen. In an instant, he was off to meet the school bus. He ran with an ungainly, one-sided lope — but he ran with joy.

Tim jumped from the high step and caught the dog in his arms, "Oh, Inky! Inky!" he cried. Inky licked Tim's face and twisted and squirmed with delight. They remained there for a time, oblivious to anything but the ecstasy of being together again.

Watching them, I knew I'd been right to let the dog live. What was it Mr. Jolliff had said?

"Life's pretty precious... especially where there's love."

~Aletha Jane Lindstrom
Chicken Soup for the Cat and Dog Lover's Soul

Now and Always

Animals can communicate quite well. And they do.
~Alice Walker

A few years ago when I was looking for a small dog to add to our family, I contacted the local SPCA (Society for the Prevention of Cruelty to Animals) and got the name of a woman who was fostering some rescued Maltese dogs for them. I called the woman, and my husband and I drove to her home. As I looked around, I noticed a cute Maltese named Casper. My husband and I decided we would like to adopt him.

The foster mom asked us if there were any way we would open our hearts to Casper's companion, Kato, as well. She told us that the two boys, who had only each other for comfort, had recently been rescued from a puppy mill, where they had spent the first seven years of their lives. When the local SPCA shut down the puppy mill and seized all the dogs, Kato and Casper had been put in her foster home.

She told us that when she first picked them up, their fur was in such terrible shape they hardly looked like Maltese dogs. They were brown, the fur on their legs was matted to their stomachs, and their paws were swollen and tender from living on the wire mesh of their cage. For seven years, the only human contact these boys had was when they were thrown their food or tossed into another cage to breed with a female. What people don't realize, she said, is that the cute little puppies in the windows of many pet stores leave parents behind who live lives of neglect and suffering.

Hearing all this, I turned and looked down at the little Maltese named Kato. But he's so ugly, I thought. And he isn't even friendly. He growled and grumbled when we looked at him. Still, I felt a tug at my heart and agreed to take Kato also. As we drove home, my husband and I worried that maybe we'd taken on too much. We'd never had dogs that had been so abused for such a long time.

The first day at our home was very difficult for the two dogs. They didn't understand anything but fear of humans. They stayed close to each other and mostly hid under tables or in dark corners. In an effort to give them a fresh start, we changed their names: Casper became Thomas and Kato became Timothy.

The days turned into weeks and weeks into months. Over time Thomas became friendlier and would wag his tail when we talked to him, but Timothy still couldn't make eye contact with us. At the sound of our voices, he'd push himself against the back wall of his crate. His plastic dog kennel — the kind used to transport dogs — was the place he felt safest. Even with the crate door left open, he preferred to spend most of the day in his crate, only emerging when we gently pulled him out to take him outside. Each time I reached for Timothy, he'd flip upside down, whimpering. One day I noticed he had a gray haze over his eyes, as though there was a film on them. I asked the vet about it and he told me that it happens to dogs that live in complete fear. They retreat to another place to help themselves live through each day.

I did everything I could think of to help this dog, but he made little progress. He would sit at the back of his crate with his head hanging down hour after hour. Nevertheless, I kept trying. When the whole house was quiet, I sat on the floor and talked to him, but he wouldn't look at me. He just stared off in another direction. One day as I sat and watched this poor soul suffering in silence, I thought about his past — the hunger, the isolation, the abuse — and started to sob. My heart aching, I began telling him how sorry I was for the pain humans had caused him. My thoughts were filled with the unhappiness and fear he had endured year after year.

As the tears streamed down my face, I felt a soft touch on my hand. Through my tears, I saw Timothy. He had come out from the back of his crate to sit near me, licking the tears that fell on my hand. Quietly, so I wouldn't scare him, I told him that I loved him. I promised that I would always love him and that no one would ever hurt him again. As I whispered over and over that he would always be warm, safe and fed, he came a step closer to me. A passage from the Bible came to my mind: Love is kind; it keeps no record of wrongs; it always protects, always trusts, always hopes, always perseveres. Love never fails. The meaning of these words was so clear as I looked at this little dog who, in spite of everything he had experienced, had opened his heart to me.

Today, I am still the only person Timothy trusts completely; we share a very special bond. When I call his name, he spins in delight and barks, his tail wagging in a frenzy of happiness. When I sit down, he climbs into my arms and licks my face. And just as I promised, I hold him, gently snuggle him and tell him I love him — now and always.

~Suzy Huether
Chicken Soup for the Dog Lover's Soul

The Game of Love

Death leaves a heartache no one can heal,
love leaves a memory no one can steal.
~From a headstone in Ireland

Dad brought him home from a fishing trip in the mountains, full of cockleburs and so thin you could count every rib.

"Good gracious," Mom said. "He's filthy!"

"No, he isn't! He's Rusty," said John, my eight-year-old brother. "Can we keep him? Please... please... please."

"He's going to be a big dog," Dad warned, lifting a mud-encrusted paw. "Probably why he was abandoned."

"What kind of dog?" I asked. It was impossible to get close to this smelly creature.

"Mostly German shepherd," Dad said. "He's in bad shape, John. He may not make it."

John was gently picking out cockleburs.

"I'll take care of Rusty. Honest, I will."

Mom gave in, as she usually did with John. My little brother had a mild form of hemophilia. Four years earlier, he'd almost bled to death from a routine tonsillectomy. We'd all been careful with him since then.

"All right, John," Dad said. "We'll keep Rusty. But he's your responsibility."

"Deal!"

And that's how Rusty came to live with us. He was John's dog from that very first moment, though he tolerated the rest of us.

John kept his word. He fed, watered, medicated and groomed the scruffy-looking animal every day. I think he liked taking care of something rather than being taken care of.

Over the summer, Rusty grew into a big, handsome dog. He and John were constant companions. Wherever John went, Rusty was by his side. When school began, Rusty would walk John the six blocks to elementary school, then come home. Every school day at three o'clock, rain or shine, Rusty would wait for John at the playground.

"There goes Rusty," the neighbors would say. "Must be close to three. You can set your watch by that dog."

Telling time wasn't the only amazing thing about Rusty. Somehow, he sensed that John shouldn't roughhouse like the other boys. He was very protective. When the neighborhood bully taunted my undersized brother, Rusty's hackles rose, and a deep, menacing growl came from his throat. The heckling ceased after one encounter. And when John and his best friend Bobby wrestled, Rusty monitored their play with a watchful eye. If John were on top, fine. If Bobby got John down, Rusty would lope over, grab Bobby's collar and pull him off. Bobby and John thought this game great fun. They staged fights quite often, much to Mother's dismay.

"You're going to get hurt, John!" she would scold. "And you aren't being fair to Rusty."

John didn't like being restricted. He hated being careful — being different. "It's just a game, Mom. Shoot, even Rusty knows that. Don't you, boy?" Rusty would cock his head and give John a happy smile.

In the spring, John got an afternoon paper route. He'd come home from school, fold his papers and take off on his bike to deliver them. He always took the same streets, in the same order. Of course, Rusty delivered papers, too.

One day, for no particular reason, John changed his route. Instead of turning left on a street as he usually did, he turned right. Thump!... Crash!... A screech of brakes... Rusty sailed through the air.

Someone called us about the accident. I had to pry John from Rusty's lifeless body so that Dad could bring Rusty home.

"It's my fault," John said over and over. "Rusty thought the car was gonna hit me. He thought it was another game."

"The only game Rusty was playing was the game of love," Dad said. "You both played it well."

John sniffled. "Huh?"

"You were there for Rusty when he needed you. He was there for you when he thought you needed him. That's the game of love."

"I want him back," John wailed. "My Rusty's gone!"

"No, he isn't," Dad said, hugging John and me. "Rusty will stay in your memories forever."

And he has.

~Lou Kassem
Chicken Soup for the Kid's Soul

Peppy

There is no psychiatrist in the world like a puppy licking your face.
~Ben Williams

I was a new graduate nurse, on probation in my first job, when I met Mrs. Oldman, a charming lady of about eighty who'd never been ill or in a hospital.

One day, I saw her staring outside with tears in her eyes.

"Are you in pain?" I asked.

She looked up, startled, and shook her head. Smiling, she apologized. "No, I'm just silly. I'm lonesome for Peppy. I must be getting senile to cry for a little dog, but he's always around me at home. I forget he's not human. I talk so much to him, and somehow he gives me the impression that he understands me." She wiped her eyes and looked helplessly up at me. "Do you think I'm silly?"

"Not at all," I assured her.

"I'd do anything if I could see and hold him for a moment." She questioned me with her eyes. Reading the hopelessness in my response, she said tonelessly, "No, I guess it's impossible."

"Some people are allergic to dogs," I tried to explain, visualizing a dozen dogs, cats and heaven-knows-what other pets chasing each other under the beds during visiting hours.

She nodded sadly. "Of course."

After that crying spell, she favored me with stories about Peppy. Her neighbor, Mrs. Freund, was taking care of him and claimed he knew she'd been in the hospital. Wasn't that smart? Then she said sadly, "Yes, Peppy, he misses me. I miss him."

She grew despondent as the days passed. I tried everything to draw her out and cheer her, but to no avail. Even the other ladies in the ward noticed my efforts and Mrs. Oldman's silence. They offered snacks, refreshments and suggested they play cards with her. She thanked them gratefully, but her eyes had that lost expression and she politely refused everything. Patients came and went every day, and soon Mrs. Oldman was an old-timer, and one who'd grown dear to me. I'd often been told that a person could die if he or she lost the will to live. I feared Mrs. Oldman would give up and die if I didn't find something to give her life meaning, a reason to live. It was then I thought of Peppy. Taking my camera, I went to Mrs. Freund's house to take a picture of him. Surely that would cheer her.

Peppy sat demurely as he was photographed. No doubt the little, black, fuzzy fellow had once been lively in his youth, but now he sat with his head on his paws staring out into nowhere.

"Poor guy," Mrs. Freund said, "he is so lonesome he could die. He hardly eats or drinks. He sits and stares out the window and whines softly for her." She looked at me beseechingly. "It would help them both if he could visit Mrs. Oldman." I shook my head. Mrs. Freund tried again. "How about just taking him to the courtyard so she can see him from her window?"

"Let's try it," I said enthusiastically. "Come between three and four tomorrow. All the head nurses will be at a meeting and I'll be in charge."

I told her to put Peppy in a shopping bag to pass the attendants at the entrance. Mrs. Freund was delighted. "Aren't we glad she doesn't own a Great Dane or a St. Bernard?"

The next day I could hardly wait for Mrs. Green to leave for the meeting. Visitors ambled into the ward. Everyone had company but Mrs. Oldman.

"Want me to pull your curtains around your bed so you have some privacy?" I suggested, knowing how she felt about the pitying stares from visitors.

"Yes," she muttered.

I closed the curtain, wondering if our plan would succeed and if Mrs. Freund would manage to keep Peppy quiet in her bag while passing by the two attendants at the main entrance. I had not dared to tell Mrs. Oldman of our plan, fearing it might fail.

My heart lifted when I saw the door of the courtyard open and Mrs. Freund lugging her shopping bag. She ambled casually around the flower border, looking right and left with a mischievous expression, as if violating some holy laws. Mrs. Oldman didn't seem to notice I'd blocked her view from the window. Mrs. Freund tapped the window lightly then reached into her shopping bag. I stood back to watch Mrs. Oldman's face. Never in my life will I forget that moment. At once she rose up, her face reddened, her eyes sparkled, and her voice broke as she cried, "Peppy! Peppy!"

"Shush — shush." I tried to keep her quiet. Outside the window Peppy jumped and whined and, before realizing what I was doing, I opened the window and lifted the little dog out of the bag and into her outstretched arms. Mrs. Freund stood with her shopping bag wide open, beaming as if she'd seen a miracle, or rather, created one.

But then my heart bunched up in alarm for I heard the voice of Mrs. Green. No doubt she was looking for me.

"Quick, he has to go now." I wrestled the struggling dog back into the shopping bag outside the window.

I could hear Mrs. Green's firm step and voice as she shouted, "What do I hear? Is there a dog on the ward?"

Quickly, I grabbed Mrs. Oldman's bedpan and stepped outside the curtain, trying to look busy and professional as I walked past Mrs. Green. "Back so soon?" I asked cheerfully.

"I thought I heard a dog," she muttered, as if questioning me.

I answered with studied indifference. "Maybe a stray dog in the courtyard."

Without a word she followed me out of the ward and into the utility room. I stopped short. The bedpan was empty. I hesitated. Mrs. Green waited. I didn't know for what. I dared not show that the bedpan was empty for fear of blowing my cover. The silence grew, and my thoughts raced. Would I be reported to the director of nursing for breaking the law? I was still in my probation months. My mouth and throat felt so dry, I thought I might choke.

Mrs. Green didn't look at me as she spoke. "Rules and regulations in a hospital are made for a reason. There are exceptions, though, and while I am against secrecy and breaking rules, there are times that it proves a better policy."

I nodded sheepishly. When a patient's call light sounded, I jumped. Mrs. Green said, "Take your bedpan. Mrs. Oldman likely needs it."

She opened the door for me, and I hurried out into the ward, utterly perplexed. Mrs. Oldman had already bubbled joyfully to all about Peppy's visit and how smart he was. I begged the other patients to keep his visit a secret, lest I lose my job. They all kept their solemn bond and that secret made them special friends with Mrs. Oldman. She thrived under their affection. She regained her interest and confidence in the future. She exercised with such eagerness and determination, it shamed people half her age.

Finally, she left the hospital, welcomed by a joyfully dancing and yelping Peppy.

Mrs. Green never mentioned the dog's visit to me, but when I occasionally had to break rules for the sake of a patient, she was always mysteriously absent.

~Lini R. Grol
Chicken Soup for the Nurse's Soul

6

Merry Christmas, My Friend

It is loneliness that makes the loudest noise. This is true of men as of dogs.
~Eric Hoffer

"I will never forget you," the old man said. A tear rolled down his leathery cheek. "I'm getting old. I can't take care of you anymore."

With his head tilted to one side, Monsieur DuPree watched his master. "Woof, woof! Woof, woof!" He wagged his tail back and forth, wondering, What's he talking about?

"I can't take care of myself anymore, let alone take care of you." The old man cleared his throat. He pulled a hankie from his pocket and blew his nose with a mighty blast.

"Soon, I'll move to an old age home, and, I'm sorry to say, you can't come along. They don't allow dogs there, you know." Bent over from age, the old man limped over to Monsieur DuPree and stroked the dog's head.

"Don't worry, my friend. We'll find a home. We'll find a nice new home for you." As an afterthought he added, "Why, with your good looks, we'll have no trouble at all. Anyone would be proud to own such a fine dog."

Monsieur DuPree wagged his tail really hard and strutted up and down the kitchen floor. For a moment, the familiar musky scent of the old man mingling with the odor of greasy food gave the dog a feeling of well-being. But then a sense of dread took hold again. His tail hung between his legs and he stood very still.

"Come here." With great difficulty, the old man knelt down on the floor and lovingly pulled Monsieur DuPree close to him. He tied a ribbon around the dog's neck with a huge red bow, and then he attached a note to it. What does it say? Monsieur DuPree wondered.

"It says," the old man read aloud, "Merry Christmas! My name is Monsieur DuPree. For breakfast, I like bacon and eggs—even corn-flakes will do. For dinner, I prefer mashed potatoes and some meat. That's all. I eat just two meals a day. In return, I will be your most loyal friend."

"Woof, woof! Woof, woof!" Monsieur DuPree was confused, and his eyes begged, What's going on?

The old man blew his nose into his hankie once more. Then, hanging on to a chair, he pulled himself up from the floor. He but-toned his overcoat, reached for the dog's leash and softly said, "Come here, my friend." He opened the door against a gust of cold air and stepped outside, pulling the dog behind. Dusk was beginning to fall. Monsieur DuPree pulled back. He didn't want to go.

"Don't make this any harder for me. I promise you, you'll be much better off with someone else."

The street was deserted. Leaning into the wintry air, the old man and his dog pushed on. It began to snow.

After a very long time, they came upon an old Victorian house surrounded by tall trees, which were swaying and humming in the wind. Shivering in the cold, they appraised the house. Glimmering lights adorned every window, and the muffled sound of a Christmas song was carried on the wind.

"This will be a nice home for you," the old man said, choking on his words. He bent down and unleashed his dog, then opened the gate slowly, so that it wouldn't creak. "Go on now. Go up the steps and scratch on the door."

Monsieur DuPree looked from the house to his master and back again to the house. He did not understand. "Woof, woof! Woof, woof!"

"Go on." The old man gave the dog a shove. "I have no use for you anymore," he said in a gruff voice. "Get going now!"

Monsieur DuPree was hurt. He thought his master didn't love him anymore. He didn't understand that, indeed, the old man loved him very much but could no longer care for him. Slowly, the dog straggled toward the house and up the steps. He scratched with one paw at the front door. "Woof, woof! Woof, woof!"

Looking back, he saw his master step behind a tree just as someone from inside turned the doorknob. A little boy appeared, framed in the doorway by the warm light coming from within. When he saw Monsieur DuPree, the little boy threw both arms into the air and shouted with delight, "Oh boy! Mom and Dad, come see what Santa brought!"

Through teary eyes, the old man watched from behind the tree as the boy's mother read the note. Then she tenderly pulled Monsieur DuPree inside. Smiling, the old man wiped his eyes with the sleeve of his cold, damp coat. Then he disappeared into the night, whispering, "Merry Christmas, my friend."

~Christa Holder Ocker
Chicken Soup for the Kid's Soul

Velcro Beau

7

When I first saw him, he looked worried. His furrowed brow and uncertain eyes gave his regal face a haunted look. I would come to know that this was a dog who was spooked by change until he got his bearings. And that day his world had been turned upside down.

The large German shepherd had been running away on a regular basis. He always showed up at a neighbor's house where they played with him and fed him—and eventually called his family, asking them to come and get him. Sometimes when the family showed up to retrieve him, they were rough with him. The neighbors noticed that the dog never seemed too excited about getting into their truck. And lately he hadn't been looking well. His coat was rough and he was losing weight.

One day, when they called the dog's family to report his whereabouts, the family said they weren't coming to get him. They'd had enough; the dog was on his own. Fortunately, the neighbors called a friend who was a volunteer at the shelter where I also volunteered as dog-intake coordinator and breed-rescue liaison. She took him home and then called me.

As I drove up to my friend's house, I saw her sitting on the porch with her children. The dog was sitting on the porch, too, but wasn't interacting with any of them. Instead, he was scanning the street and sidewalk with nervous eyes.

He was a stunning dog, in spite of his worried expression, rough coat and emaciated frame. I was told he was a little over a year and a half, still a pup by German shepherd standards. He was very tall and would be an imposing creature once he filled out. I had never handled a dog his size and was intimidated at first. But, aside from being agitated at the strangeness of his surroundings, he seemed perfectly friendly and readily jumped into the back of my car.

My plan was to take him to the vet for an exam and then take him to the shelter or arrange for him to go to the nearest German shepherd rescue group. But first I thought I'd stop and show him to my husband, Larry, as he'd grown up with German shepherds and loved the breed. (Over the years, I'd heard many stories about his favorite dog, Marc; none of our rescued mutts could compare.)

When I opened the back door of the car and the shepherd leaped out, he immediately loped over to my husband. After a cursory sniff, he lost interest and began exploring the parking lot where we stood. We watched him, and I could tell Larry was impressed. He turned to me and said, "I want him."

I was surprised. We already had three dogs—an occupational hazard of volunteering at an animal shelter—and Larry often complained that the household dog population was too high. Plus, this dog was huge—it would be like adding two more dogs to our menagerie! But I didn't argue; I was pleased that Larry wanted a dog for himself.

So Beau joined our family. It wasn't easy at first. He had physical problems that made it difficult for him to gain weight. He was too skinny, yet couldn't digest any fats. His digestion was, to put it mildly, finicky. All that was certainly difficult, but his behavioral problems were even more troubling.

To our dismay, we soon learned that Beau had been "reverse house-trained." He consistently messed in the house and then stood by the door, waiting to go outside. We figured out that his first family had not given him regular opportunities to visit the great outdoors. Then, when he made the inevitable mess inside, they would get mad at him and throw him out the door. He was an intelligent dog and made the obvious connection: Go to the bathroom and then you get to go outside. We had quite a time convincing him it actually worked better the other way.

But what was worse was his utter lack of interest in people. He loved the other dogs, but had no use for the two-legged members of his new family. In my experience, German shepherds were just like that. I thought of them as "big, impersonal dogs," and didn't feel hurt by Beau's coldness. Not Larry. He was deeply disappointed by Beau's aloof disinterest. It was the antithesis of his experience with Marc, whose devotion to Larry had been the stuff of family legend.

Over time, Beau got the hang of being housebroken and established his place within our canine foursome. His physical problems also gradually cleared up, and he eventually tipped the scales at 108 pounds. He was such a handsome dog that people constantly stopped us in the street to comment on his beauty.

Sometimes when I would see him lying sphinx-like in a patch of sun or running in the fields near our house, my breath would catch. He resembled a lion or some other majestic wild animal—his physical presence was simply magical. But still, his heart remained shut. He had no love to give to us. And when he looked at us, there was no spark of joy in his eyes. The lights were on, but no one was home.

What could we do? We did our best to love him and hoped we might reach him someday.

Then one day about four months after we got him, I glanced at Beau and was startled to see that he was following Larry closely with his large brown eyes. He seemed to be studying him—learning what actions signaled a chance to go for a ride or presented the possibility of a walk, treat or a scratch behind the ears. It was as if he suddenly realized that people had things to offer him—things that might not be half bad.

His interest in all things Larry began to snowball. Swiftly, it became Beau's mission to keep an eye on my husband at all times to make sure he didn't miss any opportunities for doggy fun or excitement.

Larry didn't let him down. He knew what big dogs liked to do and where they liked to be scratched. He threw balls and sticks and took Beau to interesting places. Beau soon started whining if Larry left him behind. And when Larry finally returned from those solo jaunts, Beau was beside himself with joy. The floodgates of Beau's love had opened. The dry disinterest fell away and his heart began to bloom.

Today we call him Velcro Beau, because he sticks so close to Larry's side. Every day when Beau wakes up, he stretches his long body luxuriously and then finds one of us to give him his morning rubdown. He lays his ears flat against his head and shyly pokes his large nose against an arm. This beautiful big dog, overflowing with affection, lets us know he is ready for some serious lovin'.

I am grateful that although he is clearly Larry's dog, he has included me in the circle of his love. Often, while rubbing his large chest, I lean over and touch my forehead to his. Then he lifts his paw, places it on my arm and sighs with pleasure. We stay that way for a while, just enjoying our connection.

When we finish, Beau jumps to his feet, his eyes sparkling and his large tail waving wildly. It's time to eat or play. Or go to work with Larry. Or have some other kind of wonderful fun.

To our delight, that skinny, worried dog has become an exuberant and devoted companion. Beau knows that life is good when you live with people you love.

~Carol Kline
Chicken Soup for the Dog Lover's Soul

8

Rescued by Love

On most days you could find him sitting on the wall in front of Saint Mary's Church next to the sign that read "Saint Mary's—A Church for Everyone." No doubt the pastor had meant to attract a larger membership with this billboard invitation, but I'm not sure he was prepared for Bobby. A towering six-footer, weighing in at over two hundred pounds, Bobby was, at twenty-something, a very large child. He spent most of his time waving and smiling at the people driving by, and shouting, "Hey, pal!" to those he recognized.

Bobby called me Goldilocks. He knew me because, as the police department's Animal Control Officer, I was as visible around town as he was. My regular duties were to uphold the leash law, patrol for loose dogs and issue tickets. Bobby had appointed himself my unpaid assistant, and he took his job seriously. Once he waved me down in traffic, ran over to the patrol car and banged on the hood.

"Goldilocks, there's a big dog up the street gonna get hit by a car! You gotta go get 'im now!"

Another time he found a litter of newborn kittens in a garbage can and made it his job to find a home for all of them—including the last one which, at his insistence, I ended up taking home myself!

At first I had loved being the "dog catcher," but as time went by, the job began to get me down. It wasn't the animals—it was the people. I dreaded having to deal with negligent owners. Especially those who no longer wanted their dogs.

In our town the city provided a dog-surrender service with the local SPCA. For a ten-dollar fee, I'd pick up a dog whose owner could no longer keep him, and, more importantly, I'd collect information about him (good with children, medical history, favorite toys, etc.) that would make it easier for him to be adopted.

Unbelievably, sometimes the people most capable of paying this fee chose not to, and abandoned the dog to be picked up as a stray instead. They gave up their best opportunity to increase the dog's chances of finding another home—just to save a measly ten dollars. At first I felt crushed by this kind of behavior, but as time passed I toughened up. Lately, I felt so cynical I was afraid of what was happening to me.

One October when the nights were already dropping below freezing, it occurred to me that I hadn't seen Bobby for a while. He usually spent his nights at the Salvation Army in the winter, so I stopped by and asked about him. No one had seen him. I looked at the phone call log at headquarters to see if he had been making his usual calls to report animals—or just talk. No calls were recorded.

A week later I got a call at headquarters. "Goldilocks," he rasped, "I need you to come." He had a bad cold.

"Bobby! Where are you? Everyone's been looking for you!"

"I'm okay. I'm out in back of the chair factory."

Within a few minutes, I was turning the car off the main street onto a gravel road behind the old chair factory. All at once the road stopped and I was in a large field strewn with debris. In the middle of the field, a rusting station wagon sat on cement blocks.

I approached the car, bent over and knocked lightly on the passenger window. Bobby was curled up tightly in the front seat with his windbreaker thrown over him. Lying next to him was a chocolate Labrador puppy with long gangly legs and ears that he had yet to grow into.

The dog looked up at my knock with bright eyes and a thumping tail. I peered in to get a closer look. The front of the car was filled with empty Styrofoam cups and potato chip bags. The back of the wagon was covered in soft blankets. Neatly stacked boxes of dog biscuits and a bag of dog food were lined up next to two jugs of bottled water and two chewed rubber balls.

"Bobby, are you okay?" His eyes fluttered open.

"Goldilocks," he croaked. He struggled to sit up and get his bearings. He looked at me and I could see his nose was red and his eyes bleary. He untangled himself and climbed from the car, wincing as he stood.

"Come on with me, Bobby. Get in the patrol car and I'll bring you to the Salvation Army, or the medical center. Okay? It's warm there." I urged.

"No, I'm okay. Social Service says I'm gonna lose my check if I don't go into housing. You gotta take Brownie."

It was true. I couldn't think of a single facility that would allow him to keep his dog. He was only out here in the cold because the Salvation Army didn't allow pets. He started unloading the puppy's supplies and carrying them over to the patrol car. Brownie watched every move he made with adoring eyes. I grabbed a jug of water out of the car and started to help, feeling helpless all the same.

Everything was packed up, except for Brownie. Bobby knelt down and put his hands on each side of the puppy's head. They looked at each other for a long moment and then Brownie started to lick Bobby's face. In one quick movement, the man picked him up and placed him gently in the front seat of the patrol car. He turned to me, his eyes even redder than before.

"Here," he said, handing me a ten-dollar bill. "For the dog pound." I stared open-mouthed at the money. I couldn't believe it. Bobby was paying the surrender fee, though it was probably all the money he had in the world.

I put out my hand and grabbed his arm, "Bobby, don't worry about any fee. They'll understand."

He looked at me. "No, Goldilocks. You told me ten dollars to get a good home, 'member? A home with a kid to play with would be good for Brownie."

He turned from me suddenly and started to walk back toward the rusty station wagon. I knew better than to try to convince him to come with me. He had a mind of his own and treasured his independence, often at the expense of his health and safety.

"Bobby! I'll find him a great home," I called after him, my voice catching in my throat.

He made a noise, but didn't turn around.

As I drove away, Brownie put his muzzle on my lap and fell asleep. There were times I couldn't see the road through my tears.

Brownie was taken home that evening by a police officer who fell in love with him the moment he saw me carry him into the precinct. A year later his Christmas photos showed his little boy and Brownie sitting together in front of a fireplace.

I tried to return Bobby's money, but the station wagon was always empty. Later, I heard that he had gone to a group home in another city and was doing fine. I dropped the ten-dollar bill into the Salvation Army donation box.

I missed my assistant and wished I could have told Bobby what a wonderful job he'd done. He had rescued cats and dogs—and my faith in people, too.

~Lisa Duffy-Korpics
Chicken Soup for the Cat and Dog Lover's Soul

Four-Legged Guardian Angels

Snow had just melted off the ground that April day at our house in Regina Beach, Saskatchewan. My husband, Doug, had just cleaned up the pool in preparation for selling our house. The year before, Doug had lost his job with the provincial government, and now our financial situation was grim. In despair, we had finally put our home on the market, and a real estate agent was due to show up later that day. Even worse, we would have to give up our two beloved Great Danes, Bambi and Brigitte, because we could no longer afford the cost of feeding them. The thought of losing our dogs and our beautiful home was almost more than I could bear.

Deep in despair, I sat typing up resumes and cover letters for Doug. Out of the corner of my eye I could see our thirteen-month-old son, Forrest, as he lay on the carpet, playing near our big, gentle nanny-dog, Brigitte. I hadn't typed more than two sentences when our other dog, Bambi, began barking furiously and running back and forth to the sliding glass door overlooking our pool.

I raced to see what was happening and noticed that the sliding door was slightly open. Suddenly, I realized Forrest was nowhere to be seen. In a panic, I opened the door and ran outside. There I was surprised to see Brigitte, who was terrified of water, splashing around in the pool. Then to my horror, my eyes caught sight of Forrest's yellow sleeper. Brigitte was bravely doing her best to keep him afloat by holding on to his sleeper with her mouth. At the same time, she was desperately trying to swim to the shallow end. I realized that Forrest had somehow opened the door, wandered out and fallen into the pool.

In a split second, I dove in, lifted my precious baby out and carried him inside. But when I realized Forrest wasn't breathing, I began to go into shock. I was trained in CPR, but my mind went completely blank. When I called 911, all I could do was scream. On the other end, a paramedic tried to calm me down so that I could follow his CPR instructions, but in my hysteria I was unable to carry it out successfully. Thankfully, Doug, who was a former Canadian Forces officer and was trained in CPR, arrived and took over. I stood by with my heart in my throat, and after about three minutes, Forrest began to breathe again.

When the ambulance arrived, I rode with Forrest to the hospital. Along the way he stopped breathing a couple of times, but each time the paramedics managed to revive him.

Once at the hospital, it wasn't long before a doctor told us that Forrest would be all right. Doug and I were overwhelmed with gratitude. They kept him for observation for a total of four days, and I stayed by his side the whole time.

While Forrest was in the hospital, Doug was often at home. When he went into Forrest's bedroom, he discovered that both Brigitte and Bambi had crammed themselves under the crib. For the entire time that Forrest was in the hospital, they ate little, coming out only to drink water. Otherwise, they remained under the crib, keeping a vigil until we brought Forrest home. Once they saw he was back, Brigitte and Bambi began to bark with apparent joy and wouldn't let Forrest out of their sight. Our two wonderful dogs remained concerned about our baby's safety, and even my first attempts to bathe Forrest were traumatic. Brigitte and Bambi stood watch, whimpering the whole time.

In time they settled down, but both remained dedicated to Forrest and followed him everywhere. When Forrest finally learned to walk, he did it by holding on to the dogs' collars.

The press discovered the story and soon Purina dog food called. They offered the dogs an award and gave us tickets to fly to Toronto for a ceremony where Brigitte and Bambi were awarded medals for their bravery. We were also given a beautiful framed picture of our dogs, which we now display proudly above our mantle. Perhaps best of all, Purina gave us a lifetime supply of dog food so the problem of keeping our beloved dogs was solved.

Those gentle giants helped raise our other two children as well. Things in our lives are much better now. Most importantly, almost losing Forrest—and then getting him back—erased any despair I might have had about losing our home. A house can always be replaced, but knowing we have each other is the greatest blessing of all.

Our two dogs are both angels now and probably guarding other children up in heaven. We miss them both, but we are eternally grateful they were part of our lives.

~Karin Bjerke-Lisle
Chicken Soup for the Canadian Soul

Bubba's Last Stand

During the four years I spent as an animal control officer, I learned that dogs are the first to know when spring has arrived. Dogs who never venture farther than their own backyards will somehow find themselves across town following the scent of spring. Bubba was no exception.

Each year, animal control received several phone calls complaining about Bubba—always in the spring. Bubba, an ancient, overweight and most often cranky bulldog with a profound underbite, snored in the shade of his yard all summer, and seemed content to stay behind his fence during the winter. But as soon as it began to thaw, Bubba began to terrorize the city.

Actually, Bubba was too old to terrorize anyone. His once tan and brindle coat was mixed with so much gray that he appeared at least twenty years old, and I noticed the beginning of a limp that had the definite look of arthritic hips. He never chased anyone; I don't think he could have if he tried. Still, his appearance and his perpetual nasal congestion, combined with his bad attitude, made people uncomfortable when he got loose.

Sometimes he would get it in his head to sit outside the local deli and glare. The deli owners tried throwing roast beef at him but he just sniffed at it, gobbled it up, growled and stayed right where he was. Most people just got out of his way when they saw him coming; then they called animal control.

His owner, Tim—a thin, silent man who appeared ageless in

that way men do after working outdoors most of their lives—usually showed up at the pound, apologized, asked someone to tell me to drop off his ticket and took Bubba home. He wrapped his thin arms around Bubba's very large middle and heaved him into the back of his pickup truck. He never complained, never asked for a court date. He just apologized and paid his fines.

Tim didn't seem the kind of person who would be interested in having a pet, especially one as difficult as Bubba. Tim lived alone in a large dilapidated Victorian house that was in a perpetual state of renovation. He had never married, and no one really remembered if he had any family. He didn't seem comfortable showing affection to anyone, least of all a fat, grumpy bulldog. And Bubba never let anyone touch him, except for Tim, and even then he didn't look too happy about it. Yet year after year Tim spent a lot of time leaving work to come and drag his grouchy, old dog home.

One spring, it seemed as though Bubba had finally gone into retirement, only growling at passersby from the comfort of his yard. That was why I was a bit surprised when I got a call on an unusually warm June day that a very ugly, old, fat and wheezing bulldog was causing a problem up at the high school. How did he get all the way up there? I thought to myself as I drove to the school. The route from Bubba's home to the high school was all uphill. I had seen Bubba recently, and he surely didn't look as if he could make a trip like that.

I pulled into the high school parking lot and saw the gymnasium doors open, probably for a cross-breeze. Bubba must have entered the school through the gym. This should be fun. I grabbed a box of dog biscuits and the snare pole and threw a leash around my neck. No animal control officer had ever actually touched Bubba. The equipment was going to be of no real use—he would likely never let me near him. I had to figure out a way to get him to want to leave. I hoped the biscuits would do the job. Entering the hallway, I saw lines of teenagers standing in suspended animation along the walls. One called out to me, "Every time we even go to open our lockers, that dog growls at us. He's going to eat us!"

Sure enough, there was Bubba—holding the entire hallway

hostage. I could see him standing, bowlegged, wheezing like I had never heard him before, and growling at any sudden movement. Uh-oh, I thought to myself. Frightening the occasional neighbor was one thing, but growling at kids on school property — Bubba was looking at some serious penalties, possibly even a dangerous-dog action complaint, which was a rare occurrence, but one with dire consequences if he was found guilty.

"Bubba," I called to him, and he managed to twist his pudgy body around to see who knew his name. He looked at me, wheezed some more and growled loudly. I reached into the box of biscuits and threw one over to him. He limped over to it slowly, sniffed it, sneezed and sat down glaring at me. So much for Plan A. I was going to have to use the snare pole on him and I wasn't looking forward to it.

Suddenly from behind me, I heard, "Hey, ugly dog. Try this." A tall teenage boy put his hand into a Baggie and threw a Froot Loop at Bubba. Bubba stared at the cereal, then up at the boy. He snuffled around it, picked it up and swallowed it. I turned to the tall boy leaning against the wall. "Can I borrow those?"

"Sure." He handed me the Baggie, and I threw a Froot Loop toward Bubba. He waddled over to suck it up off the floor. I kept dropping them as I backed toward the open doors of the gym. Bubba was in bad shape; his bowed legs seemed to have a hard time holding up his rotund body. Every step seemed to cause him pain, and the wheezing was getting worse. I wanted to pick him up, but as I started to approach, he growled and backed up. So I continued to drop one Froot Loop at a time, inching my way toward the patrol car. Finally, Bubba was at the car. He was wheezing so much I worried he would have a heart attack. I decided to just get him home and worry about the report later: Bubba was fading fast.

I threw what was left of the Froot Loops into the backseat of the car. Bubba waddled over and stuck his two front paws on the floor to finish them up. I swallowed hard and quickly pushed Bubba's rear end into the backseat. He grumbled and growled, but was mostly concerned with chewing the last bit of cereal. I couldn't believe it — I had touched Bubba and survived!

By the time I pulled up in front of Bubba's house, Tim's truck was parked haphazardly in front. Tim ran out of the house, letting the door slam behind him. "Is Bubba okay? I called the school, but you had already left. I'll pay the fine, whatever it is. Give me a couple of 'em. How did he get out of the house? I can't believe he made it all the way to the high school. He's so sick. How'd you get him in the car anyway?" Tim spoke more in that minute than I had ever heard him speak in the several years I had known him.

Before I could answer, Tim walked over to the patrol car and opened the door. Bubba was snoring loudly, sound asleep on his back covered in Froot Loop crumbs and looking very un-Bubba-like. Tim put his arms around the old dog and with a lot of effort pulled him out of the car, holding him as you would an infant. Bubba never even woke up, just grumbled a bit in his sleep.

"I, um, used Froot Loops. He followed a trail of them into the car," I said.

Tim lifted his eyes from the sleeping dog to look at me. "Froot Loops? I didn't know he liked Froot Loops."

The lines in Tim's pale face seemed deeper in the harsh sunlight. He looked tired; more than that, he looked worried. "I can't believe he got out. I had him locked in the house with the air conditioner on." Tim's voice dropped, "The vet says he has cancer. They told me to take him home from the animal hospital for the weekend, you know, to say goodbye."

I looked at Tim holding his old, fat, gray bulldog. Suddenly, I understood what I hadn't before. All those years that had etched the premature lines on Tim's sad face—Bubba had been there to share them. They had each other, and for them, that had been enough.

"I'm so sorry, Tim," I said and turned to get back into the car. "I'll talk to you later."

"What about my tickets? I know I'm getting a few this time, right?"

I turned around to look at Tim. "Let me see what the sergeant says first, Tim. You just worry about Bubba right now, okay?"

I started to leave again, but then remembered there was something else I wanted to ask. "Tim?" I called over to him as he was carrying his dog into the house. "Why do you think he went to the high school? I don't remember him going all the way up there before."

Tim smiled at me, another thing I had never seen him do. "Bubba really loves kids. I used to bring him to the playground when he was a pup. Maybe he remembered that."

I nodded and waved to them: the thin, tired man with the gray flannel shirt, carrying his twenty-year-old puppy into the house... perhaps for the last time.

Bubba died soon after that day. I never even wrote up a ticket for his caper at the high school. I figured Bubba had just been revisiting his youth, saying goodbye in his own Bubba way.

You think you know people and then you find out there is more to them than you ever could have imagined. It took Bubba's last stand to show me that loving families take many forms, all of them beautiful.

~Lisa Duffy-Korpics
Chicken Soup for the Dog Lover's Soul

Loving Our Dogs

Chapter 2

I Can't Believe
My Dog Did That!

*All my dogs have been scamps and thieves and troublemakers
and I've adored them all.*
~Helen Hayes

You Have No Message

No one appreciates the very special genius
of your conversation as the dog does.
~Christopher Morley

We were visiting our daughter when we adopted our Boston terrier, Tad. An adorable puppy, just three months old, he became the family's center of attention. Each morning, as soon as he heard my daughter Kayla moving around downstairs, he had to be taken down for playtime before she left for work. When she came home from work, we had him waiting for her at the door.

After three weeks we left for home. On the drive, we let Tad talk to Kayla on the phone each night. Once home, every time we called Kayla or she called us, we always put Tad on. He scratched the phone and listened intently and tried to look into the phone to see her.

One Saturday, Kayla called while we were out. She left a message. Tad was standing beside me when I pressed the button to listen to the message. He listened to her talking and cocked his head, grinning at me. I played it again for him.

A few days later, I was taking my shower when I heard the answering machine come on and Kayla leave a message. I thought it was strange when I heard her message repeat and the machine announce, "End of messages." A few seconds later Kayla's message began yet again.

Wondering what was going on, I climbed out of the shower,

wrapped a towel around myself and headed into the living room. There stood Tad, listening to the answering machine. I stopped and watched. When the message finished, he stood up with his feet against the edge of the low table, reached over with one paw and slapped the answering machine. The message came on again. He dropped back on the floor and listened happily.

I told him "no," and distracted him from the answering machine while I erased the message. A few days later I was in the kitchen when I heard, "You have no messages." I headed for the living room. Tad had started the machine again. I watched as he cocked his head and looked at the answering machine. Then he stood with his feet on the edge of the table and tapped the button again: "You have no messages." He walked around to the other side of the table and repeated the process with the same results. This really irritated him. He returned to his first position, took both paws and began slapping and clawing the answering machine. It repeated: "You have no messages."

I said, "Tad, leave the answering machine alone." He looked at me and then turned back to the answering machine, digging at it furiously. When it repeated the same message, he ran to me and then ran back to the answering machine, waiting for me to do something. I realized he wanted to hear Kayla talking, but I had erased the message.

I called Kayla that night and asked her to call Tad and leave him a message. I explained that Tad had listened to her message, but I had erased it. When he tried to listen to it again and didn't hear her message, he had been unhappy.

Kayla called Tad and left a special message for him that he can play and listen to whenever he wants to hear Kayla's voice. We call it puppy love, twenty-first-century style!

~Zardrelle Arnott
Chicken Soup for the Dog Lover's Soul

Obedience

Animals are such agreeable friends—
they ask no questions, they pass no criticisms.
~George Eliot

For seven years my father, who was not yet old enough to retire, had been battling colon cancer. Now he was dying. He could no longer eat or even drink water, and an infection had forced him into the hospital. I sensed that he hated being in the hospital, but he hardly complained. That wasn't his way.

One night when he had no luck summoning a nurse, and tried to reach the bathroom on his own, he fell and gashed his head on the nightstand. When I saw his wounded head the next day, I felt my frustration and helpless anger rise. Why isn't there anything I can do? I thought, as I waited for the elevator. As if in answer to my prayers, when the elevator opened, two dogs greeted me.

Dogs? In a hospital? Personally, I couldn't think of a better place for dogs, but I was shocked that the city laws and hospital codes allowed it.

"How did you get to bring dogs here?" I asked the owner, as I stepped in.

"They're therapy dogs. I take them up to the sixth floor once a week, to meet with the patients in rehab."

An idea grew stronger and stronger as I walked out of the hospital and to my car. My dad had bought a springer spaniel named Boots for my mom for a Christmas present a few years before. My mother had insisted that she wanted a dog, and it had to be a spaniel. My dad had explained this to me when he asked me to go for a ride with him to pick out a puppy.

When he picked up a wriggly kissy puppy, I saw the tension ease from my father's face. I realized the genius of my mother's plan immediately. The dog was not for her; it was for him. Brilliantly, she asked for a spaniel so he could have the breed of dog he'd always wanted, and never had, when he was a boy.

By then, all of us kids had moved away from home. So Boots also became the perfect child my father never had. She was an eager, loving and obedient pal for him.

Personally, I thought she was a little too obedient. Boots was not allowed on the bed or any other furniture, and she never broke this rule. Sometimes I wanted to tell my dad when he was at home lying on his sickbed, "Call Boots up here! She'll give you love and kisses and touch you like I'm too restrained to do... and you need it."

But I didn't. And he didn't. And Boots didn't.

Instead, she sat near his bed, watching him protectively, as the months rolled by. She was always there, a loving presence as his strength ebbed away, till he could no longer walk or even sit up without help. Once in a while, he got very sick, and went to the hospital, and she awaited his return anxiously, jumping up expectantly every time a car pulled up to the house.

I decided that if I could give my dad nothing else, I was going to give him a few minutes with his beloved dog. So I went back to the hospital and asked a nurse about it. She told me that if I were to bring his dog in, she would not "see anything." I took that as a yes.

Later that day, I came back for another visit, bringing Boots. I told my dad I had a surprise for him in my car. I went to get her, and the strangest thing happened.

Boots, the perfect dog, who was as impeccably leash-trained as she was obedient, practically flew out of the car, yanked me across that snowy parking lot to the front door and dragged me through the hospital lobby. She somehow knew to stop directly in front of the appropriate elevator (I could never find the right one myself.) And even though she had never been anywhere near that hospital before, when the elevator doors opened at the fourth floor, she nearly pulled my arm out of its socket as she ran down the hall, around two corners, down another hall and into his room. Then, without a moment of hesitation, she jumped straight up onto his bed! Ever so gently, she crawled into my father's open arms, not touching his pain-filled sides or stomach, and laid her face next to his.

For the first time, Boots was on my dad's bed, just where she belonged. And for the first time in a long time, I saw my father's broad smile. I knew we were both grateful Boots had broken the rules and finally obeyed her own heart.

~Lori Jo Oswald, Ph.D.
Chicken Soup for the Cat and Dog Lover's Soul

Moving Day

Dogs laugh, but they laugh with their tails.
~Max Eastman, Enjoyment of Laughter

He was a street dog of indeterminable pedigree. Not too big, but scrappy.

He found my husband on St. Patrick's Day, 1988. A New York City police officer, Steve was patrolling the Park Slope section of Brooklyn. The skinny blond dog with the white stripe on his face and stand-up ears he never did grow into, fairly leaped into the patrol car through the open window.

I got the call that afternoon. "Can we keep him?" My big strong husband sounded like a kid.

We kept him. Steve named him Patrick, in honor of the day he'd found him. We didn't know how he'd ended up a homeless pup. But it didn't matter. He was safe now. The vet estimated that he was about six months old and that he'd been on the streets only a few days. He was healthy, but awfully hungry.

I fed him boiled chicken and rice, easy on his stomach, and determined to start putting some meat on the ribs that were a bit too prominent. After that meal—and after every single meal I fed him for the rest of his life—he thanked me with several sloppy kisses on my hands.

Things were hectic that March. The kids were growing and we were in the process of moving into a larger apartment.

Patrick watched with an odd expression; but it was an odd

move. We didn't really pack. We simply rolled everything into the hall, loaded it in the elevator, went two floors down and rolled the stuff off and into the new place.

The new apartment gave our kids their own rooms. Patrick's space was an alcove at the end of the hall leading to the master bedroom. I cut a piece of carpet to fit his "room" and piled his toys in one of the corners. I bought "Dawn Lane" and "Michael Lane" signs for the kids, so of course I bought a "Patrick Lane" sign for him. I think he liked it. When I put it on the wall he licked the sign, then me.

March 17 became his birthday. On the first anniversary of the day he found us, I threw a "Patty Party," inviting all the grandparents. I'd done it tongue-in-cheek, but it became an annual event. We got Patrick a kelly-green birthday hat and a big matching bow tie. Another dog might have been embarrassed; Patrick wore them with pride.

To repay us for rescuing him, Patrick protected us with zeal and an unerring ability to tell good guy from bad. He could pick the "perp" out of a lineup a block long. He knew guns, too. When Steve cleaned his service revolver, Patrick would eye him strangely, from a safe distance, as if to say, "What's a nice guy like you doing with a thing like that?"

In 1992, Steve retired. We bought a house in Jersey near my folks, but couldn't close until October. The kids stayed with my parents so they could start the year in their new school. We brought them home on alternate weekends. Michael's room now became the "Box Room."

Every day I knelt in that room, placing breakables on the pile of papers, wrapping them up and tucking them into boxes. And every day Patrick watched from the room's other doorway. I told him all about "our" new house and described the fun "we" would have.

Our last night in Brooklyn approached. We'd lived in that apartment four and a half years, and in the building for fifteen. Though excited about moving into our own home, we were a bit sad to leave the city we'd lived in all our lives. Patrick understood. He patrolled the apartment restlessly, sniffing every nook and cranny as if to commit to memory the security of the only loving home he'd ever known.

We closed on the house on Friday, then drove back to Brooklyn with the kids. The "Box Room" was nearly full, but the packing paper still lay on the few square feet of remaining floor, ready to protect our last-minute treasures. I gave the kids their "Dawn" and "Michael" boxes, instructing them to finish packing their toys. We had something quick for dinner. I don't remember what. I only remember what happened after.

I walked into the kitchen and happened to glance into the "Box Room." I was stunned.

"Hey, guys," I called. "You won't believe what Patrick did." They followed me through the kitchen. Patrick poked his nose in from the living-room doorway, a very worried expression on his face.

There, nestled in the canyon of cartons, lying right on top of the newspaper used for wrapping breakables, was Patrick's favorite toy.

I said, "Patty, are you afraid we're going to move away and leave you? Is that what those other people did to you?" He didn't need words. His eyes told me.

"Well," I told him. "You don't have to worry. We're not going to leave you. You're coming with us."

Then I rolled up his toy in the paper. I'd planned to put his things in the "Patrick" box. Instead, it went in with our dishes. It seemed the thing to do.

His bushy blond and white tail wagged like mad, and if asked under oath I'd have to swear he laughed. We all wound up in a heap on that stack of papers, getting licked to death by one very happy—and grateful—dog.

I'm sorry to say I'd never considered Patrick's feelings through that whole tumultuous process; never thought he was worried as he sat day after day, intently watching me wrap up and pack away our things; never realized he didn't know he was part of the "we" I kept mentioning. After all, he'd been with us four and a half years and we'd moved with him before. But I guess the vast amount of packing required for this move dredged up old memories and threatened his sense of security. Elephants never forget; dogs don't either.

When I think about Patty now, all I can say is: I'm thrilled he picked Steve. He brought joy to our lives that we would have sorely missed otherwise. He left us in November 1997 and we still miss him. He's with us, though, in a pretty wooden urn—and he smiles at us every day from his picture, dressed so smartly in his kelly-green birthday hat and matching bow tie.

~Micki Ruiz
Chicken Soup for the Dog Lover's Soul

Seeing

Whether you think you can or think you can't —you are right.
~Henry Ford

Barkley came to me when he was three years old, from a family who just didn't want him anymore. They had badly neglected the big golden retriever and he was in ill health. After attending to his physical problems and spending some time bonding with him, I found he had a very sweet temperament. He was intelligent and eager to please, so we went to basic and advanced obedience classes and to a social therapy workshop to learn everything we needed to know for Barkley to become a certified therapy dog.

Within a few months, we began our weekly visits to the local medical center. I didn't know what to expect, but we both loved it. After I made sure a patient wanted a visit from Barkley, the dog would walk over to the bed and stand waiting for the person in the bed to reach out to him. People hugged him tightly or simply petted him, as he stood quietly wagging his tail with what seemed a huge laughing grin on his face. His mellowness made him a favorite with the staff, patients and even the other volunteers.

I dressed Barkley in something different every week. He had costumes appropriate for each holiday—he wore a birthday hat on his birthday, a green bow tie for Saint Patrick's Day and a Zorro costume on Halloween. For Christmas he sported a Santa hat or reindeer horns. Easter was everybody's favorite: Barkley wore bunny ears and a bunny tail I attached to his back end. Patients were always eager to see what Barkley was wearing this week.

About a year after we began visiting, I noticed Barkley was having trouble seeing—he sometimes bumped into things. The vet found he had an eye condition caused in part by his lack of care when he was young. Over the next year, this condition worsened, but Barkley was remarkably good at functioning with his failing eyesight. Even I wasn't aware how bad it had become until one evening when Barkley and I were playing with his ball out in the yard. When I threw the ball to the dog, he had a lot of trouble catching it. He had to use his nose to sniff it out on the ground after he repeatedly failed to catch it in his mouth. The next day I brought him to the vet and they told me that surgery was necessary. After three surgeries in an attempt to save at least some of his vision, Barkley became totally blind.

I was very concerned about how he would adjust to such a terrible handicap, but he acclimated to his blindness rapidly. It seemed that all his other senses sharpened to make up for his loss of sight. Soon he was completely recovered and insisted (by standing at the garage door and blocking my exit!) that he wanted to go along with me to the hospital and visit his friends. So we restarted our weekly visits, much to everyone's great joy—especially Barkley's.

He maneuvered around the hospital so well, it was hard to tell that he was blind. Once after Barkley became blind, someone asked me if Barkley was a seeing-eye dog. I laughed and told them that it was Barkley who needed a seeing-eye person.

He seemed to develop an uncanny ability to perceive things that were beyond the senses. One day, we went into a patient's room and to my surprise, Barkley went over to the patient's visitor, who was sitting in a chair by the bed, and nudged her hand with his nose. Barkley never made the first contact like that, and I wondered why he did it now. As I came up to her chair, it was only by the way the woman interacted with Barkley that I realized the truth. I don't know how, but the completely blind Barkley had sensed that this lady was blind, too.

It was strange, but after Barkley lost his sight, his presence seemed even more precious to the patients he visited.

When Barkley received an award for performing over 400 hours of volunteer service, everyone told me, "It's amazing what a blind dog can do!"

They didn't understand that Barkley wasn't really blind. He could still see. It's just that now, he saw with his heart.

~Kathe Neyer
Chicken Soup for the Pet Lover's Soul

Refrigerator Commando

He conquers who endures.
~Persius

A golden barrel on legs—that was our first impression of Max when my wife and I saw him at the Animal Welfare League. His unique ability to inhale a full cup of dog food in less than seven seconds had enabled Max to enlarge his beagle-mix body into the shape of an overstuffed sausage. Even after Heather and I adopted him and helped him lose weight, we were continually amazed at his voraciousness. His escapades became the stuff of family legend: his seek-and-destroy mission involving several pounds of gourmet Christmas cashews, his insistence on chasing birds away from the feeder so he could eat the seeds, his discovery (far too gross to discuss here) of the yeasty joys of Amish Friendship Bread batter. And of course the refrigerator story....

One day during her lunch break, Heather called me at work. "Did you shut the refrigerator door tight this morning?"

"Think so. Why?"

She paused just enough to let the suspense build. "Max raided the fridge."

We got off lucky: we were overdue to go to the grocery store, so there hadn't been much in there. He'd gotten the last couple of pieces of peppered turkey and maybe a third of a bag of baby carrots—no surprise there, Max loves carrots (then again, Max loves potting soil.) Still, no real damage done. We wrote it off to a sloppily closed door (probably my doing), and the next morning I made sure everything was shut good and tight before I left. After all, we had just loaded up with groceries the night before, and we wouldn't want my carelessness to help Max get himself into trouble, right?

Turns out Max didn't need my help at all.

Again a phone call to me during Heather's lunch hour, this time straight to the point: "I think he knows how to open the refrigerator," she said.

"What?!"

Max had made himself a sandwich. A big sandwich: a pound of turkey, a pound of Swiss cheese, a head of lettuce, half a tomato and an entire loaf of bread. He'd also ripped open another bag of carrots and polished off the remnants of a bag of shredded coconut (for dessert, I assume). Heather found him lying amid the flurry of destroyed plastic bags, tail desperately thumping at her displeasure, as if to say, Please don't be mad, it was just SOOOO good....

Still, we didn't really believe it. He couldn't reach the handle, and the door seal was tight. How was he doing it? I caught him that night, after putting away our second load of groceries in two days. I just happened to be passing by the darkened kitchen when I saw his stout little body wiggling, pushing his narrow muzzle into the fridge seal like a wedge. Then, with a quick flick of his head, he popped the door open.

Apparently, Max, while not understanding the gastrointestinal distress that results from eating sixteen slices of cheese, had a full understanding of the concept of the lever. Where was this dog when I'd been in science class?

This was serious. He now had the skill, the determination and, most important, the appetite to literally eat us out of house and home. The next morning, as a temporary fix, we blocked the refrigerator with a heavy toolbox. Surely he couldn't move a barrier loaded with close to twenty-five pounds of metal, could he?

Another lunchtime phone call. I think I answered it: "You've got to be kidding!"

The moving of the toolbox still remains a bit of a mystery. I'm guessing he used that lever principle again, wedging his muzzle between the box and the door and then just pushing for all he was worth. And once that barrier was gone, he got serious.

More bread, more meat, more cheese. The rest of the carrots. Apples—many, many apples. A packet of cilantro, smeared like green confetti across the kitchen floor. He'd also popped open a Tupperware bowl of angel hair pasta and had been working at its sister container of tomato sauce when Heather found him. The only items left on the bottom two shelves were beer and pop, and the only thing that saved those was his lack of opposable thumbs.

That night we decided to hit the grocery store for a third time and invest in a childproof lock for the fridge. Before we left the house to buy it, we hovered anxiously around the refrigerator for a while. There wasn't much left in there, but still, what if he tried to climb to the top shelves? What if he conquered the freezer?

But what could stop him? The toolbox had been no match. Finally, I half lifted, half dragged the seventy-five-pound safe from my office closet, dragged it to the kitchen and thudded it onto the floor, flush against the door.

Max sat behind us, watching. Calculating.

Heather leaned into me, almost whispering. "Do you think it will work?"

I said, "Well, I think we'll find one of three things when we get back. One, everything will be fine. Two, the safe will be budged a couple inches, and we'll have a beagle with a very red and throbbing nose. Or three, we may come home and find he's rigged up some elaborate pulley system that's lifted the safe out of his way. If that's the case, I say from now on, we just stock the bottom two shelves with whatever he wants."

We dashed to the store and back in record time. We practically ran into the kitchen and found him lying there, thinking deeply. No sore nose, no pulley system. We sighed big sighs of relief and got the plastic and vinyl childproof strap installed. So far it's done its job. So far....

~Sam Minier
Chicken Soup for the Dog Lover's Soul

The Golden Years

Anyone can be an angel.
~Author Unknown

My best friend, Cocoa, and I live in a senior-citizen apartment complex in a lovely small town. Cocoa is a ten-year-old poodle and I am a sixty-nine-year-old lady, so you can see we both qualify as senior citizens.

Years ago, I promised myself that when I retired I would get a chocolate poodle to share my golden years. From the very first, Cocoa has always been exceptionally well-behaved. I never have to tell him anything more than once. He was housebroken in three days and has never done anything naughty. He is extremely neat—when taking his toys from his box to play, he always puts them back when he is finished. I have been accused of being obsessively neat, and sometimes I wonder if he mimics me or if he was born that way, too.

He is a wonderful companion. When I throw a ball for him, he picks it up in his mouth and throws it back to me. We sometimes play a game I played as a child—but never with a dog. He puts his paw on my hand, I cover it with my other hand, he puts his paw on top, and I slide my hand out from underneath the pile and lay it on top, and so on. He does many amusing things that make me laugh, and when that happens, he is so delighted he just keeps it up. I enjoy his company immensely.

But almost two years ago, Cocoa did something that defies

comprehension. Was it a miracle or a coincidence? It is certainly a mystery.

One afternoon, Cocoa started acting strangely. I was sitting on the floor playing with him, when he started pawing and sniffing at the right side of my chest. He had never done anything like this ever before, and I told him, "No." With Cocoa, one "no" is usually sufficient, but not that day. He stopped briefly, then suddenly ran toward me from the other side of the room, throwing his entire weight—eighteen pounds—at the right side of my chest. He crashed into me and I yelped in pain. It hurt more than I thought it should have.

Soon after this, I felt a lump. I went to my doctors, and after X-rays, tests and lab work were done, they told me I had cancer.

When cancer starts, for an unknown reason, a wall of calcium builds. Then the lump or cancer attaches itself to this wall. When Cocoa jumped on me, the force of the impact broke the lump away from the calcium wall. This made it possible for me to notice the lump. Before that, I couldn't see it or feel it, so there was no way for me to know it was there.

I had a complete mastectomy and the cancer has not spread to any other part of my body. The doctors told me if the cancer had gone undetected even six more months, it would have been too late.

Was Cocoa aware of just what he was doing? I'll never really know. What I do know is that I'm glad I made a promise to spend my golden years with this wonderful chocolate brown poodle—for Cocoa not only shares his life with me; he has made sure that I will be around to share my life with him!

~Yvonne A. Martell
Chicken Soup for the Pet Lover's Soul

Sammy's Big Smile

You're never fully dressed without a smile.
~Martin Charnin

When I was a child, my Aunt Julie had a dog named Sammy, a little black Chihuahua mix with a tongue as long as her body. Sammy could run up one side of your body, lick your face clean and run down the other side before you knew what happened. This adorable black dog always greeted you with a "doggy smile." Sammy owned my Aunt Julie, and everyone in our family knew it.

One afternoon I was visiting my aunt. We were all dressed up and going out. I don't remember the occasion, but I do remember that we were in an awful rush. My family comes from a long line of people who feel that if you're not fifteen minutes early for an event, you are late! As usual, time was of the essence. Sammy, however, wasn't in any rush. The only thing Sammy was interested in was getting some attention.

"No, Sammy, we cannot play," my aunt scolded, "We have to go! Now!"

The problem was that we couldn't "go," because Aunt Julie had misplaced her false teeth. The longer we searched for her teeth, the later we got for the event and the angrier Aunt Julie became—and the more attention Sammy seemed to demand. We ignored Sammy's barking, as we looked frantically for the missing dentures.

Finally, Aunt Julie reached her breaking point and gave up. She plunked herself down at the bottom of the stairs and cried. I sat next to her, counseling her with that special brand of wisdom eight-year-olds possess. "It's okay, Aunt Julie, don't cry. We can still go, just don't smile," I said, which made her cry even harder.

At that moment, Sammy gave a few shrill barks, this time from the top of the stairs, and then was quiet. As we turned around to see what she wanted, we both exploded into laughter. There stood a "smiling" Sammy—with Aunt Julie's false teeth in her mouth—her tail wagging a hundred miles an hour. The message in her sparkling eyes was obvious: I've been trying to tell you for a half hour—I know where your teeth are! A vision that, thirty years later, still makes me laugh out loud.

~Gayle Delhagen
Chicken Soup for the Dog Lover's Soul

18

Jim the Wonder Dog

In 1925, Sam Van Arsdale, proprietor of the Ruff Hotel in Marshall, Missouri, purchased an English setter puppy born of pureblood champion field stock in Louisiana. The puppy was considered the least promising of the litter and was sold at a throwaway price. The dog was nothing special to look at as he had unusually big paws and an ungainly appearance. Sam decided to call him Jim.

Jim grew to be a fine companion for Sam. The dog was smart and good-natured, and Sam was pleased with his "bargain."

One day, when Jim was three years old, he and Sam were walking through the woods. The weather was hot, and Sam said to Jim, "C'mon boy, let's go and rest a little under a hickory tree."

There were many types of trees in the woods, but Jim ran straight over to a hickory tree. Sam was a bit surprised. No doubt it was just a coincidence. On a whim, Sam said to Jim, "Show me a black oak tree." When Jim ran to the nearest black oak and put his right paw on the tree, Sam was amazed. This couldn't possibly be true.

"Show me a walnut tree," he said, and Jim ran unerringly to the nearest walnut and put his paw on it. Sam continued with everything he could think of—a stump, hazel bushes, a cedar tree, even a tin can. Jim correctly identified them all. Sam could hardly believe the evidence of his own eyes. How could a dog do such things?

Sam went home and told his wife what had happened.

She said flatly, "Sam Van Arsdale, you can tell me, but don't go telling anyone else."

Sam persuaded his wife to accompany them back to the woods, where Jim put on a flawless repeat performance. She shook her head in amazement—Sam's crazy story was true!

Over the next few days, Sam couldn't help telling his friends around town what his smart dog could do. They smiled at him indulgently and moved off pretty fast.

One man did listen, although of course he was skeptical. Sam, noticing that the man had parked his car on the street a few yards away, told Jim to show the man which car was his. Jim went straight to the car and put his front paw on it.

Then another man gave Sam the license plate number of his car. Sam wrote it down on a piece of paper and put the paper on the sidewalk. He told Jim to identify the car. Without hesitation, Jim walked to the car in question.

After incidents like these, Jim's reputation spread like wildfire around the small town. Soon he was demonstrating his powers in the Ruff Hotel for amazed crowds of up to a hundred people at a time. There seemed to be no limit to what Jim could do. When people were in the lobby, he could determine what room numbers they occupied in the hotel. He could identify people according to the clothes they wore, the color of their hair—in spite of the fact that dogs are thought to be color-blind—their profession, and, in the case of the military, their rank.

In addition, he could identify objects not just by name but by function. For example, at a command such as, "If we wanted to hear Amos and Andy, where would we go?" Jim would go to the radio.

Perhaps, the skeptics said, Sam was secretly signaling to Jim. Although none of Sam's friends and associates questioned his integrity, knowing him to be a plain-speaking man who wouldn't dream of deceiving others, one woman decided to test this theory. She had the clever idea to write an instruction for Jim in shorthand, which Sam did not understand. When Sam showed Jim the paper on which the instruction was written, and told him to do whatever it said, Jim went over to a certain man. The woman shouted, "He's doing it!" Then she explained that the instruction was, "Show us the man with rolled socks."

One year, at the State Fair in Sedalia, the editor of the Joplin

Globe asked for a demonstration. Since they were near the bandstand where the musicians were putting away their instruments, Sam said, "Jim, show us who plays the tuba." Jim went to the tuba player and put his paw on him. The citizens of the "Show-Me State" had to admit Jim had abilities far beyond the normal.

By this time Jim's reputation had spread far beyond the small town of Marshall. Newspapers and magazines from all over the country sent reporters to cover the story. They went away, like everyone else, amazed. Jim became known as the Wonder Dog.

Jim's feats aroused scientific and medical curiosity. He was examined by veterinarians at Missouri State University, who said that there was nothing unusual about Jim—physically, he was just like any other dog. They could offer no explanation for his uncanny talent.

Later that same day, Jim gave an outdoor demonstration at the university, attended by students and professors. Various professors gave him instructions in different languages.

In Italian, "Show me an elm tree."

In French, "Point out this license number."

In German, "Show a girl dressed in blue."

In Spanish, "Find a man wearing a mustache."

Not once did Jim err.

Sam watched the demonstration with quiet satisfaction. His bargain pup had become his dearest treasure, an extraordinary dog whom he loved and was proud of. But he had no explanation of how Jim could do all these things. When a friend at the demonstration asked him about it, he said, "All I know is that he has the power of doing whatever I ask him to do, and there seems to be no limit to his knowledge or ability."

One man who was deeply impressed by Jim's ability was Jack L. Jolly, a Missouri state representative, who invited Sam and Jim to Jefferson City for a joint session with the legislature. The politicians tried to trip Jim up. They gave him an instruction in Morse code. But Jim had no problem indicating the person they were calling for. Anyone who harbored any lingering doubts that Jim was simply reading his master's mind, or responding to secret signals, had to put them aside, because

Sam knew Morse code no better than he knew shorthand. Sam was as astonished as everyone else by Jim's supernormal gift.

One day, some friends persuaded Sam to test Jim further. Could he possibly predict the future? Sam took an interest in the Kentucky Derby, so that year he wrote down the names of the horses on pieces of paper that he then laid on the floor. He asked Jim to select the horse that would win. Jim put his paw on one of the slips of paper, which was then put in a locked safe until after the race. It turned out that Jim had picked the winner. He repeated his success the following year, and so on for seven successive years.

Sam was not a gambling man and never attempted to profit from Jim's abilities to foretell the future. He received many letters and telegrams requesting Jim's predictions of winning horses. Some people offered to split the profits with Sam. But Sam never wavered. Nor was he interested in a lucrative offer from Paramount for Jim to work in movies for a year. Like the modest Midwesterner he was, Sam said he didn't really need the money and didn't want to commercialize Jim.

As time passed, the bond between Sam and Jim grew. Sam's love for Jim was that of a man for his greatest friend. And the dog's ability to do anything Sam asked was just one facet of Jim's deep devotion towards Sam. So when Jim died at the age of twelve in 1937, Sam was devastated. And indeed, the whole town of Marshall was stunned by the loss. Jim was buried in the Ridge Park Cemetery, where his small white headstone reads: Jim the Wonder Dog.

Many people visit Jim's gravesite every year, leaving flowers and coins in remembrance of the Wonder Dog whose mysterious powers won him lasting fame and honor and love.

~Bryan Aubrey
Chicken Soup for the Cat and Dog Lover's Soul

[*Editors' Note*: The events in this story have been confirmed by eyewitnesses and documented in numerous newspapers, magazines and other publications. The editors have checked the author's sources and are confident that they are reliable.]

19

The Telltale Woof

Perseverance is not a long race; it is many short races one after another.
~Walter Elliott, The Spiritual Life

The veterinarian's words came as no surprise. "I'll do what I can, but I'm not optimistic. Call me tomorrow morning."

I smoothed the black fur on Yaqui's head and ran my fingers across the small brown patches above his closed eyes. His normally powerful body was limp, and I could barely detect any rise and fall in his rib cage. Turning away, I reached for Frank's hand, leaving our shepherd-cross companion stretched out on the polished steel surface of the examining room table.

I barely remember the drive home. Lost in worry, I didn't realize we had reached the turnoff to our ranch until I heard the frantic barking of the dog we laughingly called "Yaqui's Great Enemy." From behind his front-yard fence, Yaqui's Great Enemy, who guarded the house at the crossroads, dashed back and forth, waiting for Yaqui's reciprocal challenge. When greeted with silence, he bounced to a standstill, stared at the car, then trotted off toward his den under the porch.

After Frank left for work I wandered about the house, picking aimlessly at chores. Yaqui's pal, Simba, a hefty mastiff, padded quietly after me, stopping every so often to gaze up at me with questioning eyes.

Dinner that night was subdued as we reassured ourselves that Yaqui would pull through. Both Frank and I privately chastised ourselves for what had happened.

Six months earlier, we had moved onto a ranch in the foothills of the Pine Nut Mountains in western Nevada. Our dogs, who had been used to the confines of backyard suburban living, thrived in their new freedom, spending their days sniffing around the barns and corrals. Often, though, we found them standing by the fence that surrounded the ranch buildings, looking out across the pastures. Yielding to their entreating eyes, we would take them for walks, letting them prowl through the sagebrush, following tantalizing scents and animal trails. In time, we all became familiar with the sparse desert landscape.

Although we made a conscientious effort to keep the gates shut, occasionally we found one open and the dogs nowhere in sight. But even when they were gone for hours, we rarely worried. There was almost no traffic, and because they were big dogs, we believed them safe from coyotes and mountain lions.

One evening in early December, Simba returned alone. We called into the darkness, listening for Yaqui's answering bark, but all we heard were the echoes of our own voices. A dozen times during the night we rose to check the circle of light on the porch, but the dawn arrived as empty as our spirits.

For three days we searched. At first we drove for miles along the ranch roads with Simba beside us in our old Suburban, hoping she might give some sign that Yaqui was nearby. Then, as gray clouds moved in from the west and temperatures dropped into the low teens, Frank and I saddled up our horses. We crisscrossed the brush-covered slopes and picked our way through boulder-clogged draws, looking for recent tracks or signs of blood.

On the second afternoon, while we scoured the upper limits of the foothills close to where Red Canyon sliced into the mountain front, we thought we heard his voice, but when the wind settled, the countryside was still. Only the rhythmic sound of Simba's panting broke the silence.

By the morning of the fourth day, snow was falling steadily. Frank stared out the window as he dressed for work. Neither one of us wanted to verbalize what we were thinking. Then as he picked up his jacket, he called out, "Come on, let's check the road to Red Canyon one more time."

Straining to see, we eased the Suburban along the barely discernible dirt track to the top of the slope. There, in the eerie silence of the swirling snow, we sat for a moment. Both of us sensed the search was at an end.

Just as Frank slipped the car into gear, Simba whined. I turned around as she leaped up and pressed her nose against the rear window. She pawed at the glass, her tail waving. It batted against the backs of the seats and stirred the air above our heads. Staring at us, the huge dog tipped her head back and emitted a long, low howl.

No more than twenty feet away was a black shadow, struggling out of the gloom. Clamped firmly on his right front paw was a large, steel jaw-trap. Behind the trap, attached by a knotted strand of barbed wire, trailed a thick, four-foot-long tree limb. The wood was gouged with teeth marks and the wire crimped where desperate jaws had torn at the rusty surface, exposing slashes of fresh steel.

All three of us piled out of the Suburban. Simba licked her friend's face. Joyfully, she romped away from him, then returning, she bowed her greeting, challenging him to play. But Yaqui only stood and shivered. Cautiously, she approached him again and sniffed at the paw that was swollen beyond recognition, engulfing the metal teeth.

Frank grabbed the trap and stepped on the release mechanism. The rusty hinges refused to budge. He stamped harder on the lever and the jaws scraped opened. Yaqui sank to the ground, whimpering softly as we pried his foot loose.

Scooping up Yaqui's emaciated body, Frank laid him gently in my arms for the trip to the veterinary hospital. When we approached the main crossroads, Frank slowed, and there as always, barking behind his fence, was Yaqui's Great Enemy. Too feeble to sit up, Yaqui lifted his head and gave one weak woof. Right then I should have known he would be all right.

The following day the doctor called to say he thought Yaqui would survive but definitely would lose his leg. The day after that, he said Yaqui would keep his leg but would surely lose his foot. The third day, the foot seemed out of danger but a few toes would have to go.

Yaqui survived with all his digits intact, but for the next ten years he wore a prominent scar across the top of his foot. On cooler days he walked with a faint limp, but his spirit was never scarred.

We identified the wood attached to the trap as belonging to a species of tree that grows only in the upper reaches of the canyons, many hundreds of feet above where we found Yaqui. Dragging the trap and its anchor, he had struggled beyond the limits of credible endurance to return to us, trusting that we would be there for him. Thankfully, we were.

~Eleanor Whitney Nelson
Chicken Soup for the Dog Lover's Soul

Loving Our Dogs

Bringing Out
the Best in Us

*The great pleasure of a dog is that you may make a fool of yourself
with him and not only will he not scold you,
but he will make a fool of himself too.*
~Samuel Butler, Notebooks, 1912

Body and Soul

I was fifteen years old when I began my long battle with anorexia nervosa and bulimia. As a teenager, I succumbed to the intense peer pressure to be thin. But when I started dieting I soon lost control, and I couldn't stop losing weight. When I dropped below ninety-five pounds, my frightened parents took me to the hospital. Back in 1969, few people had even heard of eating disorders, and neither my parents nor the doctors knew how to help me.

Finally, after four years and several prolonged hospital stays, I forced myself to get better. I managed to gain back every pound I'd lost and resolved to get on with my life. I even had a boyfriend.

Then one day my best friend told me she'd seen my guy out with another girl. "He hates me because I'm so fat," I sobbed.

And so it wasn't long before I'd all but stopped eating again. My family watched in helpless horror as I repeatedly collapsed from malnutrition. I felt so ashamed and couldn't bear the pain I was causing them.

Finally I left home, hoping to make a fresh start. I packed my car and drove until I ran out of money in Phoenix, Arizona. I liked the Phoenix climate. The warm sun felt good on my emaciated body.

Unfortunately, hot sunny weather also meant lots of short shorts and halter tops. I was painfully thin, but whenever I looked in the mirror I was horrified by what I saw. "I need to lose more weight," I panicked.

Whenever I went out with friends I ate and drank normally, but afterward I always raced to the restroom to purge. The more I purged, the more depressed I became. Depression led to binge eating, which led to even more purging. I knew I was slowly killing myself. I didn't want to die, but my illness was stronger than my will to live.

I went to psychologists and attended support groups, but they didn't help. Ultimately, I grew so weak I had to quit my job and go on disability. My health steadily deteriorated as I lost irreplaceable muscle tissue. My seventy-eight-pound body was so ravaged from malnutrition, my kidneys began to shut down and I was in constant pain.

"There's nothing more I can do," my doctor said bluntly. "Barring a miracle, you're going to die."

My brother Robert brought me home to Michigan, where I took an apartment, crawled into bed and waited for God to take me. I hated my life and could hardly wait for it to be over.

The first morning I opened my eyes in my new place, I discovered a pair of liquid brown eyes looking back at me. It was Cassie, the Australian shepherd a friend in Phoenix had given me just before I'd left town.

"I suppose you need to go out," I sighed, struggling to my feet and putting on a robe.

At the front door, Cassie just sat there gazing up at me. Ruff! "You come, too," she seemed to be saying, and grudgingly, I shuffled off to get dressed.

A few days later in a nearby field, Cassie started pouncing at my feet and barking, eager to romp. "Go on ahead," I said, but Cassie wouldn't leave my side. She barked and barked until I finally got the message and began walking with her. Daggers of pain shot through my nutrient-starved bones with every footfall. I cried out in agony, but every time I stopped moving Cassie waited at my side and wouldn't quit barking until we were again on our way. As painful as it was, I felt my blood—life—stirring in me for the first time in a very long while.

Somehow, Cassie knew there was something terribly wrong with me. She sensed my every mood and refused to leave my side. When I grew despondent, she curled up beside me. When I sobbed in pain, she licked away my tears.

Once, on one of my bad days, I asked my sister Pam to adopt Cassie. "I don't have enough strength to take care of her anymore," I explained.

Pam shook her head no. "I won't take her," she said firmly.

"Please reconsider," I begged. "Cassie needs a good home and someone who will love her."

"She already has both of those things," Pam insisted. As hot tears filled my eyes, she hugged me and said, "Don't you understand, Cynthia? Right now that dog is the only thing keeping you alive."

She was right. I needed a miracle to stay alive, and Cassie was that miracle. She was my constant companion, my best and truest friend.

For Cassie's sake, I forced myself to eat. A few raw vegetables. A dry turkey sandwich. After all, I thought, if I died, who would take care of my Cassie? Who would brush her fur, romp with her in the fields or cuddle with her on the sofa at night?

Cassie refused to let me surrender to despair. Her confidence in my ability to overcome my illness became infectious. Our daily walks made me physically stronger. Cassie's love and understanding gave me the will to fight on.

In time, I ventured out to church and made several friends. At a singles' dance, I met a man named Philip. When he asked me out I said yes. We fell in love, and a year later we were married. And even though the doctors said that because of my health it could never happen, miraculously I got pregnant—not just once, but twice.

Today, I still battle my anorexia, but now I have four more reasons to fight my disease: Philip, my teenaged stepdaughter, Corrie, and my two young sons, Trevor and Zachary.

Cassie is still my constant companion. Wherever I go, she's always right there by my side. But at ten years of age, Cassie's health has begun to go downhill.

Cassie once took care of me, but now the tables are turned; it's my turn to take care of her. Often, with an understanding look, with a gentle paw on my arm, she seems to tell me it will soon be time for her to go.

This wonderful dog once gave me the courage to live. Now she's giving me the courage to live on without her when she goes. I won't let her down.

~Cynthia Knisely as told to Bill Holton
Chicken Soup for the Cat and Dog Lover's Soul

The Joy of the Run

All the men in my family for three generations have been doctors. That was what we did. I got my first stethoscope when I was six. I heard stories of the lives my grandfather and my father had saved, the babies they'd delivered, the nights they'd sat up with sick children. I was shown where my name would go on the brass plaque on the office door. And so the vision of what I would become was engraved in my imagination.

But as college neared, I began to feel that becoming a doctor was not engraved upon my heart. For one thing, I reacted to situations very differently from my dad. I'd seen him hauled out at three in the morning to attend a child who'd developed pneumonia because his parents hadn't brought him to the office earlier. I would have given them a hard time, but he never would. "Parents want their kids to be all right so bad, they sometimes can't admit the child's really sick," he said forgivingly. And then there were the terrible things like the death of a ten-year-old from lockjaw—that I knew I couldn't handle. What troubled me most was my fear that I wasn't the son my father imagined. I didn't dare tell him about my uncertainty and hoped I could work it out on my own.

With this dilemma heavy on my mind the summer before college, I was given a challenge that I hoped would be a distraction. A patient had given my father an English setter pup as payment for his help. Dad kept a kennel of bird dogs on our farm, which I trained. As usual, Dad turned the dog over to me.

Jerry was a willing pup of about ten months. Like many setters, he was mostly white, with a smattering of red spots. His solid-red ears stood out too far from his head, though, giving him a clown-like look. Just the sight of him gave me a much-needed chuckle. He mastered the basics: sit, stay, down, walk. His only problem was "come." Once out in the tall grass, he liked to roam. I'd call and give a pip on the training whistle. He would turn and look at me, then go on about his business.

When we finished his lessons, I would sit with him under an old pin oak and talk. I'd go over what he was supposed to know, and sometimes I'd talk about me. "Jerry," I'd say, "I just don't like being around sick people. What would you do if you were me?" Jerry would sit on his haunches and look directly at my eyes, turning his head from side to side, trying to read the significance in my voice. He was so serious that I'd laugh out loud and forget how worried I was.

After supper one evening, I took him out to the meadow for exercise. We had walked about 100 yards into the knee-high grass when a barn swallow, skimming for insects in the fading light, buzzed Jerry's head. Jerry stood transfixed. After a moment, he chased the swallow. The bird flew low, zigzagging back and forth, teasing and playing, driving Jerry into an exhilarated frenzy of running. The bird led him down to the pond and back along the meadow fence, as though daring him to follow. Then it vanished high in the sky. Jerry stood looking after it for a while and then ran to me panting, as full of himself as I'd ever seen him.

In the days that followed, I noticed that his interest in hunting faded as his enthusiasm for running grew. He would just take off through the grass, fast as a wild thing. I knew when he'd scented quail because he'd give a little cock of his head as he passed them. He knew what he was supposed to do; he just didn't do it. When he'd finally come back, exhausted and red-eyed, he'd lie on the ground with an expression of such doggy contentment that I had a hard time bawling him out.

I started again from the beginning. For a few minutes he would listen solemnly. Then he'd steal the bandanna from my back pocket and race across the meadow, nose into the wind, legs pumping hard. Running was a kind of glory for him. Despite my intense desire to train him well, I began to feel a strange sense of joy when he ran.

I had never failed with a dog before, but I was surely failing now. When September came, I finally had to tell Dad that this bird dog wouldn't hunt. "Well, that ties it," he said. "We'll have to neuter him and pass him off to someone in town for a pet. A dog that won't do what he's born to do is sure not worth much."

I was afraid being a house dog would kill Jerry's spirit. The next day, I had a long talk with Jerry under the oak tree. "This running thing is gonna get you locked up," I said. "Can't you just get on the birds and then run?" He raised his eyes to my voice, looking out from under his lids in the way he did when he was shamed. Now I felt sad. I lay back and he lay down next to me, his head on my chest. As I scratched his ears, I closed my eyes and thought desperately about both our problems.

Early the next Saturday, Dad took Jerry out to see for himself what the dog could do. At first, Jerry worked the field like a pro. Dad looked at me oddly, as if I'd fooled him about Jerry.

At that very moment the dog took off.

"What in hell is that dog doing?"

"Running," I said. "He likes to run."

And Jerry ran. He ran along the fence row, then jumped it, his lean body an amazing arc. He ran as though running were all ease and grace, as though it made him a part of the field, the light, the air.

"That's not a hunting dog, that's a deer!" my father said. As I stood watching my dog fail the most important test of his life, Dad put his hand on my shoulder. "We've got to face it — he's not going to measure up."

The next day I packed for school, then walked out to the kennel to say goodbye to Jerry. He wasn't there. I wondered if Dad had already taken him to town. The thought that I had failed us both made me miserable. But when I went into the house, to my great relief Dad was in his chair near the fireplace, reading, with Jerry asleep at his feet.

As I entered, my father closed his book and looked directly at me. "Son, I know this dog doesn't do what he should," he said, "but what he does do is something grand. Lifts a man's spirits to see him go." He continued to look at me steadily. For a moment I felt he could see into my very heart. "What makes any living thing worth the time of day," Dad went on, "is that it is what it is—and knows it. Knows it in its bones."

I took a solid breath. "Dad," I said, "I don't think I can do medicine." He lowered his eyes, as though he heard at last what he dreaded to hear. His expression was so sad, I thought my heart would break. But when he looked at me again, it was with a regard I hadn't seen before.

"I know that," he said solemnly. "What really convinced me was when I watched you with this no-account mutt. You should've seen your face when he went off running." Imagining his intense disappointment, I felt close to tears. I wished I had it in me to do what would make him happy. "Dad," I said, "I'm sorry."

He looked at me sharply. "Son, of course I'm disappointed that you're not going to be a doctor. But I'm not disappointed in you.

"Think about what you tried to do with Jerry," he said. "You expected him to be the hunter you trained him to be. But he just isn't. How do you feel about that?"

I looked at Jerry asleep, his paws twitching. He seemed to be running even in his dreams. "I thought I'd failed for a while," I said. "But when I watched him run and saw how he loves it, I guess I thought that was a good enough thing."

"It is a good thing," my father said. He looked at me keenly. "Now we'll just wait to see how you run."

He slapped me on the shoulder, said good night and left me. At that moment I understood my father as I never had before, and the love I felt for him seemed to fill the room. I sat down next to Jerry and scratched him between his shoulder blades. "I wonder how I'll run too," I whispered to him. "I sure do."

Jerry lifted his head just slightly, licked my hand, stretched his legs, and then went back to the joyful place of his dreams.

~W. W. Meade
Chicken Soup for the Pet Lover's Soul

More than Medicine

I believe in prayer. It's the best way we have to draw strength from heaven.
~Josephine Baker

Tuesday was my day to make the housecalls in our multi-doctor veterinary practice—not my favorite thing to do. I felt isolated working outside the safety of the clinic, yet having to make crucial medical decisions on my own. The cats always hid, and the dogs were always meaner at home. And the people? Well, you never knew what sort you'd run into. I was uncomfortable dealing with the people on their own home turf. As a new graduate depending on textbooks and medical notes to get me through, Tuesdays were definitely a pain in my calendar.

This wasn't what I had envisioned when I'd decided to become a veterinarian. I'd had noble dreams of healing animals, which I felt at least semiqualified to do. But I was at a loss having to deal with people. Somehow my professors had failed to mention two very important facts: Every pet comes with an owner, and every case costs money. My boss, who always had one eye on the bottom line, constantly reminded me of the second.

Cheryl, our technician, had our schedule for the day and plotted our route. Handing me the clipboard, I could see she had saved the best for last, a sick dog in the not-so-affluent end of town.

Cheryl packed our supplies for the day, I packed my insecurities and a medical text, and we both piled into the house-call van for another day's rounds. The first several calls went relatively smoothly with the exception of one junkyard dog with a torn toenail. I was surprised we left with all our fingers intact.

As we parked in front of our last stop for the day, I sighed.

The house was old and rundown, and the lawn hadn't been mowed for a very long time. "Hope this dog isn't too sick." I said, " It doesn't look like these people can pay for veterinary services."

We knocked on the door that was presently answered by Mrs. Johnson, an elderly lady in a flowered-print housedress. "Oh, doctor!" she exclaimed. "I am so glad you're finally here. Blackie just ain't doin' right. He can hardly pick his head up. He's back in the kitchen. Come right this way."

Mrs. Johnson led us through a remarkably neat and tidy home to the kitchen. It was a pleasant room with flowerpots in the window and fresh-baked bread on the counter. Blackie, a black furry Heinz 57, lay on a pile of blankets in the corner.

Cheryl got the necessary information from Mrs. Johnson as I took a look at Blackie. His gums were pale, his pulses were thready and his heart was rapidly beating. This was one sick little dog.

I explained to Mrs. Johnson that Blackie was very sick and would need to be hospitalized. "The hospital stay and the tests could be very expensive," I told her. "And I can't be sure that we'll be able to save Blackie."

"Doctor, I want you to try," she replied. "I just know you will be able to help him. You see, I'm gonna be praying for Blackie — and for you too, doctor."

Cheryl took a twenty-dollar deposit from Mrs. Johnson. It was all the old lady could spare, but she promised to come up with more in a few days and to pay the rest over time.

We carried Blackie out to the van with Mrs. Johnson calling "God love ya!" after us.

I shook my head wearily as I pulled away from the curb. Here I was with a hopeless case and an owner that couldn't possibly pay the bill. I guess the clinic will just have to eat this one, I thought. I wasn't looking forward to telling my boss. And Mrs. Johnson was a Bible-thumper to boot.

I didn't place much stock in faith healing. Either we could cure the dog or we couldn't.

Back to the clinic we went and began treatment, running the necessary tests. The results were discouraging at best. I called Mrs. Johnson and told her that Blackie had a condition called autoimmune hemolytic anemia—his body was destroying its own blood cells.

At the time, dogs rarely survived this disease; I asked her as gently as I could if she wanted to put Blackie to sleep.

"No, doctor," she said. "You keep him going overnight. Tomorrow I have prayer group and we're gonna pray for you and Blackie. Just trust God on this one."

The next day Blackie began showing signs of improvement.

His blood cell count was up a bit, and he now sat upright in his cage. I felt my skepticism slip a notch as I phoned Mrs. Johnson with the surprising news.

"Oh, I'd no doubt he'd be better today. You just keep on doing what you're doing, doctor. Me and the girls will keep on a-praying."

With each day that passed, Blackie showed more and more improvement. Humbled, I had no explanation for it. And Mrs. Johnson and the girls just kept on praying. After a week of hospitalization Blackie was back to his normal happy self, eating and wagging his tail.

I was shaken. Maybe there was something to this praying Mrs. Johnson and the girls had been doing. Many other dogs I'd seen had received the same treatment as Blackie and had died. Did God really care about this little black mutt?

We brought Blackie home to a jubilant Mrs. Johnson. "God bless you, doctor," she said. "God bless you."

I felt blessed. My experience with Mrs. Johnson and Blackie gave me the pieces I'd been missing—healing wasn't just about textbooks and medications. If it were, Blackie would never have made it. Now I knew healing was a team effort that involved God, me, the animals and the people who loved them. It was about compassion and faith and serving others.

The next Tuesday I found myself humming as I helped Cheryl load the van for our house-call rounds. What would the day bring? I didn't know, but I was ready to start on this week's adventure. I knew I wouldn't be alone.

~Liz Gunkelman, D.V.M.
Chicken Soup for the Cat and Dog Lover's Soul

Things We Can Learn from a Dog

1. Never pass up the opportunity to go for a joy ride.
2. Allow the experience of fresh air and the wind in your face to be pure ecstasy.
3. When loved ones come home, always run to greet them.
4. When it's in your best interest, always practice obedience.
5. Let others know when they've invaded your territory.
6. Take naps and always stretch before rising.
7. Run, romp and play daily.
8. Eat with gusto and enthusiasm.
9. Be loyal.
10. Never pretend to be something you're not.
11. If what you want lies buried, dig until you find it.
12. When someone is having a bad day, be silent, sit close by and nuzzle them gently.
13. Delight in the simple joy of a long walk.
14. Thrive on attention and let people touch you.
15. Avoid biting when a simple growl will do.
16. On hot days, drink lots of water and lie under a shady tree.
17. When you are happy, dance around and wag your entire body.

18. No matter how often you are criticized, don't buy into the guilt thing and pout. Run right back and make friends.

~Joy Nordquist
Chicken Soup for the Pet Lover's Soul

24

An Unlikely Angel

If we were all like angels, the world would be a heavenly place.
~Author Unknown

It was just before Christmas. An angry middle-aged man stood at the counter of the animal shelter, gripping the leash of an aging German shepherd. "Why won't you take him?" he shouted. "I need to get him off my hands!"

The adoption counselor tried once more to explain. "At fourteen, Samson is too old to be a good adoption candidate," she said.

"Well, then just take him and put him down," the man yelled. "I want to be rid of him."

"We don't take animals just to put them down," the counselor explained. "May I ask why you no longer wish to keep the dog?"

"I just can't stand the sight of him," the man hissed, "and if you won't put him down, I'll shoot him myself."

Trying not to show her horror, the counselor pointed out that shooting an animal was illegal. She urged the man to consult with his veterinarian for other options.

"I'm not spending any more money on this animal," the man grumbled and, yanking the leash, he stalked out.

Concerned, the counselor wrote down the license plate of the man's truck and offered up a quick prayer for Samson.

A few days later, a German shepherd was found abandoned. He was brought to the shelter, and the staff recognized him as Samson. The town where he had been abandoned was where his owner lived.

The man was contacted by the police and, under questioning, admitted that distraught over his recent divorce, he had sought revenge through the shepherd. He hadn't even wanted the dog, but he fought to keep him to spite his wife. Once his wife was gone, he couldn't bear to see the animal. The man was charged with abandonment, and Samson came to stay at the shelter.

The wife and the couple's son were located in Pennsylvania. They were horrified to hear what had happened to their dog and agreed immediately to have him come live with them.

There was just one problem: The wife was nearly broke after the divorce and their initial move. She could take no time off from work to drive to New Hampshire and get the dog, and she couldn't afford any other method of getting him to her. She hated to have Samson in the shelter any longer but didn't know what to do. "We'll come up with something," the staff assured her, but in their hearts they didn't know what. They were concerned, as well. Samson had lived with his family all his life. Within a few weeks, his whole world had been turned upside down. He was beginning to mope, and the staff could tell by his eyes that if he wasn't back with his family soon, he would give up.

Christmas was only two weeks away when the angel arrived. He came by pickup truck in the form of a man in his mid-thirties. Through a friend of a shelter staffer, he had heard about Samson's plight. He was willing to drive Samson to Pennsylvania, and he would do it before Christmas.

The staff was thrilled with the offer, but cautious. Why would a stranger drive hundreds of miles out of his way to deliver a dog to people he didn't know? They had to make sure he was legitimate and that Samson wouldn't be sold to meat dealers or dumped along the interstate.

The man understood their concerns and, thankfully, checked out to be an upstanding citizen. In the course of the conversation, he explained why he had come forward.

"Last year, I left my dog in my van while I went to do some grocery shopping," he explained. "While I was inside, the van caught fire.

I heard people hollering and rushed out to see my van engulfed in flames. My dog meant everything to me, and he was trapped. I tried to get to the van, but people restrained me. Then I heard someone shouting, 'The dog is safe! The dog is safe!' I looked over, and there was this man I'd never seen before, holding my dog. He had risked his own life to get my dog out. I'll forever be in his debt. Just when you don't think there are heroes any more, one comes along.

"I vowed then and there that if I ever had the chance to do someone a good turn when it came to a beloved pet, that I would. When I heard about Samson and his family, I knew this was my chance, so here I am."

The shelter staff was amazed. They all knew about the van rescue story. It had been in all the papers, and the shelter had even given the rescuer a reward, but they had never dreamed that Samson's angel was connected to this earlier good deed.

A few days later, Samson and his angel were on their way. The dog seemed to know he was going home, because his ears perked up and his eyes were brighter than they had been in some time.

Just before Christmas, the mail brought one of the best cards the shelter had ever received. Along with a thank you note were photos of a deliriously happy Samson romping with his family in the snow and snuggling with them by their Christmas tree. Samson was truly where he belonged, and the staff knew he would live out his days happily there.

They also knew that Samson's journey home was a true Christmas miracle, and that angels—and heroes—may still appear when you need them, even in the most unlikely forms.

~Crystal Ward Kent
Chicken Soup for the Soul: Christmas Treasury for Kids

25

Killer Angels

*Hope begins in the dark, the stubborn hope that if you just show up and try
to do the right thing, the dawn will come.*
~Anne Lamott

I had just graduated from veterinary school, and I was volunteering at the local shelter in Twin Falls, Idaho. As I looked down at the dog napping in her run, I knew I was going to have to wake her up to put her "to sleep." What a cruel euphemism.

She was a Heinz 57 mixed-breed with no name, no home, no hope. She was horrifically malnourished, and her coat was a mass of mats and burrs.

In a way, she was lucky to be here. Found on the side of the road—like living garbage—she'd been left to die in a remote area of our county.

The kind rancher who found her brought her to the local shelter where she joined dozens of other cuties and uglies pressing against the front of the cages hoping to catch the eye of someone who had a heart and home big enough to give them another chance.

Problem was there were too many homeless pets and not enough homes. Day after day for a week the dog waited and waited, her still-wagging tail marking the time.

But on this day, her time was up. No one had adopted her; like many in the shelter, the animals were too big, too small, too hairy, too young, too old. Without enough cages to hold all that came through our doors, we were prepared to end her life quickly and without suffering. "Better than starving to death in the country," I said, finding little solace in the words.

I was inspired to enter this profession because of a deep love of animals. I had been highly trained and entrusted to save lives and prevent pain and suffering. Yet here I was about to end the life of this innocent creature. I hated this part of the job, but I had to do it. Choking back my emotions, I readied myself to perform the procedure for which I'd been trained.

I set her on the table, and she wiggled her gaunt frame with delight as I spoke some soothing words and patted her head. The tempo of her tail quickened as she looked up at my face. Looking into her eyes, I saw total trust, unconditional love and absolute loyalty. I felt the cruel irony of what was taking place. God's precious creatures, embodying the kindest virtues on the planet, being killed for the crime of not being wanted. She held out her leg for me to inject and licked my hand. She was ready. I wasn't.

I collapsed onto the dog and held her tight as I bathed her with tears. Never, ever would I do a convenience euthanasia again. I'd euthanize a pet if it was suffering terribly, or had an incurable disease, but never again because of an uncaring owner's mere request.

I took the dog back to my veterinary practice and named her G. H.—short for Good Home. I'd observed over the years that people who raised litters of puppies or kittens always said, "I just want to find them a 'good home.'"

I soon entrusted G. H. to a loving client who had a heart and home big enough to welcome yet another four-legged family member.

Saving G. H. set me on a new path as a veterinarian. Although my hands still held the power of death, my heart didn't. Now, whenever I look into the dancing liquid eyes of a pet, brimming with love, I realize that looks can save. They did me.

~Marty Becker, D.V.M.
Chicken Soup for the Cat and Dog Lover's Soul

Pets Teach Peace

I grew up on a farm in New Jersey. We had two hundred chickens, fifty pigeons, five pigs, three dogs, three cats and a cow. As a teenager, I had many soulful moments in the chicken pen, where the chickens would cluck to me and I would pour my heart out to them, expressing all my adolescent frustrations—at my parents, who wouldn't let me do whatever I wanted; at my friends, who scorned me; at my teachers, who didn't appreciate my efforts; and at the world, so full of injustices.

We physically punished our dogs when they were bad. The standard response to a soiled rug or chewed slipper was to hold it against a dog's nose and beat her with a newspaper or a hand. My favorite dog was Vixen, a collie/German shepherd mix. When Vixen would do something bad, I would let out my repressed adolescent fury at her, yelling, "You bad, bad, #$%^! dog! You're so #$%# bad." Vixen would sulk away, head lowered. Such events were an emotional release for me, and now that I reflect on it, probably confusing for her.

Many years later, I was living in the city with my wife Sara. At that time, I was starting a "Peace Studies" program at the University of Wisconsin-Milwaukee. I had been reading Dr. Martin Luther King Jr., Mahatma Gandhi and other proponents of nonviolence. I was very impressed by the promise that nonviolence would help create a better society, and I was starting to teach it to my college students.

In 1985, we acquired a puppy named Simone. I took Simone to the vet to get her first puppy shots. While I was waiting in the veterinary clinic, I picked up a pamphlet, "Caring for Your Dog." The pamphlet said in no uncertain terms, "Never hit your dog!" The reason it gave was that if you hit your dog, your pet could never be sure whether you were going to pet or beat it when you extended your hand.

Here is the perfect opportunity to test my commitment to non-violence, I said to myself as I read that pamphlet. We will raise Simone nonviolently!

When I went home and told Sara about my desire to put the theory of nonviolence into practice with Simone, she enthusiastically agreed, saying, "We don't spank our children, and they are not badly behaved."

We never hit Simone. Instead, when she did something we didn't like, we would change the tone of our voice, telling her that her behavior was bad. She became so sensitive to our verbal commands that all either Sara or I had to do was lower our voice, and Simone knew she had done something bad. Everyone who knew her said she was the most well-behaved dog they had ever seen. Simone never begged at the table because I would lower my voice and tell her, "No begging!" In fact, sometimes I didn't even have to say anything; just scowling was enough to get her to behave.

Both Sara and I teach adults nurturing parenting skills. It is very hard to convince parents that they shouldn't spank their children. Eighty percent of parents in the United States think it is all right to hit their children, in spite of solid research that shows that children who are physically punished earn less money, don't achieve as much education and are more likely to be incarcerated than children who are raised without spanking. Arguing with parents that spanking is a bad practice is fruitless. Parents insist that as children they were spanked, and they are all right. They can't imagine how a child could be raised without spanking. They say things like, "How else can you teach right and wrong to a young child? After all, a pat on the backside does not really hurt."

Often, telling parents that you don't spank your own kids doesn't help because parents tell you that maybe your kids don't need discipline, but theirs do. Instead, I always counter with the story of

Simone, who is perfectly behaved and has never been hit. I tell my students, "If I can raise a dog to be compliant without hitting her, surely we can raise our children nonviolently. After all, we have the gift of speech to communicate with children. It is much better to tell children what we want, set clear limits for their behavior, let them learn from the natural consequences of their actions and reward them for positive behavior. For, like Simone, our children want our approval. They want to please us."

Many students have told me that this story makes a positive impression upon them, more so than my citing statistics about how damaging corporal punishment is for children. One, a Baptist minister and an officer in the reserves, now preaches about nonviolent parenting in his sermons. As an adult, I use my peacemaking skills to resolve conflicts so that I am no longer a tinderbox of repressed emotions like the teenager who used to hurl obscenities at his dog.

~Dr. Ian Harris and Sara Spence
Chicken Soup for the Soul Stories for a Better World

Guiding Me Home

Attitude is a little thing that makes a big difference.
~Winston Churchill

I had to retreat to a place where I could feel safe and in control—my home, in a big comfortable chair in the corner of my living room. There I would sit, afraid to venture outside, in a newly darkened world I never chose.

A few months earlier, I was on top of the world: My daughter was about to leave for college, I liked my job, and Marie and I were looking forward to being newlyweds all over again. Then, at a surprise party for my fortieth birthday, I began to open all those cards that would rib me about the "Big 4-0," and found I couldn't read the words—I had to ask my wife to help me. "The first sign of advancing age," my friends joked. Within weeks I'd lost most of my sight, and the doctor declared me legally blind.

I was fortunate to have a supportive family and many good friends, some associated with Lions Clubs, whose mission involves helping the visually impaired. The Lions Clubs also support an organization called the Fidelco Guide Dog Foundation. My friends encouraged me to apply, but I wasn't a "dog person." How would I take care of a dog when I could hardly take care of myself?

One day my wife told me how hard it was for her to watch what blindness had done to me: how she hated to leave me alone at home every day and go off to work; how scared and helpless she felt, even guilty, because she could see and I could not. I realized then that blindness didn't just happen to me—it also happened to her, my daughter, my family and my friends. Not yet convinced, I applied for a dog.

In the meantime, a friend gave me a tape-recorded talk by a blind man named Tom Sullivan, speaking at a Lions convention. He told his audience that because he had a guide dog, he did anything he wanted to do and that nothing got in his way. "In this life," he said, "you have to change negatives into positives; you have to believe in your own human spirit and continually build pride in yourself." His definition for the word pride is "Personal Responsibility for Individual Daily Effort," and he talked about how his guide dog changed his life. Listening to that talk changed my life, too. By the time I played the tape for the fourth time, I stopped feeling sorry for myself.

The call from Fidelco came two days before Christmas. They had a dog for me and his name was Karl. My daughter, home on Christmas break from college, and my wife, Marie, who had taken a couple of days off for this monumental moment, were both standing at the window when Dave, the man who would serve as my trainer in using Karl, rang the doorbell. I heard the dog bounding into the room. He ran straight to me as if he knew who needed him most. I sat still as this huge German shepherd checked me out. When he seemed satisfied, Karl placed his head in my hands. I asked him, "Are you the one?" and he licked my face.

I petted the dog and "saw" him with my hands. He had a large head and soft pointed ears. We sat on the floor together, and I scratched his back. Then he rolled over so I could rub his belly. When he snuggled close, I realized this dog was a loving, gentle giant.

The training was tough and stressful for both Karl and me. Some days went well; others showed no progress. During our second week of training we were missing curbs and failing to walk down the sidewalk in a straight line. I felt as though Karl wasn't listening to any of my commands. I was terribly frustrated, and I could tell Dave was getting frustrated as well. Poor Karl just didn't know what to do. All of a sudden Dave yelled out, "Will the both of you just stop!" I gave Karl the command to halt, thinking, All right Karl, you're in trouble now.

Dave said, "You two have got to be the worst looking guide-dog team I've ever seen in my life. Karl goes to the left and George, you try to go to the right. Karl tries to walk you around obstacles, and you walk into them. Karl stops at curbs and you keep going." This wasn't what I expected to hear. It sounded like I was in trouble, not Karl. Dave continued, "George, you have to start trusting your dog. Follow his lead, listen to him! Karl can see and you can't. George—you're blind."

I stood there in shock as Dave continued, "Let Karl do his job. His job is to guide you and keep you safe. If you trust him he'll never let you down."

That moment marked another shift in my life. "I'll try," I said, and picked up the harness. I put all my trust in Karl and let him be my eyes. We began walking as a real team for the first time. I could sense the confidence in his stride, and for the first time we picked up our pace. I knew we had a long way to go, but I felt reborn as trust became more important than fear.

The training continued, and with Karl at my side, we went to Boston and New York. We rode in taxis, buses and subways. We visited malls, dined in restaurants and took walks in the country. Then came the last day of my training during the worst rainstorm I can remember, but that didn't bother us—we had made it. It was official: Karl and I were a team.

Before my wife and I went to bed that night, I told her of a plan I had devised to test my new skills. Marie worked in the town where I grew up. My plan was to go to work with her the next day and walk to my parents' house (just under two miles), spend the day with them and then walk back to her office. She thought I had lost my mind. Cocky and confident, I told her I could do this walk—well, with my eyes closed. "I grew up in this town; I know every turn and every street. Besides, I have Karl, so don't worry." She reluctantly agreed.

I was soon to learn this would be more than just a walk.

As Karl and I set out, the first challenge we faced was the most dangerous thing a blind person has to do: safely cross a busy street. I picked up the harness and listened for a lull in the traffic. Hearing no oncoming cars, I gave Karl the command "Forward," and our walk began. Although he and I had crossed many streets during training, this was the first time we were alone. I could feel how focused he was, even more alert to danger. As we reached the other side of the street, he halted to wait for my next command. He stopped at every curb and walked me around every obstacle.

Everything went well until we reached about the one-mile marker. On a busy, narrow street, I second-guessed myself, but even worse, doubted Karl. A large vehicle passed us and it sounded too close, as if it were on the sidewalk right in front of us. I gave Karl the command to "Halt," dropped the harness and stood there in a panic, leash in my hand. I remember thinking, What are you trying to do? You have no right to be out here!

I stood there until a man came up to me and said, "You appear to be lost. Can I help you?" Instead of accepting, I thought back to what Dave had said. Always trust the dog; he'll never let you down. I bent over and took Karl's head in my hands and asked him, "What do you think, Karl, do you think we need help, do you think we can make it?" Licking my face, he calmed me. That simple act of love reminded me I had nothing to fear as long as he was by my side. I thanked the person for his offer of help and explained, "I'll be fine. I have this dog and I trust him to keep me safe. Well, we have to get going, because a new journey begins today." It occurred to me that my dog also represents my own body, and that I have to learn to trust it as well.

In that moment, my dream of independence became reality. Karl and I crossed each street and passed the landmarks I knew were there: the church I attended as a child, my old school and the playground where I learned to play basketball.

As we crossed our last street before my parents' house, I knew their front gate would be about seventy yards ahead on the left. When I felt we had gone about forty yards, I told Karl, "Find left inside," to find an opening that would take us off the sidewalk to left inside. I repeated the command several times and started to worry we'd gone too far. What if he'd missed the gate? That wouldn't be a huge problem—we'd just have to backtrack a little. But what if I had taken a wrong turn, or miscounted streets? If that was true, I had no idea where we were. What would I do now? I thought: Trust the dog and we can do it.

All of a sudden Karl turned hard to the left, picked up his head and put his nose on the gate of my parents' front yard. We had made it! I dropped to my knees, wrapped my arms around Karl, cried and thanked God for the incredible gift of this dog.

I am now Executive Director of the Fidelco Guide Dog Foundation. Once afraid to leave home, I now travel across America speaking to a variety of groups and organizations. I help them realize their own inner strengths, and I remind them that we're all here to turn negatives into positives and learn to deal effectively with our own life-changing situations. I help others realize, as I came to realize, what an incredible difference these dogs make in people's lives. I love this job!

In many ways, my life is better now than when I could see. And it's hard to imagine life without Karl; he's so much a part of me. If given the choice of sight, but living without Karl—well, let's just say I'd have to give that a lot of thought, because I can't imagine life without him.

~George Salpietro
Chicken Soup to Inspire the Body and Soul

Rescued by a Drowning Dog

"**B**ubba, this is the last time," I bellow as the big brown dog jumps to the table, grabs the script I am working on and bolts away. He skitters across the kitchen floor as I give chase.

"No!" I shriek in anticipation of the disaster. A large clay pot crashes, its dirt-and-flower contents emptied all over the floor.

"Darn you," I say. I slide to the floor and begin sobbing.

I don't want to be here. I don't want to be alone. Hurting this much. And I don't want to be dealing with this demon dog.

Why does anyone think animals are good companions? I wonder bitterly. They're no substitute for people and certainly no solace for loneliness.

But my husband Arnie had been a believer. Two years ago, Arnie proudly lugged home a large carton. "A surprise for you," he announced, as a filthy dog sprang from the box onto our new white sofa and leaped onto the end table, scattering my prized collection of miniature glass figures.

"How could you?" I asked Arnie in disbelief. "Get that mangy animal out of this house!" With that, the dog put his teeth into my new sweater.

It was hate at first sight for Bubba and me.

Arnie liked to say Bubba had a touch of German shepherd in his mutt mix. More like a touch of the devil. When Bubba and I were alone, he destroyed my clothes, broke cherished possessions and hid whatever project I was working on. When Arnie was around, he was Mr. Nice Dog.

"I don't see why you're always so angry with this guy," Arnie would say, stroking the big, coffee-colored head. "He's such a gentle dog." On cue, Bubba would settle at Arnie's feet, wag his tail leisurely and smirk. At me.

I tolerated Bubba because Arnie loved him. As he grew to almost one hundred pounds, the dog became part of our household but not of my heart. He was 100 percent Arnie's dog. Each evening as the clock chimed seven, Bubba plopped down on the area rug in the front hall, blocking the door, to await Arnie's homecoming.

One evening, Bubba waited and waited. The clock chimed eight, then nine. I joined Bubba in his anxiousness, pacing beside him. Finally, the bell rang. A policeman stood in my doorway twisting his hat. There had been an accident. Arnie was dead.

Friends and family came and went. I sat in my chair rocking. I think someone told me they were taking Bubba home. I don't remember much about the next few weeks. Until one day, the doorbell rang again, and Bubba was back.

He growled at me and dashed past, flying through the house, in and out of rooms. After a while, he quieted somewhat, his pace slowing. He took up vigil in the front hall, getting up only occasionally to search for Arnie, eat or ask to be let out.

When he needed out, I opened the back door to the fenced-in yard I shared with my neighbor. I tried a couple of times to walk him, but he snarled whenever I came near.

I only kept the ungrateful mutt because Arnie had loved him.

One day, two hours passed and darkness came before I noticed Bubba hadn't scratched at the door to be let back in. I called. No Bubba. I tried to switch on the back light only to be reminded that the outside electric had been disconnected because lights were being installed around my neighbor's new in-ground pool. It had just been filled, not even heated yet.... No, it couldn't be! Bubba hated water!

But the pool had a black liner.... I grabbed a flashlight and approached the water, panicking as I heard a whimper. There in the circle of my light aimed at the deep end was the forlorn, sodden dog, hanging by his paws onto the edge of the pool. He'd probably chased a chipmunk and fallen into the unfamiliar landmark, paddling around until his strength gave out.

I hauled Bubba from the cold water, dragged him back into the house and wrapped him in the nearest thing I could find: my favorite afghan. The last present Arnie had given me.

I held the dog close until his shivering subsided, then held him some more. He made no attempt to leave the security of my arms until the clock struck seven. It had been almost a year since Arnie had died, yet each night Bubba faithfully took up the vigil when the bell chimed. Tonight, he left my lap, started toward the front hall, and hesitated. Turning, he looked me in the eye and came back to my chair, settling at my feet.

I don't know which of us had been more oblivious to the other's pain, Bubba or me. But it took a nearly drowned dog to pull me out of my grief-induced isolation.

I imagined Arnie was smiling.

~Carren Strock
Chicken Soup for the Single's Soul

Going to the Dogs

One day my mom and I were sitting in her office looking at a magazine called *Humane Society News*. We read a very sad story about a New Jersey police dog named Solo that had been sent into a building to catch an armed suspect. The last thing Solo did before entering the building was to lick his owner's face. A few minutes later, Solo was shot and killed in the line of duty. I knew how sad that officer must have felt because my own dog, Kela, had recently died. I felt like my world had ended when I lost Kela. She had been my best friend since I could remember.

The article went on to tell about a fundraiser that was going on in New Jersey to help buy bulletproof vests for the police dogs there. I thought every police dog should be protected just like the police. I may be a kid, but why can't I do a fundraiser to help save the dogs in our area?

Then I found out that a bulletproof vest for a police dog costs $475. My mom thought it was a lot of money for an eleven-year-old girl to raise, but she told me to go ahead and try anyway.

We called our local Oceanside Police Department and found out that their dogs needed bulletproof vests. At that point, I realized that I needed a name for the fundraiser and thought since I was trying to protect just one dog's life, I would call my program Vest A Dog.

I decided that veterinarian offices and pet stores would be really good places to go with donation boxes and Vest A Dog flyers. I used little green Chinese take-out boxes, decorated with a picture of Tiko, the dog I chose to vest, and me. I wrote on each box "Help protect the life of a police dog by donating a dollar."

One afternoon, after all the boxes had been distributed throughout our community, I got a call from a local newspaper reporter who had seen one of my fliers. The reporter decided to do an article about Vest A Dog. That ought to spread the word, I thought. I asked K9 Officer Jim Wall, who is Tiko's partner, if they would have their picture taken with me for the article and they did.

After the article came out, I waited for a few days before checking to see if there were any donations. I was really nervous when I finally went to collect the money. Would there be anything in the boxes? I wondered. I really wasn't sure that I could raise enough to buy the vest. But when I collected the first box, I couldn't believe my eyes. I realized that there are many generous animal lovers out there. The box was practically overflowing with dollar bills! I kept checking back to collect the donations every few days. After about three weeks, I counted the money from all of the boxes. It totaled over three thousand dollars! I was so excited and totally amazed at the amount of money that I had raised. Not only was there enough money to buy Tiko's vest, but Vest A Dog had raised enough to buy vests for the other five unprotected dogs on the Oceanside Police Department. I couldn't believe it!

When the officers from the K9 unit found out that they were going to be able to protect all six of their dogs, they couldn't stop thanking me. They decided to put together a presentation ceremony where I would give the six vests I was donating to the department's dogs. That's where I got to meet all of the other police dogs and their handlers. I was actually a little scared of them, but the officers assured me that the dogs were very friendly. I learned that these were not just police dogs, but also the officers' family pet. Again, I thought of my dog Kela and also about Solo. I wanted even more to make sure that these police dogs didn't die while trying to protect people.

Once I began presenting the vests at the ceremony, I kept seeing television reporters come in and set up cameras. I never expected to see so many news stations there! I was excited to talk with them about what I was doing. When they asked me if I was going to continue my Vest A Dog program to help protect the other fifty dogs in San Diego County, where we live, I replied, "Yes! We need to protect these dogs because they protect us every day."

Soon the phone was ringing off the hook! Each day, reporters from newspapers and television stations called with interview requests. They wanted more information about my Vest A Dog program and also wanted to know where donations could be made. The media is so powerful! People began to mail donations to Vest A Dog!

Looking back, the success of Vest A Dog totally surprised me at first. Then I realized that it wasn't unusual that a lot of other people felt the same way I did about these dogs. They just didn't know how to help before Vest A Dog got started.

So far, Vest A Dog has raised more than twenty-five thousand dollars and has supplied all of the law enforcement dogs within San Diego County with a protective vest! Then, just when I had achieved what I thought was my highest goal, people from all over the country began to call me to find out how to raise funds to vest dogs in their areas. So now my fundraiser is continuing nationwide, and I have a Web page to tell other people how to organize a fundraiser like the one that I did.

Knowing that more and more dogs are being protected is really rewarding. It has made all my efforts more than worth it.

Then, one day after school, my mom told me that the Society for the Prevention of Cruelty to Animals (SPCA) wanted to honor me for the work that I had done to protect police dogs. They invited my mom and me to New York so that I could receive an award and a check for five thousand dollars! That vested another ten dogs!

I'm so proud and happy that the money I have raised is all going to the dogs. I'm still amazed that I have vested so many dogs when I really wasn't sure if I could vest even one. Even though some days I was tired from schoolwork, I knew it was important to continue fund-raising to help save these special dogs. It was a lot of hard work but I learned that if you just keep going, you can accomplish anything. Don't think that just because you are a kid that you can't make a difference. Even if you think something is impossible, it can be done.

~Stephanie Taylor, eleven
Chicken Soup for the Preteen Soul

[*Editors' Note*: For more information on how to start a Vest A Dog program in your area, log on to www.dogvest.com.]

30

Lady Godiva and the Bee

L ady Godiva sashayed up the trail in front of me, the sun shimmering on her white coat. Her hips swayed and tail wagged as she sniffed the scents of hikers, other dogs and moose that had walked this trail before us. I had rescued this furry Samoyed from the Humane Society, and was going to change her name until I learned that the historical Lady Godiva had been a heroine who rode her horse in the nude to save her village from oppressive taxation.

My Lady Godiva was also a heroine: She had rescued me from depression and isolation following my divorce. I barely had the energy to work on my computer, and spent the rest of the time curled up in a fetal position on the couch, watching whatever happened to be on television. But Lady demanded at least two vigorous walks a day, saving me from life as a couch potato. Her curiosity and zest for life were contagious, propelling me into the Wasatch Mountains and back into the world.

Today, the spring air was crisp and clear, the sky too blue to be real, and aspen leaves had begun to uncurl into chartreuse circles. The spicy scent of pines and pinions was intoxicating as we hiked for more than an hour, about a third of the way up a steep mountain. I needed to get back to work and didn't feel like struggling to go higher.

I called Lady Godiva. She sat down and stared at me. Usually she was happy to turn around and get a treat, but today her reluctance was evident.

I called again, and Lady came back slowly for her dog biscuit. We walked about twenty feet downhill toward home when the bee from hell appeared. It was about the size of a child's fist — I had never seen one as large. It circled a few feet from my body, buzzing like a cake mixer. I froze.

Although startled, I wasn't afraid. I knew it wouldn't sting me unless it felt threatened. Lady and other animals had taught me that all creatures are intelligent and respond to our thoughts. If we send kind thoughts, animals won't hurt us. Native Americans know this, and they avoid rattlesnake bites by greeting snakes as brothers, not as enemies. So, standing motionless, I sent the bee a mental greeting. The bee continued to circle.

After a few minutes, I took a step down the trail again. The bee circled closer, and the buzzing grew louder. I stepped back, and its circles widened. What was going on? What am I supposed to do? I turned around and took another step up the trail, toward the mountaintop. The bee disappeared.

I turned back towards home, and the thing reappeared, buzzing a foot from my face.

The universe sends us signs, often in ordinary ways, so I decided to experiment. Toward home, and it reappeared. Up the mountain, and it vanished. Why?

Lady bounded up the trail, barking for me to follow. I obeyed. Was climbing this mountain some kind of test? I wondered. Was there someone I was supposed to help, some challenge to be overcome, a lesson to be learned? Familiar anxiety churned my stomach. What if I couldn't do it — whatever it was? What if I wasn't good enough? Worse: what if the bee doesn't mean anything, and I'm crazy?

I pushed through my fear by pumping up the trail, even as the path grew steeper and I had to stop to catch my breath. The peak still seemed far away, and I was afraid it would be too late when I reached the top — I would then have to hurry down the mountain in the darkness.

Lady ran back toward me, startling me out of my worries with a couple of sharp barks. I looked up. Bright bluebells waved in the breeze near the edge of the precipice, which overlooked a valley of aspen trees, their new green leaves dancing in the sunlight. A stream fed by melted snow gushed through the meadow below. I didn't have time to stand and appreciate the beauty; I had to get up the mountain. I had to find out what I was supposed to do.

Thoughts of that mission, whatever it might be, kept me ascending for another hour, and without warning we emerged from forest darkness into a clearing filled with sunshine at the summit.

A glorious panorama of mountains, hills and valleys in shades of greens, yellows and browns melted into a Monet painting. A hawk screeched above, the sun illuminating its red tail as it soared in lazy circles. Lady leaned quietly against my leg, letting me soak in the beauty.

Filled with unfamiliar peace and gratitude, I was afraid to move, afraid it was too good to be true. Then I remembered: What was my mission? What have I been sent here to do? Worry pushed peace aside.

A soft voice floated into my mind — the still, small voice I'd come to recognize, which was always gentle and kind, and never critical. Do nothing.

My words burst out in the golden silence: "What do you mean... nothing?"

Silence.

What does "nothing" mean? There must be a purpose.

Then the thoughts filled my body and soul like music: Enjoy. Be. Just Be. I don't have to do anything. I don't have to prove I'm good or perfect. I don't have to save the world. I just have to enjoy life and drink in the beauty around me every day. I only have to be.

Laughter erupted from deep inside, releasing fears. I yelled, "Bee, I got your message!" Lady barked with delight, and we danced together on the summit as the sun blazed from gold to red.

As we started for home, there was so much beauty to see that I forgot I was tired — I forgot to even think. I inhaled the pungent scent of sage and smiled at the carpets of wildflowers. If I missed squirrels chattering, or a robin flying to her nest with a worm, Lady reminded me. She led me home just as the indigo-sky darkened and night enfolded us.

~Lynne D. Finney, J.D., M.S.W.
Chicken Soup to Inspire the Body and Soul

Loving Our Dogs

Chapter 4

Pets Have Pets Too

The soul is the same in all living creatures,
although the body of each is different.
~Hippocrates

31

The Great Dog Walk

Maybe part of loving is learning to let go.
~From the television show The Wonder Years

lthough I was born and raised in New York City, my parents had an exuberance for the great outdoors. Every summer Dad rented a small cottage for us on the eastern end of Long Island. The cottage was nestled in a wooded area close to the beach, so my childhood encompassed fishing, swimming, boating and the pure enjoyment of the environment. After I married and had children, we lived down the street from my parents and continued to join them on their yearly retreats to Long Island.

One year shortly before summer vacation, my parents adopted a magnificent English basset hound puppy. My two daughters were overjoyed. The dog immediately became the most important thing in their lives. They named the puppy Huckleberry Hound after the television cartoon character.

Every day after school they headed to their grandparents' house to walk and feed the dog. The trio basked in the admiring glances they received as they paraded around the neighborhood. Huckleberry was certainly a sight to behold, with his elongated body and droopy ears that nearly touched the ground. His four stubby legs were attached to extra large paws that he tripped over constantly. His narrow face held two of the most soulful eyes imaginable. Huckleberry swaggered down the street as if he knew he was special and enjoyed every moment of the attention showered upon him.

Our first summer journey to the cottage with Huckleberry was a true nightmare. He disliked the motion of the car and became violently ill. He tossed and turned on the backseat, his eyes rolling and his tongue hanging from his mouth. He drooled so much that my mother got her new shower curtain from the trunk of the car and draped it around the girls who were riding in the backseat with Huckleberry. We all arrived exhausted from the trip. Even with the shower curtain, the girls were wet with slime and smelled like the city zoo.

When Huckleberry emerged from the car, he gazed at his new surroundings, standing dumbstruck for the longest time. Then he began to bark. Where were all the tall buildings, the fire hydrants and the curbs to sniff? Where were all his loyal fans?

A flock of geese flew overhead honking loudly. Two frogs jumped directly in front of the trembling animal. A butterfly landed on his head and a stray cat hissed at him in passing. It was all too much for this poor urban creature. He fled into the house and under the nearest piece of furniture.

Huckleberry was a city hound. Give him a concrete sidewalk and he was in his element. The country offered him no benefits. He became a recluse and spent his days on the screened front porch. Huckleberry would sit and watch the girls play outside, but when it was time for his walk, he hid. We all felt sorry for him but decided to let this timid animal spend his summer as he wished, curled up on his comfortable porch chair.

One morning a pipe burst in the kitchen, and my father called the plumber, Young Charlie, who was the son of one of his fishing buddies, Old Charlie. Young Charlie was accompanied by an old black Lab named George, who announced their arrival loudly from the back of the pickup truck. The girls scooted outside to greet the dog and were thrilled to see that he wanted to play. After a rousing game of catch and a romp around the property, all were in need of a cold drink.

Huckleberry had watched them play from his window seat. When they stopped to rest, he began to howl. All efforts to silence him were to no avail. The girls hooked up his leash and pulled him outside. At that moment, the black Lab stepped up, grabbed the leash in his mouth and began to walk Huckleberry around the yard. The howling stopped. Huckleberry, head held high, a spring in his step, tail wagging, followed in whatever direction George led. Both dogs were rewarded with hugs and doggy treats at the end of their walk.

The next day, Young Charlie arrived with George and announced that his dog was very anxious to return to our house. From that day on, George, who appeared to know that he was doing a good deed, took Huckleberry on his daily walk.

The summer slipped away and school beckoned: It was time to return to the city. Both dogs nuzzled each other as we packed the car for the journey home.

The following winter was harsh. Huckleberry became ill after eating something encrusted in the snow and died within a week. The entire family was horrified. We mourned, each in our own way, and my parents decided not to get another pet. Our lives continued: Winter passed, spring blossomed and summer was at hand once more.

The trip to the country was marred by the emptiness we all felt without Huckleberry. Within a few days, Young Charlie's truck pulled into our driveway and George was lifted out of the truck. Over the winter, he had lost the sight in one of his eyes and Young Charlie felt that walking Huckleberry would enrich George's life.

Dad explained the situation to Young Charlie, who was deeply saddened by our loss. "George still gets around okay, but he's getting old. Sure makes me sad that he won't have his friend to play with this summer," he said. We all felt a lump in our throats as the pair departed.

The next morning, the girls announced that they had a plan. We drove into town and visited the town's thrift store. We purchased one extra large stuffed animal, two pairs of old roller skates and one cabinet door. I cut the board to size and my mother glued the stuffed dog onto the platform. Dad bolted the skates to the bottom of the plank and the girls made a coat from Huckleberry's chair blanket. When the coat was tied around the finished product, we called Young Charlie to bring George for a visit.

We crossed our fingers as the black Lab sniffed the creation. My daughters attached the leash to it and handed it over to George. We'll never know if he humored us or if Huckleberry's scent gave him the feeling of having his friend back. However, for the next eight weeks George took great pride in walking that stuffed animal.

The story spread around town, and many of the residents came by to take pictures of the event. Shortly after returning to the city that year, we learned that George had passed away in his sleep, the stuffed animal at his side. We cried when we got the call.

A few days later, when our summer photos had been processed and picked up, our sorrow turned to joy. The pictures of George leading his "friend" around were vivid reminders of the happy times we had spent with Huckleberry and George. We knew we had witnessed a true act of love. Now, the two dogs will live forever in the telling and retelling of one of our favorite family stories: The Great Dog Walk.

~Anne Carter
Chicken Soup for the Dog Lover's Soul

32

The Princess and the Toad

A friend is one of the nicest things you can have,
and one of the best things you can be.
~Douglas Pagels

Some years ago, our family expanded to include a one-year-old Siberian husky named Princess Misha. Like all Siberian huskies, Misha had an innate love of the outdoors, and of course, the cooler the better. She would lie curled up in a ball on top of a snowdrift on the coldest of winter days with her tail flicked over her only vulnerable spot—her nose. When fresh snow fell, she would lay so still that she soon disappeared under a blanket of snow and became a part of the landscape. Every so often, she stood up, shook off, turned in a few circles, and then laid back down to keep watch over her domain.

On warm summer days, she found the coolest corner in the house and spent her days napping. Then after her nightly walk, she'd spend the rest of the evening stretched out on the cool cement of the front patio. All through the hot summers and into the fall, this was her nightly ritual.

One summer evening, as we sat on the front patio relishing a late-evening breeze, we saw a small toad hop out of the grass, then down the sidewalk to a few feet away from where Misha was lying. Suddenly Misha stood up, walked over to the toad, picked it up in her mouth and then walked back to her resting place and lay back down. She then put her chin down on the walk, opened her mouth and let the toad hop out while we watched in astonishment. The toad sat there in front of Misha's eyes, the two seeming to stare at one another for some time. Then the toad hopped down the walk and back into the grass.

On other nights that summer, we noticed this same ritual. We commented on the fact that Misha seemed to have a fondness for toads. We worried because some toads can be poisonous, but since she never experienced any ill effect and never hurt them, we didn't interfere. If she spotted a toad in the street on one of her walks, she would actually run over to it and nudge it with her nose till it had safely hopped off the street and back on to the grass, out of harm's way.

The following summer was the same. Misha enjoyed cooling off by lying out on the front patio after nightfall. Many times, we noticed a toad within inches of her face. At other times, we watched as she walked into the grass and came back to her resting spot with a toad in her mouth, only to release it. The toads always stayed near her for some time before hopping off into the night. The only difference from the previous summer was that she spent more nights in this manner, and the toads were bigger. A toad always seemed to be close at hand.

One night early in the third summer, after letting Misha out, we watched as a large toad hopped out of the grass and over to her, stopping inches in front of her. Misha gently laid her head down so that her nose almost touched the toad. That was when it finally dawned on us—perhaps there was just one toad! Could Misha have shared the past three summers with the same toad? We called a local wildlife expert who told us that toads can live three to six years, so it was entirely possible. Somehow these two unlikely companions had formed a bond. At first it seemed so strange to us. But then we realized we were very different from Misha too, but the love between us seemed completely natural. If she could love us, we marveled, why not a toad?

Misha had a minor operation that summer, and we kept her indoors for a while afterwards to recuperate. Each night she went to the front door and asked to be let out, but we didn't let her. Instead, leash in hand, we took her for short walks. One evening a few days later, I went to the front door to turn on the porch light for guests we were expecting. When the light came on illuminating the front stoop, there, to my utter amazement, sat Toad (as we came to call him), staring up at me through the screen door! He had hopped up the three steps from the patio, and we supposed he was looking for Misha. Such devotion could not be denied. We let Misha out to be with her pal. She immediately picked the toad up in her mouth and took it down the steps where she and Toad stayed nose to nose until we brought her in for the night. After that, if Misha didn't come out soon enough, Toad frequently came to the door to get her. We made sure that the porch light was turned on before dark and posted a big sign on the porch, "Please don't step on the toad!"

We often laughed about the incongruous friendship—they did made a comical sight, gazing into each other's eyes. But their devotion sometimes made me wonder if I should regard them so lightly. Maybe it was more than just friendship. Maybe in her stalwart toad, Princess Misha had found her Prince Charming.

~Joan Sutula
Chicken Soup for the Cat and Dog Lover's Soul

33

Jethro's World

"Our task must be to free ourselves… by widening our circle of compassion to embrace all living creatures and the whole of nature and its beauty."
~Albert Einstein

My dog, Jethro — a Rottweiler/German shepherd mix — was always low-key, gentle and well mannered. From the moment we met at the animal shelter when he was just nine months old, to the day he died, two things were clear: Jethro and I had a special bond, and he had a soul of exceptional kindness and compassion.

Jethro never chased animals. He just loved to hang out and watch the world around him. He was a perfect field assistant for me as I studied the various birds, including Western evening grosbeaks and Steller's jays, living near my house in the foothills of the Colorado Rockies.

One day while I was sitting inside, I heard Jethro come to the front door. Instead of whining as he usually did when he wanted to come in, he just sat there. I looked out at him and noticed a small furry object in his mouth. My first reaction was, Oh, no, he killed a bird. However when I opened the door, Jethro proceeded to drop at my feet a very young bunny, drenched in his saliva and very much alive. I could not see any injuries, only a small bundle of fur that needed warmth, food and love. I guessed that the bunny's mother had most likely fallen prey to a coyote, red fox or the occasional mountain lion around my house.

Jethro looked up at me, wide-eyed, as if he wanted me to praise him. I did. He seemed so proud of himself. But when I picked up the bunny, Jethro's pride turned to concern. He tried to snatch her from my hands, but failed. Whining, he followed me around as I gathered a box, a blanket, some water and food. I gently placed the baby rabbit in the box, named her Bunny and wrapped her in the blanket. I put some finely chopped carrots, celery and lettuce near her, and she tried to eat. I also made sure that she knew where the water was.

The whole time, Jethro was standing behind me, panting, dripping saliva on my shoulder, watching my every move. I thought he might go for Bunny or the food, but he simply stood there, fascinated by the little ball of fur slowly moving about in her new home.

When I turned to leave the box, I called Jethro but he didn't move. He usually came to me immediately, especially when I offered him a bone, but that day he remained steadfastly near the box. Hours passed and nothing could entice him away from his spot near Bunny.

Eventually, I had to drag Jethro out for his nightly walk. When we returned, he made a beeline for the box, where he slept through the night. I tried to get Jethro to go to his usual sleeping spot but he refused. His intention was clear: "No way. I'm staying here."

I trusted Jethro not to harm Bunny, and during the two weeks that I nursed her back to health, he didn't do anything to even scare her. Jethro had adopted Bunny; he would make sure that no one harmed her.

Finally, the day came when I introduced Bunny to the outdoors. Jethro and I walked to the east side of my house and I released her from her box. We watched her slowly make her way into a woodpile. She was cautious, her senses overwhelmed by the new stimuli — sights, sounds, odors — to which she was now exposed. Bunny remained in the woodpile for about an hour until she boldly stepped out to begin life as a full-fledged wild rabbit. Jethro remained in the same spot as he watched the scene. He never took his eyes off Bunny and never tried to approach her.

Bunny hung around for a few months. Every time I let Jethro out of the house, he immediately ran to the place where she had been released. When he arrived there, he would cock his head and move it from side to side, looking for Bunny. This lasted for about six months. If I said "Bunny" in a high-pitched voice, Jethro would whine and go look for her. He loved Bunny and was hoping to see her once again.

I am not sure what happened to Bunny. Most likely she simply lived out her life in the area around my home. Since then, other bunnies and adult rabbits have come and gone, and I've observed that Jethro never chases them. Instead, he tries to get as close as he can and looks at each of them, perhaps wondering if they are Bunny.

A few summers ago, many years after he met Bunny and treated her with such delicate compassion, Jethro came running up to me with a wet animal in his mouth. Hmm, I wondered, another bunny? I asked him to drop it. This time it was a young bird that had flown into a window. It was stunned and just needed to regain its senses.

I held it in my hands for a few minutes. Jethro, in true Jethro fashion, never took his eyes off the bird. He watched my every move. When I thought the bird was ready to fly, I placed it on the railing of my porch. Jethro approached it, sniffed it, stepped back and watched it fly away. When it was out of sight, he turned to me and seemed to give the canine equivalent of a shrug. Then together we took a long meandering stroll down the road leading away from my house. All was well in Jethro's world once more.

~Marc Bekoff
Chicken Soup for the Dog Lover's Soul

34

George Washington Cat and Family

We were moving into our new house. I had just opened the door to get more things from the car when "something" rushed by me. "What…?" I started. The neighbor across the way gave me a big grin, saying, "I think you have a new friend. He's a stray cat who's been hanging around here."

A cat? We already had a dog, a sweet little sable Shetland sheepdog named Greta. What would she do with a cat? In the past, Greta had shown a great affinity for all types of friends. She loved all dogs. At our old house, a parade of them had shown up on a regular basis, all of them wearing the expression, "Can Greta come out to play?" Our favorite of her friends was a little toad that used to sit on our front porch in the evenings. Greta would touch noses with him, and then sit beside him under the porch light. We even took photos of this strange friendship. But a cat?

The only cat she had known was a black-striped tabby down the street from us. We walked Greta by her house every evening. The cat would come out, arch her back and hiss. Greta would bark once or twice, the tabby would turn and leave, and Greta would continue her walk. The man who owned the cat was highly amused. "I think they like each other, but can't admit it," he told me. When Greta was hospitalized for a throat infection, the cat's owner came to our house to inquire after her. "My cat misses her," he explained.

The new house was filled with many large boxes of our things. Looking around in the rooms, all I could see were boxes and boxes—and no cat. Maybe when we finished unpacking, I'd be able to find him. In the meantime, I decided to put out cat food and leave the patio door open in case he decided to leave. The food disappeared on a regular basis. The door stayed open, but it did not seem as if anyone was leaving.

When I finally got down to the last packing box, we found him. He was the dirtiest white cat I have ever seen. His ears were a strange green hue, and his nose was black. His white coat was streaked with various shades of brown, gray and orange. Not knowing if he was feral, I reached for him gingerly. But he came to my arms as if he belonged there.

One trip to the vet's produced a bill six inches long. He had a mold infection in his ears, as well as ear mites and fleas. Plus, he had to have a bath, shots and a license. Through all this, the cat remained as patient and unconcerned as could be.

In the weeks before we found him, Greta sensed that he had been in the boxes, but didn't seem to care. When the newly cleaned and vetted cat showed up, she offered him a nose, and he nosed her back: Their relationship was cemented. We named him George Washington Cat because of the upright way he sat in our club chair with one foreleg on the arm of the chair as he regally surveyed his new home.

A few years later, we bred Greta to a wonderful working Sheltie, and she had four puppies. I was a little worried how George Washington Cat would take to the new strangers. Georgie walked over to the whelping box and sat in his Egyptian way with his tail curled around him. I watched him as he eyed the box for a while; suddenly, he started to purr. The purrs got louder and louder. Finally, he stepped carefully into the box, wrapped himself around the sleeping group and went to sleep, too. Greta came back and took a peek. From the expression on her face, I could almost hear her thinking, Babysitter! I have a babysitter! And she went to her favorite place to nap, without the puppies to nag at her.

As the puppies grew, Georgie participated with even more energy. Every morning, Greta would leave for her breakfast, and Georgie would jump into the box and start the morning wash-up. He cleaned ears (eight of them), noses (four), fronts (four), and eyes (another eight), and, when he was through, his little pink tongue hung out of his mouth. I didn't dare laugh; he took all this very seriously. When a very nice family adopted one of the puppies, Georgie hunted for him for days. Heartbroken, he meowed over the whelping box. We decided we didn't want to put him through this anguish again and never bred Greta after that.

A second puppy was given to a very dear friend, and, because Georgie could not bear to be parted from "his" brood, we kept the last two puppies. For the rest of his life, it was Uncle Georgie's morning ritual to clean them up. The now-grown dogs would dutifully come to him each morning, and he would clean their ears, eyes, face and fronts. Commenting on how wonderfully white the fronts of the Shelties were, people would ask me what I used to wash the dogs. I never told them about the boys' Uncle Georgie.

After Greta died, he looked for her constantly, and his cleaning ritual seemed a little less thorough. Georgie lingered only one short year before following his beloved canine friend. The boys missed him after he died, and, for months, went to the same spot under the table every morning for their "cleaning."

These wonderful members of our family are all gone now, but I like to think that Uncle Georgie has "his" family back, and is busy once more, cleaning all of them up with his little pink tongue.

~Peggy Seo Oba
Chicken Soup for the Cat Lover's Soul

35

The Duck
and the Doberman

A single rose can be my garden... a single friend, my world.
~Leo Buscaglia

Although Jessie, our eighty-pound black Doberman, looked menacing—she snarled at strangers and attacked backyard critters—she was extremely loyal and loving to our family. We wanted a second dog, but agreed that Jessie would be better off alone; we were afraid that jealousy might compel her to hurt any dog that got between her and us.

So when our son Ricky came home from school one day with an egg, we smelled trouble. Ricky's egg came from his second-grade class project: incubating and hatching Rhone ducks. The egg had failed to hatch at school, so his teacher allowed him to bring it home. My husband and I didn't think the egg was likely to hatch outside the incubator, so we let him keep it. Ricky placed the egg in a sunny patch of grass in the yard and waited.

The next morning we awoke to a bizarre squeal coming from the backyard. There stood Jessie, nose to nose with a newly hatched peach-colored duckling.

"Jessie will swallow it whole!" I cried. "Grab her."

"Hold on," my husband, Rick, said. "I think it'll be okay. Just give it a minute."

The duckling peeped. Jessie growled and darted back to her doghouse. The duckling followed. Jessie curled up on her bed, clearly ignoring the little creature. But the duckling had other ideas. She had already imprinted on her new "mother," so she cuddled up on Jessie's bed, snuggling under her muzzle. Jessie nudged the duckling out of the doghouse with her nose, only to have the baby squirm back to its place under her muzzle. Jessie gave a big sigh and reluctantly accepted her new role.

Ricky named the duckling Peaches and pleaded with us to keep her. Jessie didn't seem to like having a new baby, but she wasn't predatory toward Peaches either. We gave in and decided to see how things would go.

Surprisingly, over the next few weeks, Jessie really took to motherhood. When Peaches pecked at the ground, Jessie showed her how to dig. When Peaches chased tennis balls, Jessie showed her how to fetch. And when Jessie sprawled out on the leather couch to watch Animal Planet on television, Peaches snuggled right under her muzzle.

After an inseparable year of digging, sleeping and fetching together, Peaches weighed eighteen pounds. She seemed quite happy in her role as Jessie's "puppy."

Then one day something changed: Peaches' innate "duckness" kicked in. She began laying eggs once a day and became obsessed with water. During feeding times, Jessie ate while Peaches flapped and splashed in the water bowl.

One evening Jessie became frantic when Peaches disappeared. We had visions of coyotes lurking, snatching Peaches while Jessie slept. Jessie barked and howled, as would any anguished mother who had lost a child. After a thorough search of the neighborhood, we were close to giving up hope. Just then, Jessie sprinted into a neighbor's backyard. We followed her. There was Peaches, sloshing and squawking in the hot tub. Jessie hopped in to retrieve her.

As much as we wanted to keep Peaches in our family, one thing was clear: She needed to spread her wings and join the duck world. Ricky tied a red ribbon around Peaches' leg, loaded her and Jessie into the car, and we drove to a nearby pond. During the ride, Jessie curled up with Peaches and licked her head. It was as if she knew exactly what was happening and why.

As we approached the pond, Jessie and Peaches scampered toward the water. Jessie leaped in first. Peaches wobbled behind. They waded out together several yards before Peaches took off—gliding toward a flock of her own. Jessie turned around, trudged back to shore and shook off. She sat for a few minutes, watching her daughter. Then as if to say, "It's time to set my little one free," she yelped and jumped back into the car.

Back at home Ricky taped pictures of Jessie and Peaches digging, fetching and snuggling, to the inside of the doghouse. And, for a long time afterward, Jessie made weekly visits to the pond. Although we could usually see the red ribbon, we thought we could also hear Peaches' distinctive squawk, saying hello to her "birth" family.

Motherhood changed Jessie. Once unsociable and intimidating, she soon became a friend to all in the neighborhood. She snuck out at every opportunity to play with other dogs, jumped on visitors and licked their faces. Snarling was no longer part of her vocabulary.

We had feared the worst the day we saw Jessie and baby Peaches standing nose to bill. We could never have imagined that an eight-ounce ball of downy fuzz would soften our eighty-pound Doberman for life.

~Donna Griswold as told to Eve Ann Porinchak
Chicken Soup for the Dog Lover's Soul

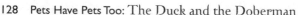

36

Puppy Love

Happiness is a warm puppy.
~Charles M. Schulz

I've heard two things for nearly most of my life. One, that animals don't have any human emotion—even though I knew they possessed fear and pain. Two, that breeders who weren't happy with imperfect dogs had them destroyed. When I became an amateur breeder myself, I would learn these things on my own.

My family and I owned one remarkable Dalmatian, Kami, who had given us companionship, warmth, love and many sloppy-tongued kisses. We loved her so much, we decided we wanted some of her pups. So we matched her with a purebred named Bo.

We had no idea exactly what it would be like to have Dalmatian pups, but we were sure we could find homes for each and every one we didn't keep. There was excitement in the air the night of their births. Kami was so large and the babies were so busy inside her that their tiny feet and heads were bulging out of her skin.

We felt like we were playing a part in 101 Dalmatians that night. The first one popped out. Then the second. We counted slowly throughout the night, ten... eleven... twelve. Twelve Dalmatian pups. We couldn't believe it. The thrill of having Kami's pups was remarkable. I felt like a dad of twelve puplets. And fortunately in this case, there was no cruel character like in the movie. Or so we thought.

The pups roamed, tumbled, wrestled and snuggled with each other. We had to help Kami nurse the twelve pups because the largest shoved the smaller guys away. We blended milk with canned puppy food and put it out in pie tins. It was always a daring adventure trying to tiptoe through twelve yapping puppies who could easily be squished with one wrong step.

It was then we noticed life's small dose of cruelty—trouble with two pups. They didn't respond to us like the others. They didn't charge me when I called out that it was chow time. They ran smack into barking pups. We soon learned that the two brother pups were deaf. It was recommended that the best option was to put them to sleep.

I pondered it for a few moments. While breeders would put them to sleep in a second, it just wasn't what I or anybody in my family wanted to do. I thought, Why should two pups die just because they were born deaf? I was rewarded for the decision at the next chow time. I stepped out into the feeding frenzy and only ten pups charged me. The eleventh looked at me and ran for the bushes. He stopped and looked back at me again.

I followed, wondering what he was doing. He'd seen me carry the pie tins filled with food. What could he possibly be waiting for? In a few seconds, I knew. Seeing me coming, he charged into the bushes. Seconds later, he reappeared, nudging his sleepy deaf brother from the brush. An overwhelming sense of loyalty and satisfaction swept over me. I learned then the puppy's sense of love, loyalty and caring. I learned then what an unselfish action the pup had taken.

The brother pups are now living happily together at a home where the family appreciates them immensely.

Last I heard, they brought their adopted family a double amount of love and happiness.

~Mark Malott as told to Diana Chapman
A 5th Portion of Chicken Soup for the Soul

37

Bullet's Dog

Piglet sidled up to Pooh from behind. "Pooh!" he whispered.
"Yes, Piglet?"
"Nothing," said Piglet, taking Pooh's paw. "I just wanted to be sure of you."
~A.A. Milne

One morning in early June, I went outside to feed our horse Bullet. Usually, Bullet waits patiently at the fence for his breakfast, but this morning he was lingering near the two tall oak trees in the center of the pasture where he liked to spend the hottest hours of the day.

Curious why he wasn't eager for his breakfast, I peered across the pasture at him, hoping he wasn't sick. Then as he began to slowly walk toward me, I noticed a blotch of red fur hunkering down in the tall grass beneath one of the trees. So this was what held Bullet's attention this morning: another stray dog had found its way onto our property. Most of them shied away from our large retired racehorse, but this dog seemed to feel safe in the shelter of the tall grass in spite of Bullet. I placed a bucket of alfalfa cubes inside the fence. After Bullet ate them, I would give him a few of the oatmeal cookies he loved more than anything.

It was a glorious morning, so I sat down on my back steps, reluctant to go back inside and start my day. As Bullet ate his alfalfa cubes, the dog rose cautiously to its feet. The dog stared at Bullet for a long moment and then slowly made its way toward the horse. It paused every few steps and looked at me intently to make sure I wasn't a threat. As the dog drew closer to Bullet, I held my breath. I didn't know how Bullet would react to an animal that approached while he was eating. Knowing that a kick from a horse can be fatal to a dog, I was about to shout at the dog to scare it away. Just then Bullet swung his head and looked at the dog for a moment. Unperturbed by the approaching animal, he turned back to his food and began to eat again.

The dog drew close enough to snag a cube that Bullet had dropped. My heart broke as I watched the dog—a female—chewing on the alfalfa. I knew she had to be extremely hungry to attempt to eat horse feed.

I went inside the house to find something that the dog could eat. I had some leftover meat loaf in the refrigerator that I had planned on serving for dinner. I put the meat loaf in an old aluminum pie tin and walked toward the fence with it. The dog ran to the safety of the tall grass near the oak trees as soon as I took one step in her direction. I put the food down on the ground and tried to coax her toward me. After several minutes, I gave up and went back inside the house. She would probably come for the food as soon as I was out of sight.

A little while later, while folding laundry, I realized that I had not yet given Bullet his cookies. I grabbed a handful from the box we kept under the sink and went back outside. To my surprise, Bullet was kneeling in the grass with the dog next to him. I smiled at the warm picture they made. Knowing that I carried his treat, Bullet got up quickly and galloped to the fence to meet me. The dog watched as I tossed the cookies over the fence. I noticed that she had not yet gotten the courage to venture outside the fence to get the meat loaf I had left for her.

Again I sat down on the back steps, trying to think of how to get the dog to overcome her fear and come for the meat loaf. For some reason, she seemed to feel safe within the confines of the pasture. Noticing that Bullet was eating, the dog began to move forward slowly, watching me all the while. He might share his alfalfa with you, but he'll never let you at his oatmeal cookies, I said to myself. But to my surprise, Bullet watched with only mild interest as the dog leaped forward and grabbed a cookie. She swallowed the cookie in one famished gulp, then darted forward to snatch another one. There were no more cookies left, but the dog stood beneath Bullet and scurried for the crumbs that fell from the horse's mouth, licking the ground furiously to get at every last morsel.

When Bullet walked back toward the shade of the oak trees, the dog trotted along beside him. All day long, whenever I looked out the window toward the pasture, the dog was always close to Bullet, either running along at his side or lying in the grass near him. The dog appeared to be devoted to the horse, who had willingly shared his food with her.

It was three days before I coaxed the dog from the pasture. She got down on her belly and crawled toward me, her large brown eyes begging me not to hurt her. Whimpering, partly in fear and partly with joy, she allowed me to gently pet her. I noticed that she was young and quite beautiful, in spite of being malnourished. I found myself calling her Lucy, and knew that this stray was here to stay.

Though Lucy eventually warmed to my husband, Joe, and me, she always preferred Bullet's company the most. She spent most of the day inside the pasture with him. They would run together with great exuberance and joy until they got tired and then drop in the grass beside each other to rest. Bullet always shared his cookies with Lucy. Often Bullet would lower his head and nuzzle Lucy, and she would reach up and lick his face. It was obvious that they loved each other. At night Lucy slept in the stall next to Bullet.

When visitors commented on our new dog, we always laughed and said, "Lucy isn't our dog. She's Bullet's."

Lucy brought joy into the life of an aging racehorse, and much amazement and wonder into ours.

~Elizabeth Atwater
Chicken Soup for the Dog Lover's Soul

The Eyes of Tex

An animal's eyes have the power to speak a great language.
~Martin Buber

Eric Seal thought the scrawny puppy at his feet was perhaps five weeks old. Sometime during the night, the little mixed-breed female had been dumped at the Seals' front gate.

"Before you ask," he told Jeffrey, his wife, "the answer is an absolute no! We are not going to keep it. We don't need another dog. When and if we do, we'll get a purebred."

As though she hadn't heard him, his wife sweetly asked, "What kind do you think it is?"

Eric shook his head. "It's hard to tell. From her color markings and the way she holds her ears in a half-lop, I'd say she's part German shepherd."

"We can't just turn her away," Jeffrey pleaded. "I'll feed her and get her cleaned up. Then we'll find a home for her."

Standing between them, the puppy seemed to sense that her fate was being decided. Her tail wagged tentatively as she looked from one to the other. Eric noticed that although her ribs showed through a dull coat, her eyes were bright and animated.

Finally, he shrugged his shoulders. "Okay, if you want to fool with her, go ahead. But let's get one thing straight: We don't need a Heinz 57 mongrel."

The puppy nestled comfortably in Jeffrey's arms as they walked toward the house. "One other thing," Eric continued. "Let's wait a few days to put her in the pen with Tex. We don't want Tex exposed to anything. He has all the troubles he can handle."

Tex, the six-year-old cattle dog the Seals had raised from a puppy, was unusually amiable for a blue-heeler, a breed established by ranchers in Australia. So, although he already shared his doghouse with a yellow cat, soon Tex happily moved over and made room for the new puppy the Seals called Heinz.

Not long before Heinz showed up, the Seals had noticed that Tex appeared to be losing his eyesight. Their veterinarian said he thought the dog had cataracts that might be surgically removed.

But when they brought Tex to a specialist in Dallas, he determined that the dog's poor eyesight was only partially due to cataracts. He made an appointment for Tex at the local college's veterinary laboratory.

Doctors there determined that Tex was already blind. They explained that no medical or surgical procedure could have halted or delayed Tex's progressive loss of vision.

As they talked on their way home, the Seals realized that over the last few months, they had watched Tex cope with his blindness. Now they understood why Tex sometimes missed a gate opening or bumped his nose on the chain-link fence. And why he usually stayed on the gravel walkways traveling to and from the house. If he wandered off, he quartered back and forth until he was on the gravel again.

While the couple had been preoccupied with Tex's troubles, Heinz had grown plump and frisky, and her dark brown-and-black coat glowed with health.

It was soon obvious that the little German shepherd crossbreed would be a large dog—too large to continue sharing a doghouse with Tex and the yellow cat. One weekend, the Seals built another doghouse next to the one the dogs had shared.

It was then they recognized that what they had assumed was puppy playfulness—Heinz's pushing and tugging at Tex while romping with him—actually had a purpose. Without any training or coaching, Heinz had become Tex's "seeing eye" dog.

Each evening when the dogs settled in for the night, Heinz gently took Tex's nose in her mouth and led him into his house. In the morning, she got him up and guided him out of the house again.

When the two dogs approached a gate, Heinz used her shoulder to guide Tex through. When they ran along the fence surrounding their pen, Heinz placed herself between Tex and the wire.

"On sunny days, Tex sleeps stretched out on the driveway asphalt," says Jeffrey. "If a car approaches, Heinz will nudge him awake and guide him out of danger.

"Any number of times we've seen Heinz push Tex aside to get him out of the horses' way. What we didn't understand at first was how the two could run side by side, dashing full speed across the pasture. Then one day, the dogs accompanied me while I exercised my horse, and I heard Heinz 'talking'—she was making a series of soft grunts to keep Tex on course beside her."

The Seals were awed. Without any training, the young dog had devised whatever means were necessary to help, guide and protect her blind companion. It was clear that Heinz shared more than her eyes with Tex; she shared her heart.

~Honzie L. Rodgers
Chicken Soup for the Pet Lover's Soul

39

Dixie's Kitten

There is something about the presence of a cat
that seems to take the bite out of being alone.
~Louis J. Camuti

Dixie was a pretty dog, an English setter dressed in a white coat adorned with black and brown markings. In her younger days she had spent many happy hours in the fields, running and hunting quail. But now Dixie was so old that she spent most of her time lying in the sun, basking in the soothing warmth of its rays. She especially loved to lie in the yard. There was a full water bucket and brimming food dish within easy reach, and her outdoor shelter was lined with clean, fragrant hay. There were times when her old bones ached and pained her, and she would groan as she stood up to move to another patch of sunlight. But sometimes there were wonderful days when somebody brought by a young bird-dog pup, and a spark would leap in her tired eyes. She adored puppies and would forget her age for a little while as she romped with the younger dogs.

"It's been a long time since you were a puppy, old girl," I told her one day, stopping to comb my fingers through her silky hair. She wagged her tail and looked toward the pup being admired in the front yard. Then with a soft whine, she eased her aching body into a more comfortable position and dropped her chin to her paws. Her eyes were fastened on the younger dog and she seemed lost in thought. Probably dreaming about the days when she was running through the fields teaching the younger dogs to sniff out quail, I decided. I gave her one last pat on the head, and went into the house.

Lately Dixie had seemed lonely. I remembered the family of ducks that used to cross the road in front of our house every evening to share her dish of dog food. Not once had Dixie growled or snapped at the ducks, and sometimes she would even move aside so they could have better access to her food. Visiting cats were always welcome to join in the meals, and it wasn't unusual at all to find her with her nose in the same bowl with several ducks, cats and whatever stray dog may have wandered up. Dixie was a gentle, social soul and nowadays there just didn't seem to be as many guests dropping by to chat over dinner.

One day there was a knock at my door. I opened it to find my next-door neighbor standing there with a concerned look on his face. "Have you seen my kitten?" he asked. "He slipped out and is missing."

It was a cute, fluffy little thing, not much bigger than a minute, and I knew my neighbor was right to be concerned. A tiny lost kitty would be no match for the coyotes and wild cats that roamed our rural area.

I told him I hadn't but that if I spotted it, I would give him a call. He thanked me, sadness etched on his face. "He's so little," he said as he headed for the next house. "I'm afraid if I don't find him soon, something bad will happen to him."

Later that afternoon I carried dog food out to Dixie. She was in her house and I could hear her tail thumping a greeting as I poured the food into her bowl. I fetched the water hose and filled her bucket, then called her out to eat. Slowly she emerged and painfully, carefully, stretched. As I reached down to pat her head, a tiny gray kitten stepped out of the dark doghouse and twined itself around Dixie's legs.

"What have you got there, girl?" I exclaimed. Dixie glanced down at the kitten, then looked back up at me with a gleam in her eye. Her tail wagged harder. "Come here, kitty," I said and reached for it. Dixie gently pushed my hand aside with her nose and nudged the kitten back inside the doghouse. Sitting down in front of the door, she blocked the kitten's exit and I could hear it meowing inside. This had to be my neighbor's lost kitten. It must have wandered through the thicket of bushes between our places and straight into Dixie's doghouse.

"Crazy dog," I muttered. Dixie wagged her agreement, but didn't budge from in front of the door. She waited until I was a safe distance away before she stood up to begin nibbling at the pile of food. I went into the house and telephoned my neighbor.

"I think I've found your kitten," I told him. I could hear the relief in his voice, then the laughter as I told him that Dixie had been hiding it. Promising to come over to collect the runaway cat, he hung up after thanking me again.

He showed up, eager to look at the kitten. "Yep, that's my cat!" he said as the little gray fur ball stepped out of the doghouse. Dixie backed away from us and nosed the kitten toward the door. Gratefully, the man reached for the cat. In the same instant, Dixie snarled at him.

I was shocked. She'd never growled at anybody before! I scolded her, and my neighbor reached for the kitten again. This time Dixie bared her teeth.

"Let me try," I said. I reached for the kitten but Dixie shoved it inside the doghouse, then followed it in and flopped down, blocking the tiny cat from us with her body. Nobody was going to take her kitten!

We could hear the kitten purring loudly inside the house. Then it stepped up, bold as brass, and rubbed itself against Dixie's face. She licked its fur and glared out at us. It was plain that she had adopted the little cat and planned to keep it. "Huh," I said. At the moment, it seemed the only thing to say.

"Well, it looks like the kitten's happy," my poor neighbor said after a few minutes. The little gray cat had curled up between Dixie's front paws and was grooming itself intently. Every once in a while it stopped to lick Dixie's face. Kitten and dog seemed perfectly content. "I guess she can keep the kitten, if she wants it that bad."

So Dixie was allowed to help raise the kitten that she had

claimed as her own. Thanks to the kindness and understanding of my neighbor, the tiny cat and the old dog spent many happy hours together. The kitten benefited from the arrangement and grew into a fine, healthy cat. And Dixie was happy to live out her days basking in the sun, dreaming of kittens and puppies and romping in the fields.

~Anne Culbreath Watkins
Chicken Soup for the Dog Lover's Soul

Man's Best Friend

No matter how little money or how few possessions you own,
having a dog makes you rich.
~Louis Sabin

40

Fate, Courage and a Dog Named Tess

There is no faith which has never yet been broken,
except that of a truly faithful dog.
~Konrad Lorenz

I had just picked up my young niece Hannah from school when I first saw the confused dog darting in and out of traffic at a busy intersection. She was a lanky German shepherd, and I cringed as I watched several cars swerve or stop to avoid hitting her. She appeared to be lost, and Hannah immediately began begging me to intervene. I resisted. I was in a hurry to get home to cook dinner for Hannah and her parents and brother. I had a schedule to maintain, and right then, helping a stray dog was the last thing I wanted to do.

However, as soon as I was able to, I turned around. As we approached the intersection from the opposite direction, we saw her again. She had moved out of the street and was now making friendly advances to everyone walking by, only to be ignored or shooed away by people in a hurry to get home at the end of their workday. With a hopeless sigh, I pulled over and parked my car.

"Okay, Hannah," I said. "This is what we'll do. I'll open the car door and give her one chance to get in, but if she doesn't, we're going home. I won't try to force her."

I got out, opened the door and made a halfhearted call to a pup more than fifty feet away. At the sound of my voice, she pricked her ears, looked directly at me and came running in our direction. In an instant she was in the car, wagging her tail and showering us with doggy kisses as if she'd known us forever. I couldn't help but laugh. What a sweet dog! And miracle of miracles, she was wearing a chain collar that I hadn't noticed before. Even though she didn't have a name tag, surely someone was missing her. A phone call or two, and with any luck, I'd be able to return her to her family. This might not be so bad after all. I took her home firmly believing she would soon be out of my life.

A week later, after running ads in the paper and making repeated phone calls to the local Humane Society and rabies control, I finally resigned myself to the hard reality that whoever had placed the collar around her neck didn't want her back. I lived in a small house and already had two dogs, so keeping her wasn't an option. I decided I would find her a home where she would be cared for and appreciated by a loving family. My first step was to make an appointment with my vet, who pronounced her in perfect health, although obviously under-weight. I named her Tess and began to teach her about in-house living, knowing she needed some better manners to increase her appeal.

With lots of food and grooming, she filled out and her scruffy coat began to glisten. She thrived under all the attention. Within six weeks she was completely housebroken and beautiful. I wrote a story about her and convinced the editor of our local paper to run it in the weekend edition. The story was typed and ready to be dropped off at the newspaper office the next day, and I felt certain we were spending one of our last evenings together.

Just as I was getting ready for bed, the doorbell rang, and because it was late, I answered wearing pajamas, thinking it was probably a neighbor wanting to borrow something. Instead, much to my dismay, an unkempt man stood before me, asking to use my phone. No way I wanted this guy in my house, but I offered to make a call for him if he would supply the number. Without another word, he opened the storm door and pushed his way into my living room. My mind raced. Why in God's name hadn't I checked to see who it was before opening the door? My two dogs—an English springer spaniel and a shih tzu—and Tess, all stopped their effusive greetings, sensing, as I did, that this guy was trouble. The three of them looked at him, then looked to me for some sign that things were okay.

But things were definitely not okay. I was too terrified to speak or move. I stood frozen, waiting, trapped in a dangerous situation from which I feared there was no escape.

Suddenly, the German shepherd I had taken in to save from a life on the streets stepped between me and this stranger who threateningly stood before us. Tess was only eight or nine months old, big, but still very much a pup, and yet, there she was, head down, hackles raised, emitting a low-pitched, menacing growl as she glared at the intruder. For maybe five long seconds we all stood there, motionless. Then, very slowly, the man took one backward step. He raised his hand slightly as he implored me to hold my dog, and he carefully backed out of my house and down the walk.

At last, finally able to move, I shut the door, locked it and turned to hug my friend, the stray dog I had rescued—and who, now, had rescued me. Magically, with the danger gone, she transformed herself back into the wiggling, tail-wagging, pain-in-the-neck pup I had come to know. The next morning I called and canceled the appointment I had to drop off the story about her. Tess didn't need a home; she already had one. Two dogs had become three, but the lack of space didn't seem nearly as important as it had before.

Since that night Tess has never once growled or shown the least bit of hostility to any other human being, and, although her muzzle is now graying, she still often acts like the pup who, without hesitation, bounded into my car—and my life—eleven years ago. I have learned a lot from Tess, especially on that memorable night when she taught me about fate and courage. But most important, she showed me how a random act of kindness can bring blessings to your life.

~Susanne Fogle
Chicken Soup for the Dog Lover's Soul

The Ugly Pupling

I n the spring of 1980, I was living in Woodstock, New York, when my Tibetan terrier dog, Shadow, had a litter of six puppies.

The one pup I couldn't sell was considered homely. Tibetan terriers are known for their lustrous double coats. The underlayer of their coat is thick and cottony, while the outer layer resembles human hair — silky and shiny. This combination makes for a very fluffy look. People also prize their well-proportioned faces. This pup had neither trait. She had a rather long nose and a terribly unattractive coat. She had no underlayer, and this made her top-coat look thin, flat and wiry. It gave her the appearance of a tramp just coming in from the rain. People who came to see her would say, "She seems like a pleasant dog," they'd say, "but she looks kind of scraggly and ugly." No one wanted our little friend, not even for free!

What amazed me was that no one recognized this dog's rare quality. She was by nature always very happy, and although most puppies are happy, she had an unexplainable inner joy about her, a sixth sense, a certain spiritual presence, as if she could read your mind and move you to a more contented place.

In June, I still had the pup with the perpetual "bad hair day." I was going back to school in less than a week and I felt hesitant to leave without finding her a proper home.

One night an idea came to me. There was a Tibetan monastery about a mile from my home, and I'd been there a few times to partici-pate in their meditations. I'd even introduced myself to some of the

Tibetan monks living there. Maybe someone there would be willing to adopt her. It was worth a try.

The following morning, I took my little friend to the monastery. When I arrived, a lot of cars were in the parking lot. I thought, Gee, this place has always been so quiet. I wonder what's going on? I got out of the car with the pup in hand and went up the stairs to the familiar front doors. I entered the foyer and found people lined up wall to wall, apparently waiting for something to occur beyond the hand-carved interior doors. Then I saw a familiar face—one of the monks I'd met on a previous visit. When he saw me holding the dog, he gave me a wide grin and said, "Ah, follow me now!"

He pulled on my sleeve and dragged me to the front of the line. Using what appeared to be a special code, he knocked on the door. The double doors swung open and we were greeted by another monk. The first monk whispered something in the second monk's ear, then the second monk also said, "Ah." With that, the pup and I were pulled to the front of yet another line of people, all bearing gifts of fruit, candy, plants, odd bowls and handmade crafts.

I turned to face the front of the room and there before me was a very bright and cheery-eyed fellow, dressed to the hilt in red and golden-yellow velvets. He glanced at my puppy, then directly at me. Then he put his hands out, fingers open, and said, "Yes, yes. Oh, yes." This magnificent-looking person placed a red string around my puppy's neck, sang a foreign chant, and proceeded to place a second string around my neck. He continued his chant while slowly lifting my puppy from my arms. He carefully embraced her within his velvet robe. He then nodded and bowed, saying something in a foreign language. He tapped me on the head and turned around as he walked toward his chair, still holding my puppy in his arms.

The monk who brought me into the room now quickly ushered me out. In the foyer, met by other monks, I was swept through the halls, pup-less and out the front door of the monastery. I was asked to stand at the top of the steps and wait until further notice.

At this point, a wave of maternal concern moved through me. Where is my dog and what will happen to her? I thought. Turning to a Buddhist onlooker for understanding, I related the events of the last fifteen minutes.

He smiled and explained that I had met the "Karmapa," a monk who is quite high in the Tibetan Buddhist tradition — second only to the Dalai Lama. He told me that I was very fortunate because today the famous and beloved Karmapa was here from Tibet to bless this monastery along with its surrounding land. People from all over the world had come to pay him their respects, but rarely did anyone enter into his private receiving room. To enter there and be blessed by His Holiness, and then for him to accept my generous gift, was an auspicious event, one that rarely happens in a lifetime! He shook his head, "You must have earned a lot of merit in past lives; you are very fortunate, my dear." Closing his eyes, he pondered for a moment, then added, "Then again, perhaps it is your dog's good fortune!"

At that moment the door flew open again, and this wondrous Buddhist monk exited from the building and down the red-carpeted exterior steps, holding his head up high while greeting the people. Women and children gathered around, holding baskets of flowers to throw at his feet.

I was so caught up in the magic of it that I didn't notice her at first. But then to my surprise, I saw my pup — the pup that was considered ugly — now looking like a beautiful star! The Karmapa held her up high with what seemed to be the greatest of pride, and the crowd roared with delight. I would swear that the puppy appeared to be smiling, too.

From that point on, everything seemed to happen in slow motion. They continued down the stairs. Slowly they entered the waiting black limousine. Through the closely-hovering crowd, I caught my last view of the dog and the monk, glimpsing them through the tinted-glass windows. Something in the way they sat together told me she was going to be all right. It wasn't just that she was with the Karmapa; it was the way she sat on the lap of the Karmapa. They seemed to have gained a great deal of respect and trust for one another in a short period of time. The limousine drove them away, leaving behind a path of colorful rose petals.

After that, the monks at the monastery kindly kept me posted on her adventures and whereabouts. Over the years, I heard that the Karmapa traveled all over the world with his Tibetan terrier. The sight of her funny face always brought him and others a feeling of joy, and therefore, he gave her a name that translates from the Tibetan language as Beautiful Happy One. She became his friend and devoted companion, and they were rarely apart during her entire lifetime.

Once considered an ugly puppy, few appreciated what she possessed, yet from the moment she was born, she emanated happiness. It was as if she knew she'd eventually meet her wonderful friend, the Karmapa, who would recognize her true beauty and love her great soul.

~Angel Di Benedetto
Chicken Soup for the Pet Lover's Soul

Devotion

To sit with a dog on a hillside on a glorious afternoon is to be back in Eden,
where doing nothing was not boring—it was peace.
~Milan Kundera

The truck chugged into the parking space beside me in front of the supermarket and shuddered to a stop. Its rusty hinges protested as the man leaned his shoulder against the door to force it open. The truck was old, its red paint so faded and oxidized, six coats of wax could not have coaxed a shine from its ancient hide. The man, too, was old, stooped and faded like his truck. His washed-out red and black checkered flannel shirt and colorless trousers were a perfect match for the aura of age surrounding him and his truck. A farmer, I thought, judging by the leathery, tanned skin of his heavily lined face and gnarled, dirt-encrusted hands. The creases radiating from the corners of his eyes bore witness to years of squinting against the sun. As he stepped out of the truck, he turned to address the only youthful thing in the whole picture, a lively young springer spaniel attempting to follow him.

"No, Lady," he said. "You stay here and guard our truck. I won't be long." He didn't roll up the window, apparently secure the dog would hold her post.

As he entered the grocery store, the dog moved over to assume a position behind the steering wheel, her eyes following the man's progress. As the door closed behind him, she settled back on her haunches, staring almost unblinking at the closed door.

The minutes passed. The dog did not move, and I began to feel her anxiety.

"Don't worry, girl," I said. "He'll be back soon."

I knew she heard me by the way her long brown ears perked up and by the sound of her tail as it thumped a tattoo on the seat beside her. Her nose twitched and the brown freckled fur covering her muzzle shivered in response, but her eyes never wavered from their scrutiny of the door through which the old man had disappeared.

No Buckingham Palace guard could have maintained a more steadfast devotion to duty. Each time the market door opened, the dog stiffened in anticipation, settling back when the emerging figure was not the one for whom she waited.

At last he appeared, carrying a laden plastic bag. The sedate little lady on guard duty erupted into a brown and white flurry of pure joy. She yipped a series of sounds that could only have been interpreted as laughter. She chased her tail in a tight circle, sending up a cloud of dust from the dirt-encrusted seats. When he finally wrested the protesting door open, she launched herself at him, standing with her front paws on his shoulders, licking his face with great swipes of her pink tongue. The spray of white lines at the corners of the man's eyes disappeared as his face crinkled in response to her pleasure. His broad smile revealed strong, slightly stained teeth, probably the result of years of smoking the scarred old pipe peeking out of his shirt pocket.

"Move over, Lady, I'll drive now," he said as he gently pushed the dog to the other side and slipped behind the wheel. That did not end her display of affection. She jumped on him again, her tongue washing his face and ears, knocking off the old misshapen hat protecting his head. From her throat rolled a garbled stream of sound, a language only he understood. Taking her face in his hands, he ruffled the hair at the base of her ears and looking into her eyes said, "I know, I know. I took longer than I expected. But guess what I brought you."

Her hips stopped their frantic swinging as she sat back, alert, watching his every move as he pretended to search his pockets and then the plastic bag, finally producing a package of beef jerky. The dog licked her lips as he slowly tore open the package, removing at last a strip of the hard, dried beef. Gripping it in his strong teeth, he let it protrude from the corner of his mouth as if it were a cigar. Her eyes never left the promised treat. She sat beside him, quivering with anticipation until he nodded. Then she stretched her neck and using only her front teeth, pulled the blackened meat from his mouth. She didn't eat it immediately. Instead, she sat back, watching and waiting, drooling, as the jerky protruded from her mouth in the same way as it had from his.

A smile twitched the corners of the man's lips as he took another piece, placing it into his mouth as he had before. They looked like two old cronies settling back to enjoy a quiet cigar. I felt a smile spread over my own face. He nodded again and the dog flopped down to begin enjoying her treat. He glanced over, seeing me for the first time.

We both grinned sheepishly. I, for having been caught eavesdropping on a private display of a man's affection for his dog. He, for having been caught in the foolish little game he played with her. He snatched the beef strip from his mouth.

As he coaxed his old truck into protesting life, I remarked, "That's a fine dog you have there."

He bobbed his head and replied, "She's a real champion, all right."

Giving me a parting smile, he backed out of the parking space, the old truck resenting every demand being made of it. I watched them as they drove away and noticed the jerky was back in the man's mouth. The dog, having wolfed down her prize, was sitting erect again, eyeing his share, too. I was willing to bet she'd get the last bite of it before they reached their destination.

~Marjie Lyvers
Chicken Soup for the Dog Lover's Soul

A Dog's Love

I think dogs are the most amazing creatures; they give unconditional love.
For me they are the role model for being alive.
~Gilda Radner

Jared had looked forward all year to the weeklong canoe trip with his dad and the other scouts. At last, they were on the Current River in Missouri, and despite his leg braces, he felt just like one of the other eleven-year-old boys.

Shortly after lunch, the scouts beached their canoes. They planned to swim across the river to explore a cave tucked behind huge granite boulders on the other side.

Putting on his life jacket, Jared studied the river that ran deep and swift and wide, but not too deep or swift for a boy with good legs. To reach the caves, the other scouts were already swimming upstream and letting the current carry them down. At the last minute, they broke from the current and kicked for the rocks, safely reaching the shore. Jared wanted to follow them.

He unstrapped his leg braces and then waved to his dad, who had let Jared's dog, Rio, off the leash to play in the water. Rio liked the water, and her shiny black coat looked slick as a seal in the sun. His dad waved back.

Jared had gotten Rio earlier that year as a gift from Canine Companions for Independence to help him get around easier. She was trained to be a guide dog, and since he'd had her, he was no longer afraid of being shoved around in the halls at school. Instead, Rio would push against his braces, helping him navigate through the stream of boys and girls. Since she came along, the other kids noticed Jared more because they liked petting Rio. Jared was glad to have her even if Rio was just doing the job she was trained to do.

Now Rio's smart eyes were on him, but Jared's look told her no. She couldn't help him swim the river; she was trained to help on land, but not in the water. Besides, this was something he wanted to do on his own.

Jared waded out and sank down, using his arms to paddle. At first it was just like at home, in his pool, where he'd taught himself to swim without the use of his legs. The water was colder than he'd thought and felt as strong as a giant's arms as it tugged at him.

When he got to the middle, Jared heard the other boys calling to him from the rocks. They didn't seem to be getting any closer. He looked back at his dad, who was getting farther and farther away.

Then he realized that he couldn't swim free of the current!

Jared only had time for one word before the giant's arms twisted him around and yanked him under. Rio! Water filled his ears and flushed up his nose. He choked and tried to swim out of the giant's grip. But it was no use. The river carried him away.

Suddenly, Jared slammed into something live and strong and sleek as a seal. It was Rio. She pushed against him, just as she did in the halls at school. She looked at him as if to say, Why did you come out here without me?

Jared grabbed onto Rio's fur and, with all her power, Rio pulled him to shore.

Safe on the beach, Rio stood over Jared, panting hard. Shivering, Jared reached up and hugged her neck. She answered with a wag of her tail. At that moment Jared understood that his dog had not just saved his life because it was her job. She'd saved his life because she loved him.

~Zu Vincent
Chicken Soup for the Kid's Soul 2

When Harry Met Kaatje

If you haven't any charity in your heart,
you have the worst kind of heart trouble.
~Bob Hope

ecember 1994. In Holland on a business trip, I had completed my assignment and was heading home. It was early morning on a cold and rainy Saturday, and I was on my way from the hotel to Amsterdam Central Station to catch the train to the airport.

Just outside the train station, I came across a homeless man. I'd seen this particular man a number of times in the past, as I'd traveled through Amsterdam quite often, and usually gave him some change. Many homeless people call Amsterdam Central Station their home, but this man really stuck in my mind because he was always so good-natured.

That day, because of the holidays, I was feeling particularly upbeat, so I handed the man fifty guilders (about twenty-five dollars) and wished him a Merry Christmas. With tears welling up in his eyes, he thanked me profusely for my generosity and asked my name. I told him mine was Dave, and he said his was Harry. We chatted briefly and went our separate ways.

As I walked up to the ticket vending machine inside the train station, I reached into my wallet, but found nothing. I realized that I had just given Harry the last of my money, and the bank was not yet open for currency exchange. I had no Dutch money left to buy my ticket to the airport. As I stood, pondering my predicament, along came Harry. He saw me standing there bewildered and asked if I needed help with the ticket vending machine, as it was entirely in Dutch.

I explained that this was not the difficulty. My actual problem was that I had no money. Without the slightest hesitation, Harry punched out the code for a ticket to the airport, and deposited the change required. Out came a ticket. He handed it to me and said, "Thank you."

I asked why he was thanking me when it was I who was indebted to him.

He said, "Because I have been on the street for many years. I don't have a lot of friends, and you are the first person in a long time that I have been able to help. This is why I thank you."

Over the next eight years, I continued seeing Harry at the train station when I passed through Amsterdam, which was almost every month. He usually saw me first and came over for some conversation. A number of times we had dinner together. Dinner with Harry isn't what most people think of as a normal meal. We would purchase pizza or fries from the outdoor vendors and sit on the curb to eat, since Harry wasn't welcome in restaurants. I didn't care; I considered Harry a good friend.

Then, starting in June 2002, I stopped seeing Harry at the train station. I thought the worst—that Harry, even though he was fairly young and healthy, had probably frozen to death or been killed.

In early 2003, I was in Amsterdam for my monthly visit. It was 5:30 on Saturday morning, and I was on my way to the train station. Suddenly, I heard a voice yell, "Hey, Dave."

I turned to see a clean-shaven, casually dressed gentleman walking a medium-sized brown and white collie-type dog. They were coming my way. I had no idea who this person was. He walked up to me, shook my hand and said, "It's me. Harry."

I was in complete shock! I couldn't believe it. I had never seen the man without ragged clothes and layers of dirt all over himself, and now he looked completely respectable. He began to tell me the story of where he had been for the last several months.

It all began with the dog he was now walking. Kaatje, his new companion, had just shown up one day and started hanging out with him at the train station. He and the dog lived on the street for a few months until one day Kaatje was run over by a car. Harry rushed the dog to a vet, who informed him that the cost of surgery to repair the dog's hip was going to be very expensive. Harry, of course, had no money. The vet made Harry an offer: if he performed the operation, Harry would take up residence on a cot in the back of the vet's office and work for him by watching the dogs during the night shift until the surgery was paid off. Harry readily accepted the offer.

Kaatje came through the hip surgery with flying colors. Harry kept his end of the bargain. Because he was so kind to the animals and was such a good worker, when the bill was paid off, the vet offered Harry a permanent position. With a steady salary, Harry was able to get an apartment for himself and Kaatje. Harry was no longer homeless. His love for Kaatje had rescued him from the streets. He stood before me now, looking like any pleasant young man out for a walk with his dog on a Saturday morning.

It was time to catch my train. Harry and I shook hands, and Kaatje gave me a nice goodbye face wash.

"Let's get together the next time I'm in Amsterdam," I said.

"I'd like that," Harry said with a warm smile.

We made plans to meet for dinner near the train station on my next trip and parted ways.

Just before going into the train station, I turned so I could watch man and dog walking happily back to a place people sometimes take for granted—a place called home.

~Dave Wiley
Chicken Soup for the Dog Lover's Soul

Daisy's Trip

Faith makes things possible, not easy.
~Author Unknown

Daisy stood on Abe's lap in the front of his faded blue truck.
She licked his face. His fingers were buried in her neck.
"I've never seen Pop so happy," said Peter Galan, Abe
Galan's son. "Since Mom passed away, that dog has been his life."

And vice versa, evidently. Ten-year-old Daisy just completed
Modesto's version of The Incredible Journey, a tracking so amazing
even dog experts marvel.

"Daisy tracked her master four miles to a place she had never
been before, over a route that her master never walked." It defied
logic, but that didn't mean a dog couldn't do it.

Daisy yaps. She's half Chihuahua. She's a soprano.

The journey began last Friday, when Daisy watched Abe's children drive away with her master. They took him to Memorial Medical
Center, where he was to undergo cancer surgery.

Another car came and carted Daisy to the house where Rachel,
Abe's daughter, lived. Daisy was supposed to stay with Rachel while
Abe was away.

No one filled Daisy in on the plan.

The first night she never slept. She paced the floor and whined.

The second night, Rachel let Daisy sleep in the yard. Daisy spent
the night digging. She tunneled out before dawn.

Rachel called all of the brothers and sisters at 6:30 in the morning and said, "My God, Daisy is gone."

The extended Galan clan gathered at Rachel's home and fanned out like soldiers.

They walked every step of the neighborhood, taping posters to all the poles. They scoured the street where their dad lived. They knew it would kill him if he lost that dog.

Darkness fell, and still no sign of Daisy.

Meanwhile, Memorial staff was mesmerized by a stray dog. Daisy just sat there by the emergency entrance, and every time the doors opened she'd run in. Someone would chase her out, and she'd turn around and run back in. For hours she did this, starting before dawn.

Employees considered calling the pound, like they do with other strays. But Daisy was different. She was clearly looking for someone. She even made it into the main hallway and was sniffing at the doors.

Paramedic Nina Torres took her to dispatch, where Lou Menton and her partner LaVonda Barker soothed her with a blanket and a Wendy's hamburger. Then she just curled and slept.

Dispatch tried to page the master. "Will the owners of a light tan dog please come to security...."

By 6:30 that night, another one of Abe's daughters—Chris Hackler—made the long walk down Memorial's hall to tell Dad the bad news.

He was coming home the next day. They had to let him know about Daisy. He went nuts when they told him. He tried to get out of bed to go look for her himself.

Chris went out into the hall to compose herself and (as is her fashion) began telling her tale to whoever would listen. Good thing because a woman overheard her and said, "Hey, they've been paging all day for the owner of a lost dog."

The woman went with Chris to call security, who called dispatch, who called the dog "Daisy" to see if it was a match.

Her ears shot right up.

A security guard told Chris she couldn't bring a dog into the hospital, "but if I don't see you do it, I guess there's nothing I can do about it."

Chris wrapped Daisy in a blanket and carried her infant-style into the elevator. A man in the lift tapped her on the shoulder: "Pardon me. Your baby's tail is showing."

Chris told everyone on the elevator the Daisy saga, so everyone on the elevator had to get off with her and watch the reunion. Twenty people were in the hall when Chris handed Abe the bundle: "Dad, I have something for you."

Daisy popped out like a showgirl.

Abe let out a yell, and Daisy started barking. The rest of them were crying like babies.

When Abe was well enough to return home, Daisy's new friends gathered outside to bid them adieu. "We like it when things here at the hospital end happy," Torres said as she planted a big kiss on Daisy's wet nose.

Abe turned to the crowd outside his truck and waved.

Daisy licked her chops and beams. Birds gotta fly, fish gotta swim and Daisy had done found her man.

~Diane Nelson
A 6th Bowl of Chicken Soup for the Soul

46

A Dog's Life

Last summer, I traveled to Rockville, Maryland, to visit with my parents. The trip was special because I had brought along my ten-year-old dog Dakota, who had been part of my family since he was a puppy. My parents had not seen him since I moved to San Jose, California, two years ago, and they were excited about seeing him again.

On the way back, my brother dropped Dakota and me at the airport. After checking in, I stayed with Dakota until an airline baggage handler came to get him. Seeing him off, I headed to the gate. When the agent announced that boarding had started, I happened to look at Dakota's ticket and noticed that it was marked for Salt Lake City instead of San Jose.

In a panic, I went to the agent and advised her of the mistake. I wanted to know if Dakota was on my flight or on a different flight bound for Salt Lake City. The agent didn't have an answer and asked a supervisor to look into it. Ten minutes later, I looked out the window and saw that a baggage handler had pulled up to the aircraft with Dakota in his crate. After seeing Dakota being placed in the aircraft, I boarded the plane.

As I walked onto the plane, I spotted the same baggage handler at the entrance to the plane. Because I was still a little worried about Dakota being on the right plane, I asked him if he had loaded my dog on the aircraft. He said yes and assured me that I shouldn't worry, that everything was okay. His words were welcome relief.

I started to relax. Dakota had been loaded on the correct plane and the flight crew knew I had a dog on board. Because the flight was half full, I switched to a seat in an empty row located in the back of the plane and pulled out my laptop to get some work done. One of the flight attendants noticed Dakota's picture on my computer screen and struck up a conversation about dogs, as she also owned a dog.

About two hours into the flight, I felt a tap on my shoulder. It was that same flight attendant. The pilot wanted to speak to me about my dog, so I followed her up to the front of the plane. I wondered what he wanted to talk to me about, and as I approached the cockpit, the captain came out to meet me.

He told me that he had received a call from the dispatcher who said that Dakota had been inadvertently loaded in the wrong cargo hold. He went on to explain that the aircraft was divided into two cargo holds — forward and rear. The rear cargo hold was designated for animal cargo, as it was lighted, pressurized and heated, while the forward cargo is not designed or used for animal cargo. He said Dakota had been misplaced in the forward cargo hold, and since it was not properly heated, he could not be sure that Dakota was okay, especially in the freezing temperatures at thirty thousand feet.

I couldn't believe what he was telling me. I turned white as a ghost as my eyes watered with tears. The captain then told me that he was going to divert the plane in order to make an unscheduled landing in Denver. Again he cautioned that he did not know if Dakota was still alive. Even though I was very upset, I was grateful that the captain was going to stop in Denver. He went on to explain that once we landed, I could go with him to check if Dakota was all right.

As I sat down in my seat, the captain made an announcement about Dakota's situation and his plan to fly the plane to Denver in an attempt to save Dakota's life. After the announcement, I looked around to see the passengers' reactions, and to my amazement, there were no signs of disapproval.

Unfortunately for Dakota and me, we still had another hour to go before we could land in Denver. It was the longest hour in my life, and as I sat in my seat, I could no longer hold back the tears. I thought about Dakota in that cargo hold and what he might have been going through. I began to think of the worst: that he was already dead, that he must have frozen to death in that cold and dark cargo hold.

I stared out the window and reminisced about my better days with Dakota, from the time he was a puppy through all that we had gone through together over the last years. I recalled the times when I was sad, when he was always there to cheer me up. I remembered the different places we had lived and the places we had visited together.

But then, the more I thought about Dakota, the more I started to wonder if, maybe, he was still alive. I thought about how stubborn and resourceful he was. If anyone could survive it would be him. By the time we approached Denver, I began to believe that Dakota might still be alive and that he would make it.

When we landed in Denver, I looked out the window and saw the ground crew waiting for us at the gate. As soon as the plane stopped, I could hear the ground crew opening the cargo hold door. Immediately, I unbuckled my seat belt and ran to the front of the plane. My heart was pounding in anticipation. As the captain exited the cockpit, we made eye contact, and I could tell that he had good news. With a smile, he told me that he had received a thumbs-up sign from the ground crew: I had not lost my best friend.

We both exited the plane and hurried down the stairs. When I reached the ground, what I saw amazed me: Dakota's crate had been unloaded from the plane and placed on the tarmac with the ground crew in a semi-circle around it. As I approached the crate, I could see Dakota sitting and looking out the wired door. Immediately I opened the door and took him out. He was very cold and shaking. While I was holding him, the ground crew was also excited that Dakota had survived, and they began to pet him. My Dakota was alive and back in my arms!

When it was time for me to put Dakota back into his crate, I couldn't do it. It was too cruel. How could I put him back into the aircraft's cargo hold after all he had been through?

I then asked the captain and the supervisor who had greeted us on the tarmac if I could bring Dakota on board. I reminded him that the plane was only half full and that I had three seats to myself. The supervisor said that it was against the rules and Dakota would have to go back into the cargo hold. The captain then interjected, indicating that since they make exceptions for Seeing Eye dogs, they could also make an exception in this case. The supervisor relented, and to my joy I was able to bring Dakota on the plane with me.

I picked up Dakota and carried him up the stairs and into the plane. As I entered the plane with Dakota in my arms, the passengers cheered and clapped. While I walked down the aisle to my seat, some of the passengers reached out in an effort to touch Dakota. I realized that they also cared and were excited that Dakota had made it.

When I got to my seat, I placed Dakota next to me, but he was still cold and shaking. The flight attendants provided several blankets, which I used to warm him up.

Soon, Dakota seemed more comfortable and was able to fall asleep. Throughout the flight, parents brought their children over to see Dakota, some even looking for him to keep their babies from crying.

And, for the passengers' troubles, the airline offered free drinks and a complimentary movie called *My Dog Skip*—a film about a boy and his dog.

~Mike Bell
Chicken Soup for the Traveler's Soul

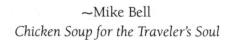

Lucky Wows the Sheriff

Instinct is untaught ability.
~Bain

Lucky was a dog of huge proportion — actually, disproportion. His neck was thick, his head was skinny, and his eyes were too close together, giving him a slightly stupid expression. I once had a friend who described his horse as a "cross between a freight train and a wire gate." When I found that big splotchy dog, stray and starving by the side of the road, I thought the description suited him, too. But in spite of his appearance, I brought him home to live with us.

Late one night I came home from work, driving up the long lane to our house in the country and — as usual — turned the car around in preparation for leaving the next morning. Lucky — also as usual — watched this routine, wagging mightily, and waited for me to open the car door. But this night, as I stepped out of the car, Lucky growled menacingly, barked and advanced toward me. I backed into the car seat and quickly closed the door against my big black-and-white, cow-spotted friend, who had now turned aggressive. In disbelief I contemplated the hundreds of cans of expensive dog food we had served him. This is how he thanks me? I sat there, safe in my metallic cocoon, puzzled. Then as my head cleared, I took heart and reasoned the dog was just playing a game and that it was silly to sit there in the dark. I pushed the door fully open. Lucky exploded, shooting up to display his full six-foot-plus "Bigfoot" imitation. Throwing his body weight across the door, he slammed it shut. Then standing guard, he never took his too-close-together eyes off the door again.

Our Tennessee fall had deepened. Though leaves would blow down from the woods for at least another month, frigid nights already frosted the leaves banked by our doorstep. Just as I was getting good and chilly, my husband drove into his parking spot beside my car. "What are you doing sitting out here in the cold?" he asked.

I cracked the window open an inch to explain that Lucky was now crazy and I could never get out of the car again.

"Well," my practical husband said, "Let's go see what's upsetting the big fellow."

Now that the mister was home, Lucky permitted me out of the car. As we approached the doorstep with a flashlight, the dog ran ahead and began a bizarre impersonation of a giraffe imitating a pointer. That's when we heard it — or more accurately, felt it — a buzzing sound from beneath a leaf pile. It could mean only one thing: a rattler. (When I encountered my first rattlesnake, what surprised me was that rattlers don't rattle; it's your teeth that rattle as the chills run up and down your spine.)

For some reason, the snake remained coiled in its chosen spot until the county sheriff arrived with his deputies and shotguns. As we raked the leaf cover aside, we saw that the timber rattler was so large that a man could not girdle it with the thumbs and middle fingers of both hands. We could also see why the snake had remained in place for so long. Picture a dozen little snakes squiggling around in all directions; with two large, uniformed deputies, armed with garden rakes and shovels, scrambling to collect the snake babies into a tall container; and a great black-and-white dog running back and forth, barking, dancing and "helping."

When the dancing was over and all the snakes caged, the exhausted sheriff said that he had worked the hills for many years, but had never seen "such a snake." Then he said, "Ma'am, it's a good thing you didn't step in that mess o' snakes in the dark. That dog saved your life tonight. I think you owe him a big Angus steak."

We all looked at Lucky who had returned to normal: a homely, friendly and slightly stupid-looking dog, wagging his tail at his team-mates. He was an unlikely hero, but a hero all the same.

The sheriff then paid Lucky the highest compliment a country dog can receive, "Yes sir, that's a fine dog you've got there."

We had to agree.

~Mariana Levine
Chicken Soup for the Dog Lover's Soul

Dusty, the Wonder Dog

Lots of people talk to animals...
not very many listen, though.... That's the problem.
~Benjamin Hoff, The Tao of Pooh

When I was a kid, my godparents, Uncle Nell and Aunt Frances, brought me a four-month-old puppy. She was half German shepherd, half collie. As her pink tongue tickled my face with wet licks, it was love at first hug.

My family named the puppy Dusty. Although I wanted to lay sole claim to her affections, in a family of seven kids, no one lays permanent claim to the family pet.

Dusty was our dog, not my dog. We soon realized that she had the patience of Buddha. My baby sister often transformed Dusty's warm fur into a nap-time pillow—falling asleep on the rug. Like a protective mother, Dusty waited—without moving—until my sister woke.

Dusty doubled as a school crossing guard, too. Monday through Friday she'd walk us kids two blocks to St. Patrick's Parochial, looking both ways to check for traffic before allowing us to cross the street. We'd wave goodbye as we entered the door, knowing Dusty would be waiting at the school door to claim us at the close of the school day.

Of all the contributions Dusty made to our family, one incident stands out far and above all others.

Late one night, Dusty rushed to my parents' bedroom. She barked and barked. When she got no response, Dusty raced upstairs to my bedroom and my brothers' bedroom and barked again and again. When she failed to fully wake us, she flew back down the steps and returned to my parents' room. Finally, she got Mom's attention.

"What are you doing, Dusty?" Mom snapped, still halfway in dreamland. Dusty persisted. Finally my mother gave in. "Okay, what is it?"

Dusty whined and rushed out of Mom's room. Thinking the dog needed to be let out to relieve herself, my mother followed Dusty to the front door.

When Mom opened the door to let her out, Dusty tore across the street, not stopping to do her business as my mother had assumed. Then she discovered what Dusty already knew. The house across the street — where my best friend, Marianne, and her family lived — was on fire. All of Dusty's middle-of-the-night craziness had served a purpose: she'd been trying to call for help.

My mother alerted the fire department immediately. Soon, the firemen in their trucks roared up the street, squelching the blaze and saving my best friend's family from harm and their house from total ruin.

My mother refused to take credit. "It was Dusty," she told the firefighters. "She saved them. Not me."

I put my arms around my dog's neck and kissed her square on the tip of her wet nose. "Thank you for saving Marianne," I whispered into Dusty's tan and black ear. "You're the bravest dog I've ever known."

Dusty wagged her tail and licked my face. That old familiar rush of puppy love overtook me. I smiled and promised to let her sleep in my bed for the rest of her life.

~Mary Saracino
Chicken Soup for the Preteen Soul

Just an Old
Golden Retriever

All God's angels come to us disguised.
~James Russell Lowell

She was just an old golden retriever. Her name was Brandy, and for eleven years she was the sole companion of an elderly woman who lived in a bungalow colony in the country. Neighbors often saw the two of them together in the garden. The woman would be hunched over picking flowers and there was that old dog, close at her heels or lying in the middle of the grass watching her pull weeds. When the woman died, some relatives came and collected anything they thought was valuable and put a "For Sale" sign on the front lawn. Then they locked the dog out and drove away.

Some of the neighbors left food out for Brandy, but mostly the dog stayed near the house that she knew and waited for her owner to come back. A young mother who lived next door noticed the old retriever, but she had never been around animals before and while she thought the dog was friendly enough, she didn't feel it was any of her concern.

However, when the dog wandered into her yard and began playing with eighteen-month-old Adam, she wanted to shoo the dirty thing away. Adam was her only child and the light of her life. But he was having so much fun feeding Brandy cookies she decided to let her stay. After that, whenever Adam had cookies Brandy came by to visit.

One afternoon, the boy's mother left Adam in the soft grassy yard to play while she answered the phone. When she returned he was gone. Just gone. The mother was frantic. Neighbors came over to help in the search. Police arrived and looked for three hours before calling in the state police and helicopters to do an extensive aerial search. But no one could find the child, and as the sun set over the horizon, whispers of abduction, injury or even death crept into conversations.

The search had been going on for six hours when a neighbor, who'd just returned home, wondered where Brandy was. Adam's mother, hysterical with worry, didn't understand why anyone was asking about the old dog at a time like this.

When someone suggested she might be with Adam, a trooper recalled hearing a dog barking deep in the woods when they were doing a foot search. Suddenly, everybody started calling for Brandy.

They heard faint barking and followed the sound until they found the toddler, standing up fast asleep, pressed against the trunk of a tree. That old dog was holding him there with one shoulder as one of her own legs dangled over a thirty-five-foot drop to a stream below.

Brandy had followed Adam when he wandered off. When she saw danger, she'd pushed him out of harm's way and held him safe for all those hours, even as the child struggled to get free.

As soon as the rescue team picked up Adam, the old dog collapsed. A trooper carried Adam back home, while his mother, sobbing with relief, carried Brandy. She was so grateful to the old golden retriever that Brandy spent the rest of her days with them. Brandy lived to the ripe old age of seventeen.

But this story doesn't end with just one life saved. In Brandy's honor, Adam's mother, Sara Whalen, founded Pets Alive, a rescue sanctuary in New York that takes in unwanted animals, including those designated to be euthanized because they are old, blind, incontinent or perhaps not cute enough to be adopted. While she can't save them all, Sara feels comforted that she can help at least some of them. She knows that if someone had put that old retriever to sleep, she could have easily lost the light of her life: her son.

Today, thirty years later, there are more than three hundred animals in her care, including birds, potbellied pigs, old horses retired from the carriage business and unadoptable pets from rescue groups across the country. The woman who used to think an old, abandoned dog wasn't any of her concern found that every life has value and has become a beacon for thousands of animals in need.

~Audrey Thomasson
Chicken Soup for the Dog Lover's Soul

Loving Our Dogs

Support Dogs

*One reason a dog can be such a comfort when you're feeling blue
is that he doesn't try to find out why.*
~Author Unknown

Daisy Love

In our early days of working together at the grooming shop, my husband, David, and I had a field day studying humanity as it passed through our door on the other end of a dog leash. Things were less hectic then. We had plenty of time to dissect our customers' personalities and discuss our observations.

George was one of these character studies. Despite his gruff personality, he was a sentimental man, an uncommon trait in cool, reserved New England where we strive to keep a stiff upper lip. George wore his heart on his sleeve, notably for Evie, his wife of forty-five years whose death after a lingering illness had been a traumatic blow to the craggy old gentleman.

Each April on the anniversary of Evie's passing, George would grace the editorial page of the local newspaper with a poem written in her memory.

"Every year about this time, we know we can count on two things," David remarked as he leafed through the paper. "Income taxes and a poem from George."

"I happen to think it's touching," I argued. "And I'll tell you something else: If George doesn't get his dog to the vet soon, he'll have somebody else to grieve for."

For almost a year, I had been upset whenever George brought his terrier mix, Daisy, in for grooming. I had noticed small lumps growing on her body, but each time I suggested he take the little Benji look-alike to the vet, he changed the subject. I agonized over the situation with David, who also worked as a psychiatric nurse. "People like George will not act until they are ready," he told me. "In the mental-health field, we refer to this as denial."

I empathized with George's dread. In his mind, if he didn't name the demon, it didn't exist. And Daisy was much more than a pet to the lonely widower. A heavy smoker and drinker in his younger years, George's retirement had been hastened by poor health, but now he worked at keeping fit. His daily walks with Daisy were a big part of his regimen.

His life revolved around the little dog. There was the morning ride to the doughnut shop where Ruthie the waitress always saved him a plain, and Daisy a coconut, cruller. "I know it's not health food, but it's my only vice," he told me. Once home, they'd relax in his recliner to watch *The Price Is Right*, then take a walk before lunch. After a nap, they arose in time to greet the school kids getting off the bus in front of their house. No matter what the chore—leaf raking, fence painting, bulb planting or lawn mowing—Daisy happily tagged along at her master's heels as he addressed her with a steady stream of chatter.

His pride in the little mongrel showed every time he picked her up after grooming. "Well, well, don't you look pretty," he'd enthuse as Daisy wagged her whole body with delight. "Show us how you dance!"

The little dog dutifully twirled on her hind legs, then yipped for a cookie. "Show Kathy how you go for a walk," he'd tell her, as she picked up the leash in her mouth and trotted to the door.

"Now let's go visit your mother and show her those pretty bows." Off they would go to tend the flowers on Evie's grave.

Another winter came and went before George got to the vet with Daisy. By this time, the lumps were harder and larger. I felt a sense of grim foreboding when he said the vet had decided not to operate. "He said she would be more comfortable if you gave her medicated baths." Somehow I did not believe those were the vet's only instructions.

As the months passed, Daisy grew less energetic. She found it increasingly hard to stand, so I took to trimming her while she was lying down. She still performed her little tricks at the end of each visit. "Show Kathy how you act shy," he told her as she ducked her head and covered her eyes with a paw.

When I returned from my summer vacation, my new assistant, Trudy, conveyed the news I had been dreading: Daisy had passed away. "George was very upset that you weren't here," she told me. "He even called the vet a quack. It got worse when he started crying."

Unable to reach him by phone, I sent George a letter expressing our condolences. Months later, when he dropped by to see us, he looked as though he had aged several years. We reminisced about Daisy, her funny tricks and endearing ways. "My son keeps telling me to pull myself together. If he tells me once more, 'Dad, it was only a dog....'" All I could offer was a hug.

"The worst part is, it was all my fault," he said tearfully. "I blamed the vet, but if I had taken her to see him when you folks told me to, I'd still have her now."

David gently placed his arm around the old man's shoulder. "We've all learned some lessons the hard way, George," he told him.

A few weeks later, fate intervened when a young woman came into the shop, dragging a dirt-caked terrier mix that was matted from head to tail. The raggedy creature's pungent odor told me it had recently gotten up close and personal with a skunk.

"This here is Fanny. She belongs to my aunt and uncle, but they wanna get rid of her."

As I reached down to examine the dog, she jerked its chain. "I gotta warn ya, she's a bad dog. She barks all day, and she don't like kids."

"She barks in the house?" I inquired.

"No, she don't come in the house. They keep her tied out in the yard."

Poor Fanny was frightened and jumpy. Grooming her was not easy or pleasant. When she emerged, de-fleaed and de-skunked, her bones jutted out from her bare skin. Yet somehow she looked eerily familiar.

"Who does she remind you of?" I asked David.

"Sinead O'Connor?" he guessed.

"No! Doesn't she look like Daisy, George's old dog?"

It would take some convincing. George had sworn he would never have another pet.

"I just can't go through it again," he told me. "I don't deserve it after what happened to Daisy."

"But, George, you know you've been lonely," I prodded, as determined as a used-car salesman.

"Everybody's lonely," he grumped. "What else is new?"

"The poor thing spends her life tied to a rusty chain in a muddy backyard. She's totally unsocialized." I warmed to my subject. "Maybe you shouldn't take her after all. She's going to need an awful lot of training, patience and love. You might not be up to it."

"I guess I could take her on a trial basis," he mumbled.

"Well, if it doesn't work out, you can always give her back," I offered brightly.

The first thing George did was to rename the dog.

Daisy II. Her coat grew out, soft and fluffy, and she learned to walk on a leash and come when called. She still got anxious when he left her for grooming, then exploded in a yapping fury when he came to pick her up.

"Watch this," he said one December day, placing his car keys on the chair beside my counter. "Daisy, want to go get doughnuts?"

In a furry flash, she raced to the chair, jumping up and then landing squarely at his feet, head cocked to one side and keys gripped tightly in her mouth. George beamed proudly.

David and I stood in the doorway, watching the happy pair walk across the snow-dusted parking lot as the church bells chimed a Christmas carol. "Merry Christmas, George!" I called after him. "And don't forget—if it doesn't work out, you can always give her back!"

~Kathy Salzberg
Chicken Soup for the Dog Lover's Soul

The Gift of Courage

Sometimes even to live is an act of courage.
~Lucius Annaeus Seneca, Letters to Lucilius

Mark was about eleven years old, skinny and slouching, when he and his mom first brought Mojo into the clinic where I worked. Baggy clothes dwarfed the boy's small frame, and under a battered baseball hat, challenging blue eyes glared at the world. Clearly we had to earn Mark's trust before we could do anything with his dog. Mojo was around nine then, old for a black Labrador retriever, but not too old to still have fun. Though recently it seemed that Mojo had lost all his spunk.

Mark listened intently as the doctor examined his dog, answered questions and asked more, while nervously brushing back wisps of blond hair that escaped the hat onto his furrowed brow. "Mojo's going to be okay, isn't he?" he blurted as the doctor turned to leave. There were no guarantees, and when the blood work came back, the doctor's suspicions were confirmed. Mojo had liver and kidney disease, progressive and ultimately fatal. With care he could live comfortably for a while, but he'd need special food, regular checkups and medications. The doctor and I knew finances were a struggle, but the moment euthanasia was suggested, Mark's mom broke in. "We're not putting Mojo to sleep." Quickly and quietly they paid their bill and gently led their old dog out to the car without a backward glance.

We didn't hear from them for a few weeks, but then one day, there they were. Mojo had lost weight. He'd been sick, they said, and he seemed listless. As I led Mojo back to the treatment room for some IV fluid therapy, Mark's little body blocked the way.

"I have to go with him—he needs me," the boy said firmly.

I wasn't sure how Mark would handle the sight of needles and blood, but there didn't seem any point in arguing. And indeed, Mark handled it all as if he'd seen it a million times before.

"Oh, you're such a brave old guy, Mojo," Mark murmured as the catheter slipped into Mojo's vein. We seldom had a more cooperative patient. Mojo only moved his head slightly during uncomfortable procedures, as if to remind us that he was still there. He seemed to take strength from the small, white hand that continually moved in reassurance over his grizzled throat.

This became the pattern. We'd get Mojo stabilized somewhat, send him home, he'd get sick again, and they'd be back. Always, Mark was there, throwing out questions and reminders to be careful, but mostly encouraging and comforting his old pal.

I worried that Mark found it too difficult, watching, but any hint that maybe he'd rather wait outside was flatly rejected. Mojo needed him.

I approached Mark's mom one day, while Mark and Mojo were in the other room, "You know Mojo's condition is getting worse. Have you thought any more about how far you want to go with treatment? It looks like Mark is really having a hard time with all this."

Mark's mom hesitated a moment before leaning forward and speaking in a low, intense voice, "We've had Mojo since Mark was a baby. They've grown up together, and Mark loves him beyond all reason. But that's not all."

She took a deep breath and looked away momentarily, "Two years ago Mark was diagnosed with leukemia. He's been fighting it, and they tell us he has a good chance of recovering completely. But he never talks about it. He goes for tests and treatments as if it's happening to someone else, as if it's not real. But about Mojo, he can ask questions. It's important to Mark, so as long as he wants to, we'll keep on fighting for Mojo."

The next few weeks we saw a lot of the quiet little trio. Mark's abrupt questions and observations, once slightly annoying, now had a new poignancy, and we explained at length every procedure as it was happening. We wondered how long Mojo could carry on. A more stoic and good-natured patient was seldom seen, but the Labrador was so terribly thin and weak now. All of us at the clinic really worried about how Mark would handle the inevitable.

Finally the day came when Mojo collapsed before his scheduled appointment. It was a Saturday when they rushed him in, and the waiting room was packed. We carried Mojo into the back room and settled him on some thick blankets, with Mark at his side as usual. I left to get some supplies, and when I reentered the room a few moments later I was shocked to see Mark standing at the window, fists jammed into his armpits, tears streaming down his face. I backed out of the room noiselessly, not wanting to disturb him. He'd been so brave up until now. Later when we returned, he was kneeling, dry-eyed once more, at Mojo's side. His mom sat down beside him and squeezed his shoulders. "How are you guys doing?" she asked softly.

"Mom," he said, ignoring her question, "Mojo's dying, isn't he?"

"Oh, honey..." her voice broke, and Mark continued as if she hadn't spoken.

"I mean, the fluids and the pills, they're just not going to help anymore, are they?" He looked to us for confirmation. "Then I think," he swallowed hard, "I think we should put him to sleep."

True to form, Mark stayed with Mojo until the end. He asked questions to satisfy himself that it truly was best for Mojo, and that there would be no pain or fear for his old friend. Over and over again he smoothed the glossy head, until it faded onto his knee for the last time. As Mark felt the last breath leave Mojo's thin ribs and watched the light dim in the kind brown eyes, he seemed to forget about the rest of us. Crying openly, he bent himself over Mojo's still form and slowly removed his cap. With a jolt I recognized the effects of chemotherapy, so harsh against such a young face. We left him to his grief.

Mark never told us anything about his own illness, or his own feelings throughout Mojo's ordeal, but when his mom called months later to ask some questions about a puppy she was considering buying, I asked her how he was doing.

"You know," she said, "it was a terrible time for him, but since Mojo's death, Mark has begun talking about his own condition, asking questions and trying to learn more about it. I think that dealing with Mojo when the dog was so sick gave Mark strength to fight for himself and courage to face his own pain."

I always thought Mark was being brave for Mojo, but when I remember those calm, trusting eyes and gently wagging tail that never failed no matter how bad he felt, I think maybe Mojo was being brave for Mark.

~Roxanne Willems Snopek Raht
Chicken Soup for the Pet Lover's Soul

Calvin:
A Dog with a Big Heart

To conquer fear is the beginning of wisdom.
~Bertrand Russell

Blinded in a Nazi concentration camp at the age of twenty-one, I arrived in America with my wife in 1951. We worked and raised two sons; now, at eighty-two, I have five grandchildren. For most of those years, I depended on a white cane as my mobility aid. I envied my blind friends who had guide dogs — they had so much more freedom of mobility than I did. My problem, although I was reluctant to admit it, was that I had a fear of getting too close to dogs.

In spite of my fear, the day I retired I decided to apply for a guide dog at the Guiding Eyes for the Blind Guide Dog School. I so wanted the freedom a dog could give me, I had to make the attempt.

When I arrived, Charlie, the training supervisor, had a few cheerful welcoming words for the twelve of us beginning the May 1990 class. After the welcoming ceremonies, I took Charlie aside and said, "I would like to have a guide dog, but because of my negative experiences with dogs, I am not sure I could ever bond with one." Charlie, curious, asked me if I minded telling him about my negative experiences.

"I am a Holocaust survivor. In one of the Nazi concentration camps I was in," I explained, "the commandant had a big, vicious German shepherd. Sometimes when he entertained guests and wanted to show how cruel he could be, or how vicious his dog was—or both—he told a guard to bring a group of prisoners into his courtyard. Once, before I was blinded, I was in that group. I watched as he chose one of us to stand apart. Then he gave the dog the command, 'Fass!' meaning, 'Fetch!' With one leap, the dog grabbed the victim by the throat. In a few minutes, that man was dead. The dog returned to his master for his praise and reward, and the audience applauded the dog for a job well done. More than four decades later, nightmares about this still torment me," I confided to Charlie.

After a moment of reflection, Charlie said, "No human being is born evil; some become evil. No dog is born vicious; some are trained to be vicious. Give us a chance to prove to you that the dogs we train and the one you get will guide you safely, love you and protect you."

His words strengthened my resolve. I was determined, I told Charlie, to give myself a chance. Should I fail, it wouldn't be for lack of trying. Charlie called a meeting of his staff to reexamine my file and decided Calvin would be the right match for me. Calvin was a two-year-old, eighty-pound chocolate Lab. Following our four-week training period, I went home with Calvin and found myself struggling to forge a bond with him. I was in the process of learning to love him, and although I understood the helpful role Calvin was to play in my life, I was still cautious around him, never fully relaxing and accepting him. This struggle affected Calvin as well. During this period, Calvin ate, but lost weight, and the vet told me it was because the dog could sense my emotional distance. I often recalled Charlie's words: "No human being is born evil, and no dog is born vicious...." My instructor called me several times, offering advice and giving me encouragement.

Slowly but surely, Calvin and I began to break down the invisible barrier between us. Finally, after about six months—twice as long as the average human/guide dog team—I began to trust Calvin more fully. I went with him anywhere I needed to go and did so with confidence.

Any lingering doubts I had about Calvin were dispelled one day as we stood at a busy intersection, waiting to cross the street. As we had been trained, when I heard parallel traffic start to move, I waited three seconds, then gave the command, "Calvin, forward." When we stepped off the curb, a motorist suddenly and unexpectedly made a sharp right turn, directly in front of us. Calvin stopped on a dime, slamming on the brakes! He had reacted exactly as he had been trained to react in such a situation. Realizing that he had saved us both from serious injury, I stepped back onto the sidewalk, crouched down, gave Calvin a hug around the neck and praised him for a job well done.

It was the turning point in our life together. After that, the love between us flowed freely and Calvin blossomed.

Out of harness, Calvin became as playful and mischievous as any other dog. When my granddaughter Hannah, a one-year-old just starting to get steady on her feet, came to visit, Calvin let her painstakingly position herself to grab his silky ear. Then he moved deftly to the side, his tail wagging a mile a minute, as Hannah reached in vain for him. Calvin's game made Hannah squeal with delight.

Calvin also formed a loving relationship with my wife, Barbara. She was coping with several chronic physical conditions and was homebound, and they became inseparable pals and playmates. At her periodic visit to the doctor, he noticed that her blood pressure was lower than it had been for a long time. Barbara asked the doctor if Calvin's companionship could have anything to do with her lowered blood pressure. "Most unlikely," he replied. "I'll change your prescription, though, since your blood pressure is better. Come back in two months." The blood pressure stayed down. The doctor, although unconvinced, grudgingly accepted that Calvin's companionship might have had a favorable effect. Barbara and I had no doubt. The facts spoke for themselves.

Time and time again, Calvin proved he had a big heart, big enough for Barbara and me: He not only gave me the extra measure of independent and safe travel I had craved for many years, he also became a beloved member of the family.

Yes, Charlie, you were right. "Give us a chance," you said. "Your dog will love you, guide you, protect you." Calvin did all that and then some.

~Max Edelman
Chicken Soup for the Dog Lover's Soul

53

Pop Pop's Promise

Of all the attitudes we can acquire, surely the attitude of gratitude is the most important and by far the most life-changing.
~Zig Ziglar

When I was a little girl my grandfather, Pop Pop, used to tell me that every part of life held the promise of something good. He said if I believed in that promise, sooner or later I would find a good thing even in life's roughest situations. When I was young, it was easy to believe what my grandfather told me, especially when the two of us spent time together on his farm in Virginia's Shenandoah Valley. The gentle greeting of a milking cow, the fragrance of freshly turned earth in the garden and the unspoiled sweetness of a newborn kitten taught me the truth in my grandfather's words.

Still, as a child born with cerebral palsy, I thought I'd found something my Pop Pop had gotten wrong. He had said "everything in life holds the promise of something good."

His words made sense when it came to newborn kittens and fresh gifts from the garden, but not when it came to cerebral palsy. I couldn't find a single good thing in my disability. It meant physical pain, frightening operations, difficult therapy and the frustrating realization that no matter how hard I tried, there were things that I just could not do. I used to watch other children walk smoothly across a room, but when I tried to do the same, my muscles refused to cooperate. My body behaved like a complicated toy that never worked the way I wanted it to. I underwent my first operation before I was two. By the time I was sixteen, I had endured a dozen surgical procedures on my feet, ankles, thighs, calves and even my eyes. Cerebral palsy did not fade away with surgery, therapy or braces, and it didn't fade away with prayers hung on every star in the heavens.

Walking was an overwhelming task. It demanded determination, concentration and luck. If I had all of these, I could usually move across a room without crashing into anything. For me, that was graceful. Far too often, my poise faltered in midstride and I'd tumble to the ground like some weary, wind-tossed butterfly.

With time and practice, I learned to manage—somewhat. Still, my greatest struggle was that cerebral palsy had a terrible hold on my heart. I tried to act happy and secure, but beneath my smile I felt guilty and afraid. Even saying the words "cerebral palsy" made me redden with shame. I believed my worth was measured not by the way I lived, but by the way I walked. I was afraid that other people would see my disabled body and decide there wasn't enough to love in the person they saw. That fear surrounded me like a huge stone wall, and I couldn't open up to other people. I could not believe in the person I was created to be—I could only hide behind that wall of fear.

Since my grandfather said that everything in life held the promise of something good, I wanted to believe him, but after many years of trying, I couldn't find anything good about having to live in my body. Then, when I was twenty-three, something good found me.

Slugger was a lively young Labrador, a handful of sunshine-colored fluff. Doggy delight bubbled up inside him and escaped in a constant stream of puppy wiggles. When Sylvia Fisher of Caring Canine Companions saw Slugger, she knew he was destined to make a difference. Sylvia enlisted the help of Vicki Polk and many other Caring Canine Companions volunteers. Thanks to the tireless dedication of these people, the bright-eyed puppy was transformed into a skilled service dog.

I'll always remember the moment when I met Slugger for the first time. His tail waved an easy hello and his brown eyes sparkled with friendly curiosity. At that moment I fell in love. He was the most incredible animal I could have imagined, but I soon discovered there was even more to him than I could have guessed. Much more! As a certified service dog, Slugger had mastered basic obedience. He knew how to retrieve dropped items, open doors and bark on command. He had even learned to provide support while navigating steps and hills with his handler.

It had taken two years for Slugger to learn the skills essential for a service dog; it took the two of us several months to uncover the secret of successful teamwork. We graduated together in 1993, and although he and I still had a lot to learn from each other, I knew this dog would make a difference in my life. At the time, I had no idea how great that difference would be.

My partnership with Slugger brought a new freedom to my life. When we began our career as a service dog team, I was completing my master's degree at James Madison University. With Slugger by my side, tasks like carrying heavy textbooks and walking across a crowded campus became easier than I had ever dreamed they could be. I no longer had to rely on other people to give me a hand when I was going up a hill. If I dropped a pencil during one of my classes, he quickly retrieved it. On many occasions, Slugger even kept me from falling on icy steps and rain-soaked sidewalks.

My service dog brought me the gift of physical freedom. Even more precious than that, however, was the gift he brought to my heart. Slugger touched me with an extraordinary love — a love that kept pace when my heart danced, and held steadfast when I stumbled. In sweet, unspoken ways, that love eased the pain in my heart, and his devotion taught me to believe in the person I was created to be. I learned to define myself not by what I had to overcome, but by what I had the courage to become.

Slugger and I have lived and worked together for nine years. In his gentle way, my service dog continues to share his Labrador lessons, and they have made me a wiser person. Thanks to him, I understand that blond fur on a dark skirt makes a wonderful fashion statement. I've discovered that every good partnership requires give and take. I have learned that a gift is most beautiful when it is shared. And now, at last, I understand what my grandfather meant when he said that every part of life holds the promise of something good.

~Leigh B. Singh
Chicken Soup to Inspire the Body and Soul

54

Agnes and Mattie

Our perfect companions never have fewer than four feet.
~Colette

In her ninety-third summer, Agnes, her mind still sharp as an eagle's eye, was wheeled down the dim hall of the nursing home to the last room on the left. Number 109.

"It's a good room, Auntie," her niece, one of two living relatives, said softly. "Nice and clean."

Agnes took in the white walls, the gray linoleum floor and was silent. That night, as she lay on the strange bed, trying to shut out the sounds of the TV from the room next door, she felt as if her real life had ended in that careless moment when she'd tripped over a tree root, shattering her hip and her freedom.

She hung her wooden crucifix above the metal nightstand. Into the top drawer she stuffed old letters, pictures, a box of candy and a broken old dog biscuit she found in the bottom of her purse. In her real life, she'd walked every day, and the neighborhood dogs greeted her eagerly, just as her own dog Rusty used to. She couldn't bear to throw out the biscuit.

Agnes refused to leave her room. She refused to make this place home.

This is not my home, she thought fiercely. This is nothing like my home.

She read. She napped. She traveled a worn path in memory back over the years to the big yellow house at the end of the street. Rusty always trotted at her heels as she strolled. She saw the towering shade trees that her beloved Papa had planted as saplings for her and her husband Jack when they first got married.

She and Jack had enjoyed a good marriage. There'd been no children. Just the dogs. The last was Rusty, a tall, proud mutt, who was with her when Jack died of pneumonia. Rusty had slept on the floor by her side of the bed, and every morning she'd reach down first thing to pet him. Now, curled in her bed, she hung an arm over the mattress; for a heart-stopping second, she thought she felt Rusty's mink-soft head and heard the thump of his long, fringed tail. Then the clanging of the meal carts and the bland smell of institutional food brought her back to reality. She cried into her pillow.

The activities director of the nursing home, a woman named Ronnie, was concerned about Agnes. There must be a way to reach her, she thought. Every day Ronnie came to Number 109, pulled up a chair and showed Agnes the activities schedule.

"Look at this," Ronnie would say, her finger sliding down the list. "We have current events, bingo, women's issues, music, sweet memories. Won't you just try one? Or maybe you'd like to go down the hall and meet some people?"

But the elderly lady with the girlish bangs shook her head. "I'm fine," she said, her eyes cloudy with sadness.

One day, in late autumn, Ronnie walked into Agnes's room and spied a dog calendar on top of the nightstand.

"What a handsome dog," Ronnie said, tapping the picture. For the first time she saw a spark in the faded blue eyes.

"I love dogs," Agnes said.

Ronnie's mind started racing. She'd tried in the past to arrange for a dog to visit the nursing home, but it had never worked out. Now it was time to try again. Back in her office, she dialed the number of a local shelter and talked to the shelter director, a woman named Mimi. Halfway through Ronnie's story, Mimi broke in and said, "We have the perfect dog. Her name is Mattie."

For weeks Mimi had been wondering what to do about

Mattie. She thought back to the blustery winter night when Mattie, a large black mutt, had been brought in as a stray. She shivered in the doorway, her coat mud-caked and wet. Despite her appearance, she was dignified, like a lady who'd fallen on hard times.

"Here, girl," Mimi called. Shyly the dog came, placing a dirty paw on Mimi's knee, then removing it, as if to say, "I'm sorry. I forgot about the mud."

They bathed her and combed out the mats, from which they took her name—Mattie. No one claimed her. She lived in a kennel run with four to five other dogs, waiting to be adopted. Months turned to years. Each time people came to look, competing canines raced to the gate, barking and furiously wagging their tails. Mattie trailed modestly behind, shyly raising trusting brown eyes. Like a gem that doesn't shine, she was passed over. She became a lonely, institutional survivor. Like Agnes.

Now, Mimi walked down the long, noisy kennel aisle to a large run. "Mattie," she called into the maze of barking, wriggling canines. The big, long-haired mutt padded to the gate, calmly easing herself through the crush of younger, excitable dogs. She pressed her setter-type nose into the wire mesh.

"Hey, old girl," Mimi said, getting down to eye level. "A lady named Agnes needs you." Mattie's ears perked.

Not many days later, Mimi walked Mattie down the dim hall of the nursing home to the last room on the left. Number 109. The dog was freshly bathed and groomed. Her ears were erect, and her tail was raised high with anticipation. They turned the corner of the doorway and Mattie's nails clicked on the gray linoleum. Agnes looked up from her chair; the book she'd been reading slipped off her lap. Her mouth dropped. Tears filled her eyes and spilled down her cheeks.

"I thought I'd never see a dog again," she sobbed.

"Her name's Mattie," Mimi said.

"Here, Mattie. Here, girl," Agnes called. Mattie trotted over, leash dragging, waving her long, fringed tail just as Rusty used to. Agnes buried her face in the soft fur. Mattie scrunched as close as she could get and placed a paw on Agnes's lap. She looked up adoringly, her eyes begging friendship.

Agnes stroked her silky head, whispering, "Hello, Mattie, girl. There's a good girl." Her wizened face was soft and glowing. Mattie laid her head in Agnes's lap and sighed as Agnes scratched behind her ears.

Suddenly, Agnes remembered something. With the aid of her walker, she hobbled eagerly to the nightstand, Mattie trotting at her heels. The old lady opened the drawer, retrieving the crumbling dog biscuit she hadn't been able to throw away. Mattie's ears lifted. Daintily she took the biscuit, then cleaned the crumbs from the floor.

Before they left, Mimi promised Agnes they'd come every week. Agnes flipped through the dog calendar, marking in all the Tuesdays with Mattie's name.

Now when Mattie arrived for her visits, the drawer of the metal cabinet was always stocked with favorite treats. Ever the lady, Mattie would ask politely by sniffing the drawer, then sitting and waiting. She never had to wait long.

As the months went by, Agnes began to show an interest in the events around her. Soon Mattie was accompanying Agnes to drawing classes, flower-arranging workshops and gospel songfests. She sat with her head in Agnes's lap as Agnes talked with friends, and she thumped her tail at Agnes's happy chuckle.

Encouraged by the change in Agnes, Mimi took Mattie to visit residents at other nursing homes. Mattie's days became full as well. Before long, many volunteers were taking dogs to visit old people and children throughout the area. The successful Golden Outreach Program was officially launched.

When Agnes celebrated her one-hundredth birthday, Mattie, herself a senior citizen and still a regular visitor, came to celebrate. As Agnes ate her cake and visited with her many guests, she stroked the now-grizzled head resting in her lap and frequently returned the old dog's devoted gaze. Finding each other had transformed their lives, as well as the lives of others through Golden Outreach—a program born of the love between one elderly lady and a gentle dog.

~Shari Smyth
Chicken Soup for the Cat and Dog Lover's Soul

55

The Perfect Dog

Everything has beauty, but not everyone sees it.
~Confucius

During summer vacations, I would volunteer at the vet's, so I'd seen a lot of dogs. Minnie was by far the funniest-looking dog I'd ever seen. Thin curly hair barely covered her sausage-shaped body. Her bugged-out eyes always seemed surprised. And her tail looked like a rat's tail.

She was brought to the vet to be put to sleep because her owners didn't want her anymore. I thought Minnie had a sweet personality, though. No one should judge her by her looks, I thought. So the vet spayed her and gave her the necessary shots. Finally, I advertised Minnie in the local paper: "Funny-looking dog, well behaved, needs loving family."

When a young man called, I warned him that Minnie was strange looking. The boy on the phone told me that his grandfather's sixteen-year-old dog had just died. They wanted Minnie no matter what. I gave Minnie a good bath and fluffed up what was left of her scraggly hair. Then we waited for them to arrive.

At last, an old car drove up in front of the vet's. Two kids raced to the door. They scooped Minnie into their arms and rushed her out to their grandfather, who was waiting in the car. I hurried behind them to see his reaction to Minnie.

Inside the car, the grandfather cradled Minnie in his arms and stroked her soft hair. She licked his face. Her rat-tail wagged around so quickly that it looked like it might fly off her body. It was love at first lick.

"She's perfect!" the old man exclaimed.

I was thankful that Minnie had found the good home that she deserved.

That's when I saw that the grandfather's eyes were a milky white color—he was blind.

~Jan Peck
Chicken Soup for the Kid's Soul

Finders Keepers

W hen my daughters reached the third and fourth grades, I occasionally allowed them to walk to and from school alone, if the weather permitted. It was a short distance, so I knew they were safe and no trouble would befall them.

One warm spring day, a small friend followed them home after school. This friend was different from any other friend they had brought home. She had short stumpy legs and long floppy ears, with a fawn-colored coat and tiny freckles sprinkled across her muzzle. She was the cutest puppy I had ever seen.

When my husband got home that evening, he recognized the breed—a beagle puppy, not more than twelve weeks old, he guessed. She took to him right away and after dinner climbed into his lap to watch TV. By now the girls were both begging me to keep her.

She had no collar or identifying marks of any sort. I didn't know what to do. I thought about running an ad in the lost-and-found but I really didn't want to. It would break the kids' hearts if someone should show up. Besides, her owners should have watched her more closely, I rationalized.

By the end of the week she was part of our family. She was very intelligent and good with the girls. This was a good idea, I thought. It was time the girls took responsibility for another life so they would learn the nurturing skills they'd need if they decided to become mommies when they grew up.

The following week something told me to check the lost-and-found section in the local paper. One particular ad jumped out at me and my heart pounded with fear at what I read. Someone was pleading for the return of a lost beagle puppy in the vicinity of our grade school. They sounded desperate. My hand shook. I couldn't bring myself to pick up the phone.

Instead, I pretended I hadn't seen the ad. I quickly tucked the paper away in the closet and continued with my dusting. I never said a word about it to the kids or my husband.

By now we had named the puppy. She looked like a Molly, so that was what we called her. She followed the girls everywhere they went. When they went outside, she was one step behind them. When they did chores, she was there to lend a hand (or should I say, paw).

Homework proved a challenge with her around. More than once, the teacher was given a homework page that the dog had chewed on. Each teacher was understanding and the girls were allowed to make it up. Life was definitely not the same at the Campbell household.

There was only one problem with this otherwise perfect picture: my conscience was bothering me. I knew in my heart I had to call that number and see if our Molly was the puppy they were desperately seeking.

It was the most difficult thing I've ever done. Finally, with sweaty palms, I lifted the receiver and dialed. Secretly I was praying no one would answer, but someone did. The voice on the other end was that of a young woman. After describing the dog to her in detail, she wanted to come right over.

Within minutes she was at my door. I had been sitting at the kitchen table, head cradled in my hands, asking God for a miracle. Molly sat at my feet the whole time, looking up at me with those big puppy-dog eyes—eyes the color of milk chocolate. She seemed to sense something was wrong.

A thousand thoughts crossed my mind before the woman rang the bell. I could pretend I wasn't home or tell her, "I'm sorry, you have the wrong address." But it was too late; the bell rang and Molly was barking. I opened the door, forcing myself to face my fear.

One look at Molly and the woman's face lit up like a Christmas tree. "Here, Lucy," she called. "Come to Mamma, girl." Molly (Lucy) instantly obeyed, wagging her tail in delight at the sound of the woman's voice. Obviously she belonged to the woman.

Tears stung at the back of my eyelids and threatened to spill over at any moment. I felt like my heart was being ripped from my chest. I wanted to grab Molly and run. Instead I smiled faintly and asked her to please come in.

The woman had already bent over and scooped Molly up into her arms. She awkwardly opened her purse and stretched out a twenty-dollar bill toward me.

"For your trouble," she offered.

"Oh, I couldn't." I shook my head in protest. "She's been such a joy to have around, I should be paying you." With that she laughed and hugged Molly tighter to her bosom as if she were a lost child and not a dog.

Molly licked her face and squirmed with delight. I knew it was time for them to go home. Opening the door to let them out, I noticed a little girl sitting in the front seat of the van. When the child saw the puppy, a smile as bright as a firecracker on the Fourth of July exploded across her face.

My glance turned to a small wheelchair strapped to the back of the van. The woman saw me look at the chair and offered an explanation without my asking. Molly (Lucy) was given to the child to promote emotional healing after a car accident had left her crippled for life.

When the puppy disappeared from the yard, the little girl had gone into a deep depression, refusing to come out of the shell she was in. Molly (Lucy) was their only hope their daughter would recover emotionally and mentally.

"She formed a special bond with the puppy and Lucy gave her a reason to live," her mother explained.

Suddenly I felt very guilty and selfish. God has blessed me with so much, I thought. My heart went out to this family that had been through such a terrible time. As they pulled out of the drive, the smile on my face was genuine. I knew I had done the right thing—that puppy was exactly where she belonged.

~Leona Campbell
Chicken Soup for the Pet Lover's Soul

Delayed Delivery

S tella had been prepared for her husband's death. Since the doctor's pronouncement of terminal cancer, they had both faced the inevitable, striving to make the most of their remaining time together. Dave's financial affairs had always been in order. There were no new burdens in her widowed state. It was just the awful aloneness... the lack of purpose to her days.

They had been a childless couple. It had been their choice. Their lives had been so full and rich. They had been content with busy careers and with each other. They had many friends. Had. That was the operative word these days. It was bad enough losing the one person you loved with all your heart. But over the past few years, she and Dave repeatedly coped with the deaths of their friends and relations. They were all of an age—an age when human bodies began giving up. Dying. Face it—they were old!

And now, approaching her first Christmas without Dave, Stella was all too aware she was on her own.

With shaky fingers, she lowered the volume of her radio so that the Christmas music faded to a muted background. To her surprise, she saw that the mail had arrived. With the inevitable wince of pain from her arthritis, she bent to retrieve the white envelopes from the floor. She opened them while sitting on the piano bench. They were mostly Christmas cards, and her sad eyes smiled at the familiarity of the traditional scenes and at the loving messages inside. She arranged them among the others on the piano top. In her entire house, they were the only seasonal decoration. The holiday was less than a week away, but she just did not have the heart to put up a silly tree, or even set up the stable that Dave had built with his own hands.

Suddenly engulfed by the loneliness of it all, Stella buried her face in her hands and let the tears come. How would she possibly get through Christmas and the winter beyond it?!

The ring of the doorbell was so unexpected that Stella had to stifle a small scream of surprise. Now who could possibly be calling on her? She opened the wooden door and stared through the window of the storm door with consternation. On her front porch stood a strange young man whose head was barely visible above the large carton in his arms. She peered beyond him to the driveway, but there was nothing about the small car to give a clue as to his identity. Summoning courage, the elderly lady opened the door slightly, and he stepped sideways to speak into the space.

"Mrs. Thornhope?"

She nodded. He continued, "I have a package for you."

Curiosity drove caution from her mind. She pushed the door open, and he entered. Smiling, he placed his burden carefully on the floor and stood to retrieve an envelope that protruded from his pocket. As he handed it to her, a sound came from the box. Stella jumped. The man laughed in apology and bent to straighten up the cardboard flaps, holding them open in an invitation for her to peek inside.

It was a dog! To be more exact, a golden Labrador retriever puppy. As the young gentleman lifted its squirming body up into his arms, he explained, "This is for you, ma'am." The young pup wiggled in happiness at being released from captivity and thrust ecstatic, wet kisses in the direction of the young man's face. "We were supposed to deliver him on Christmas Eve," he continued with some difficulty as he strove to rescue his chin from the wet little tongue, "but the staff at the kennels start their holidays tomorrow. Hope you don't mind an early present."

Shock had stolen Stella's ability to think clearly. Unable to form coherent sentences, she stammered, "But... I don't... I mean... who...?"

The young fellow set the animal down on the doormat between them and then reached out a finger to tap the envelope she was still holding.

"There's a letter in there that explains everything, pretty much. The dog was bought while his mother was still pregnant. It was meant to be a Christmas gift."

The stranger turned to go. Desperation forced the words from her lips. "But who... who bought it?"

Pausing in the open doorway, he replied, "Your husband, ma'am." And then he was gone.

It was all in the letter. Forgetting the puppy entirely at the sight of the familiar handwriting, Stella walked like a sleepwalker to her chair by the window. She forced her tear-filled eyes to read her husband's words. He had written the letter three weeks before his death and had left it with the kennel owners, to be delivered along with the puppy as his last Christmas gift to her. It was full of love and encouragement and admonishments to be strong. He vowed that he was waiting for the day when she would join him. And he had sent her this young animal to keep her company until then.

Remembering the little creature for the first time, she was surprised to find him quietly looking up at her, his small panting mouth resembling a comic smile. Stella put the pages aside and reached for the bundle of golden fur. She thought that he would be heavier, but he was only the size and weight of a sofa pillow. And so soft and warm. She cradled him in her arms and he licked her jawbone, then cuddled into the hollow of her neck. The tears began anew at this exchange of affection, and the dog endured her crying without moving.

Finally, Stella lowered him to her lap, where she regarded him solemnly. She wiped vaguely at her wet cheeks, then somehow mustered a smile.

"Well, little guy, I guess it's you and me." His pink tongue panted in agreement. Stella's smile strengthened, and her gaze shifted sideways to the window. Dusk had fallen. Through fluffy flakes that were now drifting down, she saw the cheery Christmas lights edging the roof lines of her neighbors' homes. The strains of "Joy to the World" floated in from the kitchen.

Suddenly Stella felt the most amazing sensation of peace and benediction wash over her. It was like being enfolded in a loving embrace. Her heart beat painfully, but it was with joy and wonder, not grief or loneliness. She need never feel alone again.

Returning her attention to the dog, she spoke to him. "You know, fella, I have a box in the basement that I think you'd like. There's a tree in it and some decorations and lights that will impress you like crazy! And I think I can find that old stable down there, too. What d'ya say we go hunt it up?"

The puppy barked happily in agreement, as if he understood every word. Stella got up, placed the puppy on the floor and together they went down to the basement, ready to make a Christmas together.

~Cathy Miller
Chicken Soup for the Christian Family Soul

58

Sandy, I Can't

Out of difficulties grow miracles.
~Jean De La Bruyere

As long as Jeremy could remember, he had wanted a dog. For his eleventh birthday, his parents gave him a large box that wiggled and yapped.

"A dog! I know it's a dog!"

Jeremy hurriedly opened the loosely wrapped container and out tumbled a wagging, licking cocker spaniel whose tail was flipping from side to side so quickly that its whole rump seemed to jump from the floor.

"Is it a boy or a girl?" Jeremy asked, as the puppy tried to climb into his lap, lick his face and chew the box all at the same time.

"It's a girl."

"She's beautiful! Her color reminds me of the sand on a beach. I'm going to call her Sandy."

One of their very favorite times together was when Jeremy would ride his bike in the park with Sandy running alongside. She would stop, sniff, toss her floppy ears and then zoom ahead of Jeremy. She would then wait for him to catch up and then zoom off again. She just thought this was the greatest game. When Jeremy stopped and got off his bike, she would then run up to him, barking happily and then sit looking at him with her tongue hanging out. Sandy always looked so silly Jeremy would have to laugh. She then would tumble into his lap proudly as if she had just told a very funny joke.

A year went by. That summer, at the end of a busy day swimming at the beach, Jeremy complained to his mother that he had a headache and stiff neck. The next morning, Jeremy was worse. He could not get out of bed. When the doctor was called, the stiffness had gotten so bad he could hardly move.

"I'm afraid Jeremy has polio," the doctor said.

Jeremy spent three months in the hospital. When he finally came home, he had a brace on one of his legs and needed crutches to walk. Sandy was so happy to see him, she refused to leave his side.

"Every time Sandy saw someone ride by on a bike, she would bark and run back and forth in the yard, then she would whine and whine," his father told Jeremy.

"Well, I can never ride a bike now," Jeremy half whispered.

The next morning, Jeremy limped out to the garage with his crutches to look at his Schwinn-Flyer, all red and chrome and shiny. Sandy immediately began to jump and yap and wag her tail.

"No, I can't Sandy. I can't," Jeremy cried. Sandy just whined. She did not understand.

Every day after that, Sandy would run out to the garage and back to Jeremy, barking and wagging her tail.

Sandy did not understand the word "can't."

Finally, Jeremy said, "Okay, okay, Sandy, but my leg is so weak."

As Jeremy climbed on the bike, Sandy barked happily, ran furiously around the bicycle and wagged her tail like a fan. Jeremy started to ride, then suddenly fell! He started to cry, and immediately Sandy ran up to him where he lay sprawled on the ground and started to lick his face. His crying turned to laughing because Sandy's tongue tickled him.

"Okay, I'll try again!" The second time, he fell again but not as hard. The third and fourth time, he fell and started to laugh.

"Sandy, now I'm getting mad!"

Finally, after a number of tries, he did not fall.

Sandy sat on the ground and if she could talk, she would probably have said, "I knew you could do it."

It was a slow process but after three months Jeremy was slowly riding his bicycle again. After another four months he was walking with a cane and no brace on his leg.

Sandy never knew that she was one of the main reasons that today Jeremy is a normal grown-up who does not even limp. She was only a dog and did not understand.

Or did she?

~Lawrence A. Kross
A 6th Bowl of Chicken Soup for the Soul

59

An Angel in the Form of a Service Dog

He has told me a thousand times over that I am his reason for being:
by the way he rests against my leg;
by the way he thumps his tail at my smallest smile.
~Gene Hill

The start of my life in a wheelchair was the end of a very long marriage.

In 1989 I had a serious truck accident, which shattered my lower back. Though I was considered an incomplete paraplegic, as the years passed, my back got progressively worse. At the end of 1999, my doctor ordered me to use a wheelchair at all times. My wife walked out.

Suddenly on my own, I decided to relocate to California where the weather was warmer, there was more to do, and, most important, things there were more handicapped-accessible than in the rural area where I was living. Even so, adjusting to life in a wheelchair, alone in a new place, was no picnic. After six months in California, my doctor felt that a service dog would be an immense help to me and put me in touch with Canine Companions for Independence (CCI). I went through the application process, but when I was finally accepted I was told that I was looking at nearly a five-year wait. Disappointed but determined to make a life for myself, I continued to struggle through each day, at times becoming so tired that I'd be stranded somewhere until I found enough energy to continue.

So the call from CCI only three and a half years later came as a complete surprise. They'd had a cancellation for a class starting in two weeks—would I be available on such short notice? Without hesitation I said, "Yes!" I felt a rush of emotion. I'd pinned all my hopes on this, and now it was finally happening, almost too fast.

The very next day I headed to the CCI campus as requested, just to be sure they had a possible match for me. This preliminary session was to test my handling skills and to see which of three potential canine partners might "click" with me. I was taken into a dog-filled room, and was surprised when a very fat black-and-white cat, threading his way calmly through the dogs toward my wheelchair, decided my lap was the perfect resting spot.

A trainer brought the first dog, a petite black Lab named Satine, to meet me. We had only a minute to get acquainted before starting basic commands such as "heel" to see how she would respond. Despite the feline riding shotgun on my lap the entire time, Satine responded amazingly well to everything.

Next, a much larger dog, a black Lab-mix called Hawk, took Satine's place—and the cat left my lap in a rush. But Hawk didn't give chase. In fact, he ignored everything to focus on me. Although his headstrong personality initially tested my commands, I held to my guns and soon Hawk started working for me—opening doors, picking up dropped items and a long list of other things. I was awestruck by his sheer presence, not to mention his skills and obedience.

The third candidate was a lively golden retriever named Tolarie. She was very pretty and smart, but no matter what I did, she didn't want to work for me.

When asked which of the three dogs I would choose, I named the more easygoing Satine as first choice, but really, I wanted Hawk. I was totally in love with that dog from the word go!

The next day, CCI called to tell me that I had impressed the trainers with my handling skills with Hawk and that they hoped to place me with him. My heart soared! I thanked them profusely and made arrangements to attend the two-week training course at CCI's campus in Oceanside, California.

I arrived early and spent the first day doing paperwork and meeting the three trainers and five other people in my class. When we entered the classroom, I immediately found Hawk. He came to the door of his crate and licked my fingertips as if to say, "Hi there, I remember you." I could hear his tail thumping in eager anticipation.

Then came the moment we all were waiting for: working with the dogs. The trainers brought Hawk to me, and we spent the first few minutes in a joyful exchange of greetings.

The next four days were nerve-wracking. Pairs wouldn't be assigned until Friday, after we'd each worked with enough dogs for the trainers to determine the best matches. By the second day, though, most of us had already chosen our favorites and felt jealous if "our" dog was working with someone else. On Friday, Hawk was paired with me, but the match still wasn't permanent. Trainers needed to be satisfied that the dogs had bonded with us, and that we felt comfortable with each other and worked well together. By then, I couldn't imagine having any other dog but Hawk—especially after what happened the first night we spent together.

Since my accident I'd always had a very hard time sleeping at night. Every time I moved, the pain roused me, and falling back to sleep was next to impossible. For me, three hours was a good night's sleep. The first night with Hawk, I was supposed to crate him while I slept. But as Hawk and I lay on the bed watching TV together, I dozed off. I woke at five the next morning—and Hawk was still there. He had stretched himself across my body in a way that was comfortable for me but kept me from painful motion. I had slept the whole night through!

I was amazed. With the renewed energy and sharpness that comes with a full night's sleep, I realized Hawk had done similar things all week that I'd written off as part of his training. He'd bonded with me from the start, and in a remarkably short time, had figured out my abilities and limitations and adjusted to them to make the whole training process easier on me. Every time the pain got unbearable, he had done something silly or sweet to take my mind off the pain and help me get through that day. He had done all this with no instruction—just his innate love for me and his desire to please me and make my life easier.

Hawk and I passed our final test with flying colors. We returned home and started a new and very different life—together.

Now when I go out in public, people no longer avoid me or give me weird stares. When people hear the jingle of Hawk's collar and see this team on the move, they smile and come over to meet us. Hawk does so many different things for me: he pulls my wheelchair when I'm feeling tired, opens doors and picks up things I might drop. People love to see my beautiful black dog rear up on a counter and hand a cashier my cash or credit card—what a crowd-pleaser!

Hawk's "fee" for all this? A simple, "Good boy." He loves to hear those words because he knows he is doing something that makes me happy.

His other rewards come when we get home. We both enjoy our nightly cuddle on the floor, followed by a favorite tennis-ball game. It still amazes me that Hawk, who can pick up a full bottle of water and not leave a single tooth mark, can pop a tennis ball in no time flat.

I would never have believed that I could feel this way about my life again. Each day I look forward to getting up after a full night's sleep, grooming Hawk, going out somewhere new and being a part of the world around me, then coming home to cuddle, play and relax for the evening.

Thanks to this wonderful dog and all the people who worked so hard raising and training him, my life has started all over. Hawk, my angel in the form of a service dog, truly shares his wings with me.

~David Ball
Chicken Soup for the Dog Lover's Soul

Of Dogs and Angels

You think dogs will not be in heaven?
I tell you, they will be there long before any of us.
~Robert Louis Stevenson

During my years in animal welfare work—I served as the president of the American Society for the Prevention of Cruelty to Animals—I have heard wonderful stories about the power of the human-animal bond. One of my favorites is about a girl and her very special dog.

When the girl was born, her parents were stationed with the U.S. Army overseas. The tiny baby spiked a fever of 106 degrees and when they couldn't help her at the military base, the baby and her family were flown home to the United States where she could receive the proper medical care.

The alarming fever kept recurring, but the baby survived. When the episode was over, the child was left with thirteen different seizure causes, including epilepsy. She had what was called multiple seizure syndrome and had several seizures every day. Sometimes she stopped breathing.

As a result, the little girl could never be left alone. She grew to be a teenager and if her mother had to go out, her father or brothers had to accompany her everywhere, including to the bathroom, which was awkward for everyone involved. But the risk of leaving her alone was too great and so, for lack of a better solution, things went on in this way for years.

The girl and her family lived near a town where there was a penitentiary for women. One of the programs there was a dog-training program. The inmates were taught how to train dogs to foster a sense of competence, as well as to develop a job skill for the time when they left the prison. Although most of the women had serious criminal backgrounds, many made excellent dog trainers and often trained service dogs for the handicapped while serving their time.

The girl's mother read about this program and contacted the penitentiary to see if there was anything they could do for her daughter. They had no idea how to train a dog to help a person in the girl's condition, but her family decided that a companion animal would be good for the girl, as she had limited social opportunities and they felt she would enjoy a dog's company.

The girl chose a random-bred dog named Queenie and together with the women at the prison, trained her to be an obedient pet.

But Queenie had other plans. She became a "seizure-alert" dog, letting the girl know when a seizure was coming on, so that the girl could be ready for it.

I heard about Queenie's amazing abilities and went to visit the girl's family and meet Queenie. At one point during my visit, Queenie became agitated and took the girl's wrist in her mouth and started pulling her towards the living room couch. Her mother said, "Go on now. Listen to what Queenie's telling you."

The girl went to the couch, curled up in a fetal position, facing the back of the couch and within moments started to seize. The dog jumped on the couch and wedged herself between the back of the couch and the front of the girl's body, placing her ear in front of the girl's mouth. Her family was used to this performance, but I watched in open-mouthed astonishment as the girl finished seizing and Queenie relaxed with her on the couch, wagging her tail and looking for all the world like an ordinary dog, playing with her mistress.

Then the girl and her dog went to the girl's bedroom as her parents and I went to the kitchen for coffee. A little while later, Queenie came barreling down the hallway, barking. She did a U-turn in the kitchen and then went racing back to the girl's room.

"She's having a seizure," the mother told me. The girl's father got up, in what seemed to me a casual manner for someone whose daughter often stopped breathing, and walked back to the bedroom after Queenie.

My concern must have been evident on my face because the girl's mother smiled and said, "I know what you're thinking, but you see, that's not the bark Queenie uses when my daughter stops breathing."

I shook my head in amazement. Queenie, the self-taught angel, proved to me once again how utterly foolish it is to suppose that animals don't think or can't communicate.

~Roger Caras
Chicken Soup for the Cat and Dog Lover's Soul

Meant to Be

A few years ago, we had a Lab puppy named Blue whom we loved very much. But because everyone in the family spent so much time at work or at school, it soon became obvious Blue wasn't getting the attention and training she needed. It was a difficult decision, but we decided to see if we could find her a better home than we could provide at that time.

I asked around at our church and at work, looking for a special home for Blue. A coworker told me that she had a friend whose old dog had recently died. The family was looking for a puppy. I knew of the family: the husband was named Frank and his wife, Donna, was a Lamaze instructor who worked at a local hospital. Their children, my friend told me, were crazy about dogs and missed their old dog tremendously. It sounded like the perfect place.

I spoke to Donna on the phone, and she was thrilled about taking Blue. I arranged for my husband to deliver the puppy the following day, which was a Friday. Frank gave my husband their address, 412 Adams, and told him that he would be home all day, doing work on the house, so my husband should look for ladders in the front yard.

The next morning, my husband took Blue and set off in the car. Our sad goodbyes were lightened by the knowledge that she was going to a wonderful home.

Donna and Frank lived an hour away, on the other side of the nearest big town. My husband found the house; the number 412 was clearly displayed and there was a ladder in the front yard. Taking the puppy in his arms, he went up to the house and knocked on the door. There was no answer. He waited a moment and knocked again.

A man in the next yard called over to him, "Who are you looking for?"

My husband said, "Frank."

"Oh, Frank went to the hospital," he said. "I don't know when he's coming back."

My husband was irked. Frank had said he'd be home all day. Maybe he'd had to give Donna a ride to work at the hospital. But my husband couldn't wait around. He had made appointments for the rest of the day and had to get going. Something of this must have shown on his face, for the man in the next yard said, "What's the problem, young fella?"

My husband explained his predicament and the neighbor offered to keep the puppy at his house until Frank returned. The neighbor had a fenced yard and said it'd be no trouble at all. He was a nice man with dogs of his own, and my husband decided it would be all right. He gave the puppy to the neighbor and left for his appointments.

The following Monday when I returned to work, my co-worker said to me, "Did you change your mind about giving away Blue?"

Surprised, I answered, "No. Why?"

"Well, Donna told me you never delivered her on Friday. They figured you'd had a change of heart when it came time to really say goodbye."

I told her we certainly had delivered Blue. I called Donna and told her about the neighbor taking care of Blue until Frank returned.

"But Frank was home all day!" she insisted. "And we haven't heard from any of our neighbors."

What on earth was going on? We finally figured out that my husband had made a wrong turn and had gone to 412 on the next street over. There had been a storm not long before and many people had ladders out to do roof and gutter repairs. Could it possibly be that the man in that house was also named Frank?

My husband and I got into the car and drove over to see what had become of Blue. We saw immediately that that he'd gone one street too far and we knocked on the door of the house where he'd left Blue.

A red-faced man in his sixties answered our knock. When we explained that we were looking for a puppy that had been delivered here last week, the man answered, "Oh, you mean the one that Frank ordered."

Realizing that the man at 412 on this street was also named Frank, we explained the mix-up. The man's face grew somber.

"What's wrong?" I asked. "Is the puppy all right?"

"Oh, the puppy is fine. In fact, I'm sure the puppy is great. But... well, I hope you don't want it back," he said seriously. Seeing the question in our eyes, he continued, "When you came with the puppy on Friday, my neighbor Frank was at the hospital. He'd been out in the yard working and had started having chest pains, so his wife took him to the hospital. Frank never did come home. He died of a massive coronary Friday afternoon. It was a terrible shock for his family, and I decided not to bother them until things had settled down a bit. Yesterday, I brought the puppy over and knocked on their door. Frank's eldest daughter came out. I told her that her father had ordered a puppy and since he hadn't been home, that I'd taken delivery on it for him. I said I didn't know what to do with the little dog now that 'things had changed' at their house.

"The daughter just couldn't believe it. She said, 'My father ordered a puppy? This is Dad's puppy?' Then she reached out and I gave her the pup. She hugged that little dog real tight, stuck her face in its fur and just began to cry.

"I wasn't sure what to say, so I just stood there. After a while, she looked up at me and thanked me. She said, 'You don't know what this means to me. I'm so glad to have my father's dog.' The puppy was wiggling around, trying to kiss the daughter any way it could and her face was just lit up with love."

Amazed at the story I turned to my husband, "We can't take Blue back now."

The man nodded in agreement. "Folks, some things are just meant to be. I'd say that puppy is in exactly the right place."

~Cindy Midgette
Chicken Soup for the Grieving Soul

That's Why I Am Here

I have often thought what a melancholy world this would be without children;
and what an inhuman world without the aged.
~John Duke Coleridge

My children have always been involved in 4-H. Heavily into the animal divisions with a few other projects, they took their county fair presentations very seriously. I was a professional dog trainer and handler and one year my two youngest children entered our registered dogs in the Beginner Obedience class. My fourteen-year-old son, Jeremy, wanted to do something with the dogs too, but he was very independent and didn't want something that everyone else was doing. He came to me in the spring, several months before fair, and said, "I've decided to make my dog project count." He proceeded to show me his detailed plan for his Citizenship project — providing canine therapy dog visits to local nursing homes.

In the north central portion of Minnesota where we lived, this was an unheard of concept. Jeremy told me he had already done some of the legwork by asking his brother, sister, and two members of the 4-H club to come along and assist. What he needed from me most was to choose the appropriate dogs and teach the handlers how to present a dog to an elderly and perhaps bedridden person. We contacted several nursing homes and finally found one that agreed to allow our therapy dogs to visit. Jeremy called his buddy 4-Hers and set up a training schedule. When all five kids were comfortable presenting the dogs, we made an appointment with the nursing home.

The first day we visited I went along as driver, photographer and supervisor. We went from room to room, sharing our smaller trained therapy dogs and puppies and with as many as possible. Each child carried a dog and a towel to place on the bed in case someone wanted the dog there. We were a hit! The joy these folks exhibited was genuine and wonderful. They all asked us to visit again.

On our next outings, we left earlier so we could visit more residents. Jeremy enjoyed watching people's faces light up as we entered a room, but there seemed to be something disturbing him. I asked if he was having a problem with the project. He became solemn. "I love coming here but I want to make an even bigger difference. I'm not sure how, but I know there is something more I can do."

Each time we visited, the residents anticipated it with greater enthusiasm. Some even had family members bring in photos of their own dogs to share with us. We listened to stories about their pets, their families, and their lives when they were young. Each sat constantly petting one of the dogs, gaining the comfort and unconditional love only an animal can give so freely.

One day we ventured into an area we hadn't been to before. As a nurse's aide led the way, we came upon several rooms that were quieter than most and not decorated. The aide motioned for us to continue following her to the residents who requested visits further down the hall. Jeremy stopped and peered into one of the rooms. The aide reprimanded, "There is no use going into that room; that lady hasn't moved or spoken in months. She is unresponsive and pretty much alone." Jeremy looked at her and then at the French bulldog he held in his arms. Calmly he replied, "That's why I am here." He proceeded into the room and stood hesitantly. The woman was ghostly white and showed no signs of life. She lay prone and didn't move so much as her eyes when we entered. Jeremy took a deep breath and moved to the side of the bed. "My name is Jeremy and I am here with my therapy dogs. I brought a dog to see you. Since you can't come to see the dog, I'd like to place it on your bed. I have a towel so no hair will get on your blankets."

The woman did not move. Jeremy looked to me for approval. I nodded. He moved to the side of the bed where her arm was exposed and placed the towel on the bedspread. While all this was happening, the aide left to get a nurse. By the time Jeremy was ready to put the dog beside the woman, two nurses and the aide were in the doorway. As one began to tell me we were wasting our time, I raised my hand to silence her. She huffed, but remained quiet.

Jeremy placed the dog against the woman's arm. He spoke softly, "She won't hurt you. She came here just to see you." As he spoke the woman's head shifted slightly. The glaze in her eyes seemed to disappear. Jeremy allowed the dog to nestle in close. The woman raised a weak arm and placed it on the dog's back. Although she had no words, she began to make sounds. Tears brimmed her eyes as she moved her hand along the hair. The nurses rushed to the bedside and began pressing the nurse call button. More people rushed into the room. There was not a dry eye in the group. Jeremy looked at the aide and reiterated, "This is why I am here." Then he looked at me, tears flowing unashamedly down his face and he said, "I made a difference." I hugged him and acknowledged that he certainly had. When it was time to leave, Jeremy gathered up the dog and the towel and said to the woman, "Thanks for letting us come into your room — and into your life." She smiled at him and touched his arm.

Jeremy received the highest award for his Citizenship project, and went on to the state level where he earned Grand Champion. But for Jeremy, the ribbons were nothing compared to his biggest award — the touch of a hand and the smile from a woman who was said to be a waste of time.

~Loretta Emmons
Chicken Soup for the Caregiver's Soul

Loving Our Dogs

It's My Family Too!

Dogs love company.
They place it first on their short list of needs.
~J. R. Ackerley

The Promise

He that can have patience can have what he will.
~Benjamin Franklin

For the past twelve and a half years, I have been an animal control officer (ACO) for Polk County, Iowa. In this profession, you learn early on to toughen your skin, otherwise the stress and emotional drain that come with this job will bring you down. There have been a lot of dogs over the years that I would have loved to take home and make a part of my family, but in this line of work, it's not realistic to believe you can do that with each one—there are just too many dogs in need of good homes. Still, there is always that one that gets through your defenses. For me, that dog was Buddy.

Buddy was the most elusive dog I ever encountered in my years as an animal control officer: I spent an amazing sixteen months trying to catch the big black dog.

I first received a phone call in November 2002 from a lady who said, "There is a dog lying in a field near my home. He has been there for a couple of days, and it is supposed to get really cold tonight. Could you try to catch him?" I told her I would head out there and see what I could do.

As I drove up to the area, I could see that the dog was lying on his side next to a small hillside that served as a sort of break from the cold wind. I got out of my truck with a leash in hand and walked toward him. The dog was asleep and did not hear my coming, so as I got within twenty feet of him, I whistled because I did not want to startle him. He immediately got up and started barking at me. Then he turned and ran away, into the middle of the snow-covered field where he lay down to keep a watchful eye on me. I knew there was going to be no catching him that day, so I left to answer another call that had come in.

That night it did get very cold. I just couldn't keep my mind off the black dog and wondered how he was doing out in that large, cold field all alone.

The next morning I headed to the Animal Rescue League of Iowa. This is where the county sheriff's department houses the animals I pick up, and it is the largest animal shelter in the state. I wanted to check the reports to see if anyone had called in saying they had lost their black dog. I hoped that someone was looking for this dog, so I would be able to ask the owners to come out to the field; I figured if it were their dog, the dog would come to them. There were no such lost reports.

On my way home that night, I couldn't help but drive by the field. There he sat, right in the middle of it. Again, he wouldn't let me get close to him or come to me when I called.

We played this game for a few weeks. I would get calls from different people reporting that a black dog was sitting in a field. I could not get this dog out of my mind, and even on my days off, I would drive by the field to leave food and see if I could get a look at him. He was always there, usually lying right out in the middle so no one would be able to sneak up behind him. I tried over and over to gain his trust with no luck. I could not get closer than a hundred yards from him — too far to use a tranquilizer dart. If I tried to come any closer, he would get up, bark and move to an adjacent field. I wondered sadly what could have happened to this dog to make him so fearful of people.

Finally, I spoke to Janet, one of the animal-care technicians at the Animal Rescue League. She had a reputation of being able to get close to dogs that would not let anyone near them. I told her about the black dog and asked her if she would try to catch him. She agreed, and she did try — to no avail.

It was now late December and the nights were very cold,

dropping to ten or twenty degrees below zero. The woman who had called me originally about the dog continued to call, checking in to see what I was doing to help him. I assured her I had been trying to catch him and that I was leaving food for the dog. At this point I told her I was pondering a way to set a live trap to capture the dog. Privately, I worried how he would live through the nights given the bitter cold temperatures of Iowa winters.

The weeks passed. I checked on him regularly, driving by in the morning on my way to work, cruising by during the day and making my final round on my way home at night. It was odd—just seeing him out there made me smile. I was thankful he had made it through one more night and was still alive.

Janet and I talked constantly about this dog. A live trap hadn't worked. We simply could not come up with a way to catch this dog. One day we decided that we would take some shelter out to the fields, line it with blankets and put some food beside it; perhaps he would use it. We got an "igloo" type of doghouse and went out to the field to set it up. The dog watched us intently but wouldn't come near. That was the day that I named the dog Buddy. Looking at him, I made a promise to myself and to him: "Buddy, if I ever catch you, I'm going to adopt you and show you what 'good people' are like."

We went through the rest of the winter like this, as well as the following spring and summer. One day Buddy just seemed to vanish. No more sightings, no more concerned calls about him. I continued to think about him, fearing the worst: that he had been hit by a car and was no longer alive.

That fall, however, I received a call about a black dog standing by the road close to the field where I had first seen Buddy. I couldn't believe it. It had been seven months since I had last seen him, but I immediately hopped into my truck and drove to the area. There, standing by the road, was my friend Buddy. He looked just as he had the last time I saw him. I stopped my truck and got out. I tried to approach him, but as usual he started backing up and barking at me. This time, however, when I turned to walk away, instead of turning and running, he just sat down. He was letting me get closer.

We started the game all over again. I kept leaving treats for him in the same spot. This went on for months until one day he did something he hadn't done before — he slept next to the spot where I had been leaving his treats. I decided I would leave a live trap for him on that spot along with some barbecued pork. When I went back first thing the next morning, it looked like he'd tried to get the food out by digging around the trap, but he was nowhere to be seen.

I tried again the next night. This time I put a slice of pizza in the trap, hoping it would do the trick. I couldn't sleep that night and rose early to go check the cage. It was still dark out, and as I approached I heard Buddy bark. I figured he had heard me and was already retreating, but as I squinted my eyes I could make out the outline of a black dog caught in the cage of the live trap. Overwhelmed with relief and joy, I started to cry. Then I called my wife. "I got Buddy," I told her. "I got him!"

Buddy growled at me as I loaded the cage into my truck and drove to the Animal Rescue League. As I drove in, Janet was just coming into work. I yelled to her, "You are never going to guess who I've got!"

Janet replied, "Buddy?" and started to cry.

Janet and I unloaded the cage and took Buddy to a kennel. I crawled into the kennel with him, keeping my distance. Once I realized he wasn't going to bite me, I just started petting him and loving him. I spent the next few hours trying to build the bond that I knew would last a lifetime. To everyone's surprise, after running from us and being alone for sixteen months, he was a very affectionate dog. All Buddy wanted at this point was to be petted, and if you stopped too soon, he'd let you know by gently nuzzling your hand until you started petting him again.

Over the next few days, I spent almost every free moment with Buddy. I would go to the Animal Rescue League before work, during lunch breaks and after work just so I could spend time with him. A few days later I brought my yellow Labrador, Hershey, to the shelter to meet Buddy. From the moment they met, they got along just fine.

Soon I was able to take Buddy home. Buddy fit amazingly well into our family. He had no "accidents" in the house and didn't destroy anything. Then one day my wife called me and told me that Buddy had gotten into the refrigerator. At first, I didn't believe her, but I suppose all that time scavenging for food had made him highly resourceful. Because it's true—I now live with a dog that can open a refrigerator!

We have to use bungee cords to prevent Buddy from opening the refrigerator door. There have been a few occasions when we have forgotten, only to come home to find that he's emptied the fridge. We've nicknamed him "Buddy, the Fridge King."

It's been four months now since I adopted him, and he is truly a bright spot in my life. I still can't believe this dog survived for sixteen months on his own, through two Iowa winters! He is an example of the true spirit and determination of the species we call "dog."

My long days at work are still challenging, but I am comforted by the thought that I get to go home and lavish Buddy with the love I wish all dogs could have. I kept my promise to Buddy and have shown him that people can be good. It was a happy ending worth waiting for.

~Bill King
Chicken Soup for the Dog Lover's Soul

Dogs Just Wanna Have Fun

Go forward confidently,
energetically attacking problems, expecting favorable outcomes.
~Norman Vincent Peale

My husband Daniel and I travel frequently. When we first got our dog, Buddha-tu (we call him Buddhi), we were concerned that he would be lonely or perhaps feel that we'd abandoned him when we left him at home during our trips away.

When we left, we always had someone stay in our house and look after Buddhi, so we knew he was well taken care of, but we still felt guilty. I even used to leave my husband's t-shirt for Buddhi to sleep with and made sure he got extra goodies each day we were gone. Still, I used to wonder what he made of the whole thing—did he miss his lovin's, "his rub-a-dubs and belly pats," sleeping by our bed, taking walks with us—and who was going to play ball with him while we were away? Was our absence too traumatic for him? I supposed I would never know.

But then one night when we called home, Buddhi made it quite clear what he missed the most when we were gone.

We reached our housesitter, Barbara, and had her put us on the speakerphone, so that we could talk to Buddhi. He immediately started barking and howling when he heard our voices. We were jabbering at Buddhi like a pair of fools, when we noticed we couldn't hear him anymore. Barbara told us that he had run out of the room.

What was he doing? I wondered uneasily. Maybe it hadn't been such a good idea to call home—perhaps Buddhi was confused and was searching the house for us. When he couldn't find us, would he become upset and try to get outside to continue the search? What if he tried to jump through a window? My imagination ran away with me, and I couldn't stop it. I thought, Poor baby, he misses us so much, hearing our voices had just made it worse. I urged Barbara to go and find him. My husband and I decided to try and coax him back into the room by continuing to talk to him.

Barbara ran after him to see what was going on and almost tripped over him as he raced back into the room, holding something in his mouth. He bounded to the phone, where we were still spouting endearments in a highly embarrassing manner.

We heard Barbara laughing in the background, and then she picked up the phone and told us that Buddhi had approached the phone, and had stood for a moment, head cocked. Then he carefully put his front paws up on the desk and set down the object in his mouth. It was his favorite ball. He put it directly on top of the speakerphone and stepped back—waiting for us to throw it.

~Susan White
Chicken Soup for the Cat and Dog Lover's Soul

Nothing
That Can't Be Fixed

Kindness, like a boomerang, always returns.
~Author Unknown

"Oh, no! Look out!" I shouted as I watched the truck in front of me narrowly miss the little black dog on the highway. Startled, my children, ages one and two, looked at me from their car seats.

Cringing, the dog ran away, limping on one leg. It made it to the shoulder of the road and then turned to stare hopefully at my car as I drove past. I didn't feel that I could stop with the children in the car, but something in that earnest stance stayed with me well after the stray was out of sight.

Stray dogs were a problem in the rural community where I lived. My husband, a veterinarian, often spoke about the plight of these forgotten animals. Most did not survive long. If they were not killed on the roadways, they died of starvation or disease.

I kept thinking about the black dog as I drove home. Then I made a decision to do something I'd never tried before. I dropped the children off at home, asking a neighbor to watch them, then drove to my husband's veterinary clinic. I found him inside and began to tell him about the injured dog.

"If I can catch it, would you put it to sleep?" He didn't seem very pleased with my plan, but he knew the dog was probably suffering.

There were no animal shelters in our area, and we both knew there was no way for us to keep the dog—besides having two small children, we had no yard or place for a pet. My husband thought for a moment, then answered quietly that he would do what I asked.

Armed with a blanket and some dog biscuits, I drove back along the highway. I found the dog once again on the shoulder of the road. I pulled over and parked, grabbed some biscuits and stepped out of the car. When I walked to where the dog lay, I got my first good look at just how miserable such an existence can be.

The little black dog was painfully thin. Its hair was missing in patches and roughened, raw skin showed through the bare places. A tooth caught on an upper lip gave the dog's face the appearance of a snarl. One eye seemed to be gone, and the dog's leg had been injured. It was so hungry that it was gnawing on the bottom half of an old turtle shell it held between its paws.

Kneeling down in front of it, I fed it the treats until they were gone. Then I carefully picked up the dog and set it on the blanket in my car.

During the drive back to the veterinary clinic, I kept telling myself that what I was doing was the right thing. This animal was badly injured and starving. A quick, painless euthanasia was better than the fate that awaited it otherwise.

I glanced down at the dog and saw it studying me. The look in that one brown eye was unnerving.

Just don't think about what's ahead, I told myself.

My husband was waiting for me when I pulled back into the parking lot. He opened the car door, picked up the dog and carried it into the clinic. Reluctantly, I followed him inside.

Instead of taking the dog to the kennel area, he carried it into the exam room. There, he started looking over his newest patient.

"It's a young female, about a year and a half old. She has mange, that's why her skin looks so bad. Probably hit by a car, but this leg's not broken. Her jaw is fractured, though, and starting to heal itself. This eye needs some corrective surgery and the other eyelid needs to be closed...."

While my husband continued to examine the black dog, she sat quietly on the table. Her gaze never left my face. Why was she staring at me? Did she understand why I had brought her to this place?

His examination completed, my husband turned to me. He looked at me meaningfully and said, "There's nothing here that can't be fixed."

I looked once more at the dog. She was still watching me with her single brown eye. I felt heartsick about this dog's sad life, but the decision had to be made, and I was the one who had to make it.

• • •

It's been twelve years since that day. I think about it often, especially on days like today when I'm sitting in the yard watching my hens peck around in the grass. My orange cat stretches lazily in a sunny spot on the patio. The summer's last hummingbirds are fussing about the feeders.

An old dog leans against my leg. She lays her gray muzzle, once so black and shiny, on my knee and looks up at me. I give her silky head a pat. Now I understand the expression in that solitary brown eye. And I answer her, "I love you, too, Daisy."

~Pamela Jenkins
Chicken Soup for the Dog Lover's Soul

One Cold Winter's Night

My son Ryan wanted a dog—desperately. He was a preschooler and had just lost his favorite person in the world, his grandpa. I wanted to say no. I was a single parent working full-time. Ryan had special needs. When did I have time for a dog?

Nonetheless, I called the Humane Society and described our lifestyle and Ryan's disabilities to the woman on the other end of the line. She told me that all their puppies had been adopted but a mother dog was available. The woman insisted that Ginger was just what we needed. The dog was half border collie and half sheltie. I went down to the shelter, paid my twenty-five dollars, signed a document that said we would have her spayed and left with our new dog.

Immediately, Ginger became Ryan's best friend and protector. She slept in his room at the foot of his bed. I would often find them sleeping together, heads side by side on the pillow, bodies under the colorful quilt. Ryan held her ears with one hand as he sucked the thumb on his other. He told her stories, gave her supporting roles in plays where he was the hero and dressed her in capes and hats. When he was learning to latch the hook on her leash, a task difficult for his hands affected by cerebral palsy, it could sometimes take five to ten minutes. She sat through it all, calmly and patiently, waiting for him to get it right. She looked mournful when he was upset, and consoled him by letting him bury his little face in her fur and cry when other children wouldn't play with him. She knew what her job was, and she made it her vocation. She never abandoned him.

She was a teacher for Ryan and a respite provider for me. When Ryan played with Ginger, I knew he was relatively safe — after all, she had bloodlines from two major herding breeds. If Ryan tried to leave the house on his own, Ginger sat in front of the door and yipped to alert me. If Ryan jumped on the bed she "rode" on the bed, too. She taught him laughter, friendship and silliness. She taught him loyalty and trust.

One winter, I came down with a severe case of strep throat. My symptoms had gotten progressively worse, until one evening, my fever had risen so high, I was truly a little out of my head. I wanted to go to the hospital emergency room, but it was twenty degrees below zero outside. My car was old. I didn't want to take a chance that it would break down, exposing Ryan or me to those temperatures for even a short amount of time. Everyone I knew was out of town, busy or had small children of their own. I decided to "tough it out" until my appointment at the clinic the following day.

Ginger must have kept Ryan busy most of the evening while I faded in and out. I don't even remember giving him dinner. I know he ate because I found cookie crumbs, chips and cheese slice wrappers on the kitchen counter the next day. I had set the oven timer to ring every hour that evening, so that if I did doze off I could wake up and check on Ryan. But the oven timer wasn't waking me up; the dog was. Every time I dozed off, Ginger barked or pulled at me to wake me. She sat with Ryan, eyeing me anxiously. The third time I went to set the oven timer, I gave up on it. I looked at Ginger, and I swear we had a telepathic moment. I knew that she would continue waking me and keep an eye on Ryan as sure as I knew that my eyes are brown. This knowledge flooded me with relief.

About ten o'clock that night, after Ryan was in bed, his "blankie" in one hand and Ginger's fur in the other, I had a moment of lucidity and realized that I had not taken the dog out since seven o'clock that morning. I motioned for her to go out and she came to the door, looking at me dubiously. I slipped my arms into my coat, hooked up her leash and led her out. As we reached the stairs on the deck, she whined and turned to go back into the house, all the while watching me.

With a wind chill factor of thirty-five degrees below zero, what dog wouldn't whine? I think she might have saved my life that night because I am not sure that I would have made it back into the house. I remember feeling suddenly very confused and wondering what I was doing outside. I do not remember going back into the house; I believe she herded me back inside. That night, she slept in the hall between the bedrooms instead of her usual spot on Ryan's bed.

The next morning when I woke, I was still sick, but my fever had abated. My son was still sleeping. I went to fill Ginger's food dish and water bowl. I stared at them in amazement. Both dishes were full. She had not eaten or drunk anything the day before. Ryan knew that he was not supposed to give her table food, so I doubt if she had even snacked with him. All I know for sure was that my baby was safe because a little brown dog named Ginger had kept him safe, and had kept me from harm.

After I went to the doctor, got my antibiotics and started to feel better, I cooked Ginger a hamburger—a great big one with gravy, changing the table-food rule a bit!

The whole experience taught me a valuable lesson. I had been so busy trying to be supermom that I had inadvertently isolated myself. In a time of crisis, I found myself with a limited number of people I could count on for help. I needed to get out more and allow myself to be a person, not just Ryan's mom. I needed to meet more single parents and more parents of disabled children so that I would have more support and resources when I needed them. I joined parent support groups and reestablished contacts with friends. I made new friends who were in similar situations. I reduced my work hours and still managed to pay the bills. My life became more balanced than it had been. We were happier.

Ginger is no longer with us, but each year we hang an ornament on the Christmas tree for her. After Ryan goes to bed I look at the tree and remember the little brown dog and that cold winter night. Our new dog, a retriever mix named Poppie, sleeps in the hall outside Ryan's room.

~Karen J. Olson
Chicken Soup for the Single Parent's Soul

Canine Compassion

If I had to sum up Friendship in one word, it would be Comfort.
~Adabella Radici

A rather unusual overnight guest stayed at our home recently. When I was asked to provide overnight accommodations for a rescued dog being transported to her new home in Boston, I readily agreed. Though I was a tad worried that my own two dogs might not like this new intruder in our home, I wanted to help and figured I could manage if it became a problem.

The visiting dog's name was Meadow, and she was an extremely sweet old canine soul. She had been rescued from an abusive animal-hoarding situation, and a kindhearted person had agreed to adopt her, even though she was a special-needs dog. Poor Meadow had suffered some type of severe head trauma before being rescued, and when our guest arrived at my front door that afternoon, her acute neurological ailment was painfully obvious. She teetered precariously on four wobbly thin legs, and her aged, furry brown face incessantly wobbled back and forth, as if she were suffering from Parkinson's disease. Immediately, I thought of the great actress, Katharine Hepburn, who had also suffered from Parkinson's. Katharine Hepburn had not allowed her illness to get the better of her, and obviously, neither had this sweet old girl.

As Meadow gamely tottered into my unfamiliar living room, she heard my two dogs growling, snarling and scratching incessantly at the inside of the closed bedroom door upstairs. Stopping, she peered nervously in that direction. I was afraid that the getting-acquainted canine ritual that was coming might be extremely painful for our already stressed overnight visitor. While I contemplated the best method to introduce my two dogs to our special guest, they somehow managed to pry open the bedroom door themselves. Before I could stop them, they both came charging down the steps with only one thought in their collective canine minds: the urgent need to rid their home of this unwanted intruder. But then, instead of witnessing a vicious canine attack, I witnessed something truly remarkable.

Suddenly, both my dogs stopped in their tracks on the long wooden stairway and gazed wide-eyed at the quivering, wobbly-kneed stranger below. Instantly, they instinctively knew that this new guest of ours was not a threat to anyone. They came down the stairs and stood looking at the unfamiliar dog. Blanca, my tiny female Chihuahua/spitz mix, who can be quite mean to other female dogs at times, approached Meadow first. She slowly walked up to our elderly visitor, sniffed her and quickly planted an affectionate kiss of greeting on Meadow's tremulous left cheek. I was immediately reminded of the kisses I, as a child, had lovingly set on my aged grandmother's quivering cheek so many years ago. My large male dog, Turbo, soon followed suit—although his wet slobbery kisses on Meadow's chin were much more exuberant than Blanca's had been. After all, our overnight guest was a female. I was delighted that my dogs had so readily accepted our guest, and I felt a little sheepish that I had been so worried about it.

Soon it was afternoon nap time, that part of the day when both my dogs always find a comfortable piece of furniture to do their snoozing on. Today, however, they had other plans. They both had watched in silence as Meadow wearily plopped down on the blanket I'd set out for her on our cold living room floor. They seemed to know that our special guest could not crawl up onto any comfortable bed or sofa as they so easily could. To my utter amazement, my two pampered pooches immediately plopped down on the blanket next to her, one on each side. And soon three tired, newly acquainted canine comrades were dognapping and snoring away on my living room floor — together.

I was extremely proud of my two lovable mutts that afternoon, but there was more to come.

When bedtime finally arrived, my two dogs sped upstairs to their usual cozy spots in our bedroom: Blanca perched next to my pillow, Turbo at my wife's feet, gently mouthing and licking his beloved teddy bear, just as he does each and every evening before falling fast asleep. As I was about to crawl into bed myself, Turbo suddenly jumped off the bed with his teddy in his mouth. Curious, I followed him out of the bedroom.

There he stood in the dark, at the top of the long staircase, silently gazing down at our overnight guest below. After several seconds Turbo silently carried his favorite teddy bear down that long flight of stairs. He slowly approached Meadow and then gingerly dropped his prized possession next to Meadow's head, as if to say, This teddy comforts me at night; I hope it does the same for you.

Our canine guest seemed to sense how truly grand a gesture this was on Turbo's part. She immediately snorted her thanks and then, quickly placing her wobbly head on the teddy bear's plush softness, she let out a loud contented sigh. As my generous pup turned to head back upstairs to bed, he stopped abruptly, turned around and looked back at Meadow once more. Then he walked back to her and plopped down on the floor at her side. My gallant Turbo spent the entire night huddled there with Meadow on the cold living room floor. I know that our overnight visitor, somewhat stressed and frightened in yet another strange new place, must have been extremely grateful for both his noble gift and for his comforting overnight company.

The next morning, as we all watched Miss Meadow happily departing in her new loving owner's car, I bent down and gave each of my dogs a big hug. Why had I ever doubted their canine compassion? I knew better now.

~Ed Kostro
Chicken Soup for the Dog Lover's Soul

King of Courage

*Courage is not the absence of fear, but rather the judgment that something
else is more important than fear.*
~Ambrose Redmoon

"Go away, King," Pearl Carlson said sleepily as her German shepherd dog pulled at her bedding, attempting to rouse her. "Not now, I'm trying to get some rest."

Pearl vaguely wondered what King was doing in her bedroom at three o'clock in the morning, since he usually slept on the enclosed porch at night. It was Christmas night and the sixteen-year-old girl had been looking forward to a good night's sleep after an exciting day.

Pearl sat up in bed to give the barking dog a good push and realized that smoke was filling her room—the house was on fire. Bolting out of bed, she ran in panic to her parents' bedroom and awoke them both.

Her mother, Fern, got up at once and told Pearl to escape through her own bedroom window while she helped her husband, Howard, out of their window. Howard Carlson had a lung condition and could not move quickly. They realized that Pearl had somehow wound up in the living room where the fire was at its worst.

"I'm going after her," Howard said, but his wife, knowing his health made this impossible, told him to escape through the window while she went for Pearl. Fern led her dazed daughter to safety but saw that neither Howard nor King had gotten out of the house. Fern ran back into their bedroom and found Howard collapsed on the floor with King by his side. Fern and King struggled to lift Howard and finally the two of them managed to get the nearly unconscious man to safety. Fern later said she could not have moved Howard without King's help.

King and the Carlsons were saved. King had badly burned paws and a gash on his back, but seemed otherwise healthy. Yet the day after the fire, King would not eat his dog food.

The neighbors had come by with sandwiches and refreshments and were helping to rebuild what they could of the house. Then King did something he had never done before: He stole one of the soft sandwiches. Something was wrong.

They looked in King's mouth and saw that his gums were pierced with painful, sharp wooden splinters. Now the family knew how King had gotten into the house. That terrible night, King had, with sheer desperate force, chewed and clawed his way through the closed plywood door that separated him from the Carlsons. The splinters were removed and eventually King recovered fully.

What was most striking about the dog's heroic act was that night he had easy access to the porch door, left open to the outdoors. King could easily have just saved himself. Instead, he chose to gnaw and smash through the door to the house, and face blinding fire and choking smoke, all to rescue his family.

~Stephanie Laland
Chicken Soup for the Cat and Dog Lover's Soul

Busted!

Our beagle, Samantha, was a real clown. She kept us laughing all the time, making it hard to scold her when she got into mischief. That dog had us wrapped around her finger—or should I say paw?

Samantha was really my husband Al's dog, or more accurately, he was her human. I was the one who fed her, walked her and took care of her, but as far as Samantha was concerned, the sun rose and set on Al. She adored him. The feeling was mutual; when she gave him that soft beagle "googly-eyed look," he melted.

We lived in a place called Yellowknife in the Northwest Territories, three hundred miles from the Arctic Circle. Al was in the army and away a lot. I managed on my own and was thankful for good friends, an enjoyable working environment and, especially, Samantha to keep me warm at night. She would crawl under the blankets and curl around my feet—what bliss.

It had been a long arctic winter and Samantha had waited patiently for the sunshine and warm weather to come and was raring to get out and about. A typical hound, she loved running, chasing rabbits and squirrels, and swimming in the lake. When the first warm day of spring finally arrived that year and we went out for a walk, in her exuberance, Samantha overdid it—running at top speed over the rocks that are the landscape in Yellowknife. By the time we reached the house, she was limping quite pronouncedly and appeared to be in significant pain. Her injury was diagnosed as sprained ligaments, and she was ordered to keep still: no running for several weeks. It was not welcome news for this beagle. Now she was confined to the porch while I was away at work, and then took short, quiet walks on a leash when I was home. As the weeks passed, her limp slowly but surely diminished; I was pleased with her progress.

During that period, Al was away from Monday to Friday. On his return Friday evenings, there were hugs and kisses all around, and Samantha would be plastered to his lap. She followed him everywhere all weekend, lapping up the attention she received because of her "hurtie." It was clear to me that her limp became even more pronounced when Al was home.

By the end of the summer her leg was all healed and she was back to normal. She ran and played and chased her ball for hours on end—during the week. When Al came home, her hurtie mysteriously came back, and she was placed on the sofa for the weekend with lots of hugs, a blanket and treats.

I told Al that this was just an act for his attention. "Of course it isn't," he said. "Can't you see her leg is still bothering her? How come it's not healing like the vet said it would?"

I sighed but let it drop.

The following weekend when Al returned, Samantha's limp was as bad as ever. Friday and Saturday, Al pampered his little injured princess while I tried not to roll my eyes.

Like most people, Al and I love to sleep in and snuggle on Sunday morning. We chat about the events of the past week, reload our coffee cups, chat some more, nap and generally laze around. Samantha lies at the bottom of the bed enjoying this special time as well. Eventually, we get up, shower and head to the kitchen to start making breakfast. It was our routine to cook an egg for Samantha, too. She usually waited on the bed until it was ready and we called her to come and eat. That morning when breakfast was ready, Al started down the hall, intending to lift Samantha off the bed and carry her into the kitchen because of her hurtie.

"No," I told him. "Stand where she can't see you and watch what happens next."

I called Samantha. We heard her jump off the bed and run down the hall. She was running like there was no tomorrow, and surprise, no hurtie—until she saw Al. She stopped on a dime and immediately began limping. We watched as she took a few steps. You could see the wheels turning in her beagle brain: Was it this leg or the other? Then she started limping on the other leg. Caught in the act!

Al and I laughed, both at Samantha and at each other, over what we called the Academy Award performance of the summer. In Hollywood, Samantha would have been given an award for "Best Actress in a Leading Role." Instead, we wrote, "The Best Beagle in the Northwest Territories Award" on a piece of paper and gave it to her. She seemed so proud of her performance and the award. Actually, we knew that she was the only beagle in the Northwest Territories, but we didn't tell her—we didn't want to spoil the magic.

~Lynn Alcock
Chicken Soup for the Dog Lover's Soul

Loving Our Dogs

Chapter 8

Dogs and Their Soldiers

I talk to him when I'm lonesome like; and I'm sure he understands.
When he looks at me so attentively, and gently licks my hands;
then he rubs his nose on my tailored clothes,
but I never say naught thereat.
For the good Lord knows I can buy more clothes,
but never a friend like that.

~W. Dayton Wedgefarth

Friends in Arms

"Have you a pet who would make a good War Dog?"

The message went out by radio and newspapers to citizens of England in July 1942 at the height of the Allied struggle with Germany during World War II. "The British War Office needs strong, intelligent dogs to be trained for guard and patrol duty, rescue work, as messengers and mine detectors," the message continued. "If you have such a dog and would consider lending him to the service of your country, please call the war office."

Eight-year-old Barry Railton heard the appeal at his home in Tolworth, Surrey. He looked at his six-year-old cream-colored German shepherd Khan, whom he had owned since the dog was a puppy. "Would you like to be a War Dog?" he asked Khan.

He went to his father, Harry Railton. "Could I volunteer Khan to be a War Dog?"

Railton had heard the radio appeal. "Are you sure you want to volunteer Khan? He is intelligent enough and has always been eager to learn, but remember, he would be gone for a long time."

"How long?"

Railton shook his head. "Who knows when this war will end? I can't say how long he would be gone."

Barry patted the dog's head. "Khan is smart. If the country needs him, I think he should go."

"Think about this, Barry. He might not come back."

"He'll come back, all right." Barry spoke with the optimism of a child.

Harry Railton phoned the war office, and soon papers arrived for him to fill out. In a few weeks, it was time for Khan to leave his Norfolk home for the War Dog Training School. Barry kissed the top of Khan's head and cried as he said goodbye, but the boy remained steadfast in his confidence that Khan would return.

The training school requirements were a breeze for Khan, and on graduation he was assigned to the 6th Battalion Cameronians, based in Lanarkshire, Scotland.

Corporal Jimmy Muldoon was assigned to work with Khan. Right from the beginning, they became good friends. They worked together on guard patrol for two years.

Then in 1944, Khan and Muldoon were assigned to take part in the Allied forces invasion of German-held western Europe. In boats, men of the 6th Battalion were to outflank a causeway leading to a Dutch island and then wade ashore along a mile-long stretch of mud bank.

An assault craft, packed with men and equipment, was launched at high tide, in the early hours of the morning. As the boat approached the shore, enemy guns fired. A shell hit the boat amidship and men, dogs and equipment catapulted into the air. Muldoon and Khan were thrown into the icy water as the boat, riddled by gunfire, broke in two and sank.

Men struggled to keep afloat and hold their rifles above the water. Khan rose to the surface and swam toward the lights on the shore. When the dog neared the bank, he sank into the mud, but he was able to scramble up onto firmer ground. He stopped and stood still.

The flash of searchlights and the blasts of gunfire raked the struggling men in the mud. In spite of the cracking of artillery and the screams of injured and dying men, Khan must have heard the voice of Johnny Muldoon calling to him. Unable to swim, Muldoon was desperately battling to stay afloat two hundred yards from the shore. Khan plunged back into the frigid water and, guided by Muldoon's calls, swam to his master. Grabbing the collar of Muldoon's tunic, Khan paddled through the water and mud and at last dragged Muldoon to the shore. Man and dog collapsed on the bank.

Litter bearers found Muldoon and carried him to a field hospital. Khan stayed right beside his bed the entire time the corporal was in hospital. When Muldoon and Khan returned to the regiment, the battalion commander nominated Khan for the Dickin Medal, named for Maria Dickin, founder of the People's Dispensary for Sick Animals, a British charitable organization. The Dickin Medal was awarded to eighteen dogs, eight horses, thirty-seven pigeons and one cat during World War II and its aftermath for service to the armed forces or civil defense.

Khan's medal was presented March 27, 1945, by the commanding officer at a full battalion parade. The citation on the medal read, "For rescuing Corporal Muldoon from drowning under heavy shell fire of the assault at Walcheren November 1944, while serving with the 6th Cameronians."

Corporal Muldoon wrote many letters to the war office, asking to be allowed to keep Khan after the war ended. The Railton family, however, asked for their dog to be returned.

When the war ended, Corporal Muldoon was demobilized, and he returned to civilian life in Strathaven, Scotland. Khan was sent for six months to the quarantine station not far from the Railton's home in Surrey. Barry Railton, now twelve, visited the quarantined Khan three times a week. At the end of six months, Khan returned to the Railton home.

The following year, Khan was invited to participate in the National Dog Tournament. Harry Railton wrote to Muldoon, asking him to lead Khan in the Special War Dog Parade.

Muldoon was ecstatic at the thought of seeing Khan again, even if only for a little while. Two hundred of the most intelligent, skillful dogs in Great Britain, including sixteen Dickin medalists, were to appear in the parade.

On the day of the parade, Khan was one of a huge crowd of dogs milling around on the grounds. Suddenly he stopped, lifted his head, his ears at the alert. He sniffed the air. His legs tensed. He jerked the leash from Mr. Railton's hand and bolted, a streak of fur, across the parade grounds, barking loudly.

Ten thousand people in the spectator stands saw the joyful reunion of man and dog. Applause thundered as Muldoon and Khan took their places in the parade line.

Afterwards Harry Railton searched out Muldoon in the crowd. He watched as Muldoon, tears bathing his cheeks, buried his head in the dog's fur. Sobbing, he held out the leash to Railton.

Railton shook his head. "Barry and I talked it over during the parade," he said. "Tell him, Barry."

"We think Khan belongs with you," said Barry, the tears shining in his own eyes. "He's yours. Take him home."

A grateful Muldoon left with Khan on the overnight express for Glasgow. Next morning when they left the train, they were welcomed at the station by a crowd of press members. At the end of the interview, Johnny Muldoon told the reporters, "Pray God we will live out our lives together."

His prayer was answered.

~Rosamond Young
Chicken Soup for the Cat and Dog Lover's Soul

71

Dog of War

In Vietnam, we all made choices with which we now must live. How many bullets do you carry versus how much water? When the rescue chopper says "only three" and there are four of you left, do you leave a guy or "lock and load" on the Huey driver, hijacking the craft? Worst of all, when it's dark and nobody can help you, do you let some fatally injured kid die slowly or just get it over with?

Not all my decisions were ones I regret. And not all my memories are the kind that jerk my breath away at three in the morning and leave me waiting with clenched fists for the first blessed light of dawn. In the darkness of that time, there was one bright spot: a big German shepherd named Beau.

Beau was a scout dog attached to my infantry unit. His job was to sniff out Viet Cong tunnels, ammo caches and booby traps. Like many of us, he was a soldier on the outside and a puppy in his heart.

When we had to wait for our next move, which was often, Beau was a great source of entertainment. His handler would tie a thin monofilament line across a path, then dare someone to step over it. Beau's job was not to let anyone trigger a booby trap. He'd been taught it was better to attack one GI than have a mine pop into the air and detonate at the level of everybody's head.

I would spend a minute petting Beau and sharing my C-rations with him. Then I'd start walking toward the string. Beau was never won over by my offers of food. As I approached the trip wire, he'd race to get between me and it, then flatten his radar station ears and roll out an awesome set of glowing white, bone-crushing teeth. His eyes looked straight into mine as his huge torso sank into a crouch, preparing to spring. We dealt with pretty scary stuff, but when Beau told you to stop, no one had the guts to take a step.

After nearly getting shredded by the big guy, I'd go back to my food. Immediately we were pals again.

One steamy, miserable day, my unit was moving through an area of light jungle and tall trees. I was about fourth from point; Beau and his handler were behind me. Gunshots, their sharpness blunted by the smothering heat and humidity, exploded overhead. We hit the vine-covered jungle floor. Beau crouched between me and his handler. "In the trees," someone hissed. As I looked, there were more shots, louder this time. Beau flinched but gave no other sign of injury. I emptied three twenty-round clips in the direction of the noise. My frantic and scruffy peers did likewise. In a moment, it was over.

I looked at Beau. He seemed okay. We made him roll over, then stand up. It was then I caught that line of slick, dark blue-red we all knew too well. A bullet had pierced his foreleg. It appeared to be a clean hole, bleeding only slightly. I patted him and he wagged his tail. His sad, intelligent eyes expressed, "It's okay, Joe. I'm not important. I'm just here to protect you."

A chopper took the dog and his handler away. I patted him and wondered if they would send the big guy home. What a naive kid I was. Some weeks later they were back. Beau had learned even more ways to con me out of my dinner.

Mid-summer, 1967. We were a thousand meters from a huge field outside a tiny hamlet called Sui Tres. In that field was an American artillery unit. Around them were 2,500 Viet Cong. Our job was to shoot our way through and secure the Howitzer guys.

We slept on the jungle floor, lying with our heads on our helmets. Just before dawn we heard the unsteady rumble of machine-gun and heavy-weapons fire erupt from the direction of Sui Tres. Time to face the enemy.

I put on my helmet and reached for the rest of my gear. Beau wandered over to see if we had time for breakfast. The dark jungle was filled with the normal din of muttered curses and rustling equipment. Overhead, Russian-made rockets were about to burst in the treetops around us. The approaching rockets sounded like escaping steam, followed by what seemed like a long moment of silence. Then deafening, lung-crushing thunder.

Dust filled the air. I was face down on the ground, not knowing how I got there. People were screaming for medics. My helmet was split open by shrapnel and would no longer fit on my head. Beau's long black tail wagged near me in the confusion. He was crouched by his handler, waiting for orders. But it was no use; the young soldier had given his last command.

I pulled Beau gently away and stroked the fur on his back. Sticky liquid covered my hand and ran down the side of his body. A tiny piece of shrapnel had penetrated his back just below the spine. Again he seemed not to notice, and tried to pull away to be with his handler. "He didn't make it," I said, kneeling and holding him against my chest. "He just didn't make it."

Each GI is issued a large cloth bandage in an olive-drab pouch attached to his web gear. The rule is to use your buddy's bandage for him and save yours for yourself. Beau didn't have a bandage, so I wrapped him with mine.

They took the dog away with the other wounded. I never saw Beau again.

September 18, 1967. After eleven months and twenty-nine days in Vietnam, I was going home. Malaria had reduced me from 165 pounds to 130 pounds. I looked and felt like a corpse in combat boots. My heart was filled with death—the smell, the look, the wrenching finality of it.

I was standing in line to get my eyes checked. We all had clipboards with forms to fill out. The guy in front of me asked if he could use my pen. He'd been a dog handler, he said. Now he was going home to his family's farm in Iowa. "It's a beautiful place," he said. "I never thought I'd live to see it again."

I told him about the scout dog I'd befriended and what had

happened to him and his handler. The soldier's next words took my breath away.

"You mean Beau!" he exclaimed, suddenly animated and smiling.

"Yeah, how'd you know?"

"They gave him to me after my dog got killed."

For a moment I was happy. Then two miserable thoughts popped into my brain. First, I'd have to ask him what had happened to Beau. Second, this handler was on his way home, leaving that loyal mutt to stay here till his luck ran out.

"So," I said, looking at the toe of my jungle boot as I crushed out an imaginary cigarette, "what happened to that dog?"

The young soldier lowered his voice the way people do when they have bad news. "He's gone."

I was so sick of death I wanted to throw up. I wanted to just sit down on the floor and cry. I guess this guy noticed my clenched fists and the wetness in my eyes. He lowered his voice and looked around nervously.

"He's not dead, man," he said. "He's gone. I got my company commander to fill out a death certificate for him and I sent him back to my parents' house. He's been there for two weeks. Beau is back in Iowa."

What that skinny farm kid and his commanding officer did certainly didn't mean much compared with the global impact made by the war in Vietnam, but for me, it represents what was really in all our hearts. Of all the decisions made in 'Nam, that's the one I can live with best.

~Joe Kirkup
Chicken Soup for the Pet Lover's Soul

Letters from Vietnam

One of the least pleasurable aspects of a military career are the extended family separations. The agony of saying goodbye to my wife, Mycki, and my son was compounded by the fact that I nearly always had a favorite dog that required (or at least I thought so) my sitting on the floor and explaining that Dad had to go away for a while, but would surely return. Such was the case in 1970 when military orders directed me to Vietnam and I had to break the news to Roulette, our one-year-old miniature poodle.

Non-dog people raise their eyebrows when I tell them that dogs understand more of our speech than animal behaviorists give them credit for. Roulette understood. I watched her eyes and expression as I told her I was going away and she showed a sadness that I didn't see again until the final days of her life. When I promised to write often and return in a year, she acknowledged this with just one slow and deliberate wag of her tail. Then she sighed deeply and laid her head in my lap. That moment remains indelibly imprinted in my mind.

After my arrival in Vietnam, I wrote home two or three times a week. But Mycki soon began to complain that I wasn't writing very often. She told me that at first my letters arrived at intervals of a week to ten days, but now there were often no letters for two weeks at a time.

I was puzzled and began to imagine all sorts of things, including the idea that the Viet Cong were shooting down all mail planes carrying my letters.

My wife knew from previous experience that I was a pretty faithful correspondent. Even when sent to remote areas, I always managed to find a postal drop somewhere. So she was as puzzled as I was about what was happening to my letters.

Over time, Mycki began to notice something odd. It became clear that if she was actually at the front door of our house when the mail came through the slot, the probability of a letter from me was greater. Puzzled, she decided to experiment by monitoring the front door more closely around mail delivery times. Things began to fall into place when she noticed that a little four-legged critter seemed very irritated when "momma" got to the mail first.

Our postman usually arrived between eleven o'clock and noon, and the next time he came up the walk to the front door, Mycki hid behind a partition where she had a good view of the front door and the floor of the entryway.

As Mycki peeked around the edge of the wall, she saw Miss Roulette saunter up to the several pieces of mail that had fallen on the floor beneath the slot. Roulette sniffed at a couple of items and then gently, with one front paw, pulled an envelope out from the stack. She gave a quick glance around and then scooped up the letter in her mouth. With a mixture of mild outrage and stifled hilarity, Mycki followed Roulette into the living room. She was close behind the pom-pommed tail as the poodle rounded the end of the couch and slipped in behind it with the letter.

"The game is over, Missy—get out from behind the couch," Mycki ordered. But Roulette was not a dog that responded immediately to orders. Moving the couch away from the wall, Mycki sternly requested, "Come on Rou, out of there." Reluctantly, like a momma dog protecting her pups, Miss Roulette rose and cautiously left her clandestine lair, revealing a number of letters where she had been lying.

The mystery was solved, but for Roulette, the game wasn't over, not by a long shot. With each subsequent mail delivery, it became a race to the door between Mycki and Roulette to pick up the mail. If Roulette won, a chase ensued, unless of course, Mycki was busy or not at home when the postman arrived. Then it became a matter of search and seizure.

Roulette tossed in another twist that made the game even more interesting. Whenever Mycki received a letter, she would retire to her recliner in the living room to read it. But if she left the letter on the end table afterwards, the artful dodger would strike again. Even when Mycki left the letters on the kitchen table where she did much of her writing, Roulette managed to appropriate them as soon as Mycki's attention was elsewhere. No place Roulette could reach was safe for my letters. Mycki finally resorted to storing them in a shoebox and putting the box inside her armoire.

Roulette retaliated by attempting little hunger strikes. Mycki really became concerned until she found out that Roulette was actually conning her—our son was sneak-feeding the little letter-napper at night in his room.

When Mycki explained all this to me in one of her letters, I had to laugh. It was rather nice to have two ladies fighting over me.

But things reverted to normal pretty quickly when I returned home. Roulette suddenly lost interest in the mail. However, while packing and preparing to move to our next duty station, we did discover a few more postal hideaways containing unopened letters from Vietnam—a reminder that as far as a dog's nose is concerned, a small object sent by a beloved human that travels nine thousand miles, though handled by dozens of other people, still bears a treasured message. I had never realized during all those months when I thought I was writing just to Mycki that I was also sending a uniquely personal greeting to one smart and sharp-nosed little poodle.

~Joe Fulda
Chicken Soup for the Cat and Dog Lover's Soul

73

Boom Boom

In Vietnam, I served as a helicopter pilot with the A Company, Helicopter Assault Battalion, 101st Airborne Division. During the summer and fall of 1968, we spent an inordinate amount of time in an area called the A Shau Valley. We had two basic missions: performing combat assaults and resupplying the troops in the field. The days following a combat assault were known as "log days:" logistics missions where our helicopters brought supplies to the field troops. We carried out all the essentials needed to conduct a war. During these resupply missions, we also brought back the wounded and the dead.

The first thing we did on log day was land at the logistics point and load the aircraft with the material to be taken to the field positions. One memorable day, as we were being loaded, a small dog jumped into the back of the helicopter and settled among the boxes and bags as if he owned the place.

"What's with the dog?" I asked the officer in charge of the loading detail. He explained that the dog was the mascot of the unit I was assigned to, and he always took the first log bird that went out to the troops in the field. He did, however, always manage to return on the last flight from the field to the base camp. Apparently, he didn't want to spend his evenings in the A Shau Valley. I thought to myself that this dog had more sense than a lot of people. I asked the logistics officer what the dog's name was, and he replied, "Boom Boom."

As soon as we landed at our first site in the A Shau Valley, the dog leaped from the aircraft and was treated like a celebrity. There were smiles all around from the troops as they played with Boom Boom, and I felt that I had really done these people a favor. The dog was a definite morale booster.

As evening approached, we received a call from one of our units that they had a trooper who had been injured in an explosion and the resulting fire. This man needed an immediate medical evacuation. We proceeded to the location at our best speed. I felt quite calm at the time, because after nearly a year of doing this sort of mission, you learn not to become too emotionally involved with the wounded. My job as a pilot was to transport the injured soldiers to medical help as soon as possible, and not be distracted by their distress.

Since this young soldier's injuries were quite severe, I had to take him to the nearest medic, who was in a forward base in the mountains bordering the A Shau Valley. Berchtesgaden was a difficult place to get into, mainly because of the updrafts and windy conditions. But the injured soldier needed immediate treatment. If he didn't receive it, he might not survive the thirty-minute trip to the nearest hospital.

Just as we were loading our patient into the helicopter's empty cargo bay, in jumped Boom Boom for the trip back to the rear area. I paid little attention to him since my thoughts were on the task at hand; I just knew Boom Boom was in the back with the wounded soldier.

Just before beginning the approach into Berchtesgaden, I looked back at our patient. The man was burned quite badly, and his arms and chest were blackened; but he was conscious, so I motioned back at him to grab onto something, knowing that the trip was about to get very rough. He grabbed onto a support in the rear of the helicopter, and I started our descent.

I was having a very tough time controlling the aircraft. At one time, the collective control was bottomed out, which should have had us dropping like a rock, but instead of descending, we were climbing at five hundred feet per minute. I took a quick look at our patient. The burned trooper seemed to be doing okay. But, then, I caught sight of Boom Boom, and I was horrified: The little dog was slowly sliding toward the open cargo door! He was frantically trying to stop himself by digging his claws into the metal floor, but it wasn't doing any good. He couldn't hold onto anything.

I was powerless to save him. This friendly dog was going to go out the door of my helicopter and fall five hundred feet to his death in the jungle below. Instead of flying my aircraft with total concentration, I was staring at little Boom Boom, this dog that had done nothing but make people happy. I thought of the joy I saw on the faces of the men that morning when I brought their dog out for a visit. How could I face these people again? For me, this incident would probably be the last straw. After nearly a year of missions, in which I had heard the cries of the wounded and looked into the unseeing eyes of the dead, I was going to be emotionally destroyed by a small dog's death.

Boom Boom was whining with fear and still struggling to save himself, but it was no use. Nothing he or I could do would prevent disaster.

Then, at the very moment Boom Boom was about to go flying out the cargo door, I saw a blackened arm reach out. The arm grabbed the flailing dog firmly and pulled him back from the edge.

I breathed an immense sigh of relief. "Thanks, trooper," I whispered as I focused my mind back on the task of landing the helicopter. For the remainder of that roller-coaster landing, Boom Boom was held close to the blackened chest of a badly injured man who still had it in him to save a small but precious life.

As soon as we landed, the young trooper received medical attention from several skilled people. I was informed that he would remain at the forward base until the next day; he needed a lot of attention before he could make the ride back to a hospital. Boom Boom stayed with him. I guess the dog wasn't about to risk another ride in my chopper, and I can't say I blamed him.

~James R. Morgan
Chicken Soup for the Veteran's Soul

74

Soldier Dog

During the monsoon season of 1968, after several months of combat following the Tet Offensive, my army unit was moved from the mountains of northern South Vietnam to the coastal plain, north of Da Nang. We had been assigned to provide security for a battalion of Seabees. It rained torrentially for most of each day and night, but we tried to stay as warm and dry as we could.

As a medic, my life was pretty good at this assignment. I didn't have to pull guard duty, just hold sick call and do radio watch for a couple of hours each night. Sure, I was halfway around the world, separated from my family and my home, but the Seabees had supplies. We even got fresh food, which sure beat the freeze-dried and canned rations that were issued for consumption in the jungle. But best of all, I could buy a beer each evening and relax and try to forget the terror that had been with me since the beginning of the Tet Offensive.

I was aware of the dramatic changes my personality had undergone in the short time I had been in Vietnam. I distrusted everything and everyone I came in contact with. Like the times when I treated Vietnamese civilians in their villages for their ailments.

This was an attempt by the army to win the hearts and minds of the local population. The army's public information officer wanted some photographs showing that the First Brigade of the 101st Airborne, the toughest of the tough, was also the most caring. On such occasions, the villagers would lay out a meal, sometimes consisting of rice and meat, with great formality. This was intended as a respectful greeting to me, and courtesy demanded that I eat first. But I was suspicious, and fearing that the food might be poisoned, I always insisted that the Village Chief be the first to take a bite, thus managing to thoroughly offend our hosts. But I didn't care; my sole concern at that time was surviving to make it home.

One night, after some revelry in the galley, I walked back to our camp and knelt down to slide into my damp living space. As I crawled in headfirst, I felt a wet, furry body brush my forehead. I grabbed my pistol and my flashlight and prepared to kill the rat in my bedroll.

But it wasn't a rat. In the light, I saw before me a shivering brown puppy that looked like a Chihuahua. Its big eyes were imploring, as if it knew that its life was almost over. I reengaged the safety catch and picked up the little body, so cold, so wet and so scared. We're a lot alike, I thought.

I dug around in my gear and found a can of beef slices from an old meal unit. I opened the can, broke up the meat into little bites, and put it in front of this intruder, who snapped it up quickly. Then I rinsed the can out and filled it with clean water so he could drink.

That night, when I curled up to go to sleep, I wasn't remembering the girl back home; I had a living, breathing being snuggled next to me trying to gain security and warmth from my existence. And I didn't dream of the girl back home, either. Instead I dreamed of my beagle, who always curled up at the foot of my bed when I came home from school on vacations, and who went with me everywhere.

The next morning, I went to breakfast and got extra eggs, bacon and sausages. My new little friend wolfed them down.

I decided to name him Charger, after our battalion commander. Every time I called out "Charger!" I offered him a tidbit of food, so he learned his name in no time. He also learned some simple tricks, and seemed to grow very attached to me. Wherever I went, that little ring-tailed mutt of dubious parentage was right there with me, and I grew very fond of him.

One day I was in the nearby village of Lang Co, where I went every day except Sunday, to treat the villagers for their various ailments, which ranged from ringworm and pinworm to elephantiasis. While I dispensed different pills and salves, I noticed my little friend frolicking with the fire team that had accompanied me for security. As I watched him darting after the sticks they threw for him and prancing proudly back with the stick clamped firmly in his teeth, I had to smile. I turned back to the Vietnamese child I was examining, and I saw an answering smile light up his small face. Little Charger was effecting a remarkable change in my personality. I realized that I had begun to care about the local people. I really wanted to cure their illnesses, whereas earlier I had just been going through the motions to please the army public relations machine. Charger was helping me to recover some of the humanity that I feared I had lost.

I was soon to be separated from my new friend, however. After a few short weeks, my company was ordered back to the mountains. After numerous inquiries, I was able to find someone in the mortar platoon at our battalion fire base to adopt Charger. I left him there, knowing that I would miss him but trying not to look back as I walked with my company toward the jungle, returning to the harsh reality of war.

I served more than seven months with the infantry, before I was reassigned to a medevac unit. I had not forgotten Charger, and as I came through the fire base on my way to my new assignment, I had already decided that I would bring my little friend with me to my new unit. We recognized each other instantly, and our reunion was ecstatic.

I spent the day at the fire base and soon noticed that something was different there. Talking with the soldiers, I registered that the level of profanity and vulgarity had dropped. And the men seemed more caring towards each other. A large number of them called to Charger as he trotted by, often stopping to scratch his head or give him a treat or two in passing. Charger was working the same magic for his new friends in the mortar platoon that he had worked for me.

With my heart breaking, and on the verge of tears, I left Charger with his newfound friends, for they seemed to need him even more than I did.

That was the last time I ever saw Charger. My medevac chopper was shot down about two months later. I was evacuated, and regained consciousness in a hospital in Japan. I tried to find out about Charger, but only heard a vague rumor that he had been taken back to the States. I hoped it was true.

I still remember him now, more than thirty years later. He lives on in my heart. And whenever I think back to that rainy and miserable night in Vietnam when our paths first crossed, it seems impossible to know just who rescued whom.

~Ron St. James
Chicken Soup for the Cat and Dog Lover's Soul

Loving Our Dogs

Great Dog Moments

*If there are no dogs in Heaven, then when I die
I want to go where they went.*
~Will Rogers

Beau and the Twelve-Headed Monster

When a dog barks at the moon, then it is religion;
but when he barks at strangers, it is patriotism!
~David Starr Jordan

The bicyclists are clad in black Lycra shorts and tight-fitting, bright-colored jerseys. They ride in a disciplined pace line. Sweat glistens on lean forearms and bulging quadriceps. They talk and joke and laugh as they ride. It is just past six on a warm Sunday morning in July.

A mile ahead at the top of a short steep rise is Beau's yard. Beau is a heavyset, sinister-looking black Labrador retriever who protects his yard and his family with unswerving diligence and a loud round of barking whenever strangers approach. If the threat is especially menacing, Beau supplements his barking with a swift hard charge that invariably sends the intruder packing. This morning Beau is stationed in his usual place under the porch. It is shady and cool there, and he can see all the territory he must defend.

The cyclists slow as they ascend the hill that leads to Beau's yard. As they labor against gravity, the only sound is the whirr of the freewheels and the hoosh of hard exhalations.

Beau sees the cyclists as they crest the hill. He has seen cyclists before and takes pride in chasing them from his territory. But this is something new: a dozen cyclists moving as one. To Beau it is a twelve-headed monster with twenty-four arms and twenty-four legs. He has to protect his family. He has to be brave. He explodes from his hiding place under the porch and charges across the yard, hackles raised, fangs bared, barking his fiercest bark.

The cyclists are taken by surprise. It isn't the first time they've been attacked by an unrestrained dog. They usually avoid a confrontation by outrunning the beast. But this dog is unusually fast and is very nearly upon them. It is too late to run for it. The cyclists reach for the only antidog weapons they have: water bottles and tire pumps.

When Beau reaches the edge of his yard, he hesitates for a moment. He isn't supposed to go out of the yard, and the street is definitely off-limits. But this is a twelve-headed monster with forty-eight appendages. There is no telling what it will do to his family. He has no choice — he has to break the rules, and he clears the sidewalk and the curb with one great leap.

Among the cyclists is a man who has a Lab a lot like Beau. Instead of reaching for a water bottle or tire pump, he looks at Beau and says, "Hey, where's your ball? Where's your ball?"

A few minutes later one of the other cyclists says, "Man, I couldn't believe it. He just stopped and went looking for a ball. It was amazing. How did you know he had a ball?"

"He's a Lab. Labs are nuts about tennis balls. I had a friend once who swore he was going to name his next Lab 'Wilson' so all his tennis balls would have his name on them."

The cyclists laugh and then fall silent. The only sound is the whirr of the freewheels and the hoosh of hard exhalations.

Beau is back in his favorite spot under the porch. He has a soggy green tennis ball in his mouth. If the twelve-headed monster with forty-eight appendages comes back, he's ready.

~John Arrington
Chicken Soup for the Dog Lover's Soul

76

An Answer to Prayer

Labradors [are] lousy watchdogs. They usually bark when there is a stranger
about, but it is an expression of unmitigated joy at the chance
to meet somebody new, not a warning.
~Norman Strung

My daughter Lori, fully clothed in winter attire, prepared to take Clancy, one of her two black labs, out for their Sunday evening walk. She had promised him that if the rain stopped they'd stroll down by the creek, his favorite destination.

Clancy and Duke had been there for Lori time and time again. They were there when the neighborhood ruffian climbed a tree to peep into Lori's bedroom. He learned first-hand that Clancy certainly was not his best friend. All he left behind was his telltale baseball cap beneath the tree, dropped as he scampered for home with Clancy on his heels.

Twice daily, in the darkness of cold winter mornings and evenings, Lori fed her horses and Toughie, the yellow barn cat. As she trudged knee-deep in the snow to the barn, Duke and Clancy eased her loneliness with their comical actions, bounding and barking between mouthfuls of snow. For their unselfish loyalty, unequivocal love and companionship, Clancy and Duke expected nothing in return but a pat on their heads, Lori's praising soft voice, and a dish of dog chow.

Lori's relationship with Clancy became stronger when Duke

developed arthritis. Now gray-faced, he could no longer take part in all their activities, such as playing stick or taking long walks. Too many winters and trips through the deep snow had taken their toll. Those swims in the icy creek didn't help either.

Lori looked out the kitchen window and noticed it had quit raining for the first time in several days. She pulled on her down filled jacket and laced up her heavy boots.

Clancy, along with Duke, was lying on the back porch—sleeping bundles of black lab, love and loyalty. Lori nudged Clancy gently and spoke enthusiastically, "Come Clancy, we're going for a walk before it gets too dark."

Needless to say ol' Clancy only had to be asked once. He almost knocked her down in his effort to get out the door before her. She smiled at his joyful enthusiasm. Duke gave them a lab smile but remained on the porch.

Lori and Clancy started their walk along the road, deserted as usual, in the direction of the nearby creek. They had gone only a short distance when black clouds began to roll in and darken the sky. Once more it began to spit rain.

She yelled at Clancy, who had bounded ahead to the bridge that crossed the creek. "Come on Clancy, we have to head for home." Clancy, busy chasing a mouse, paid her no mind.

Lori yelled again, "Come on Clancy, we have to head home, no swim for you today."

Clancy leaped off the bridge and into the tumultuous water. Lori raced to the bridge, calling his name all the way. Under normal circumstances, his dive into the stream would have held no consequences for this strong-swimming lab. But these were not normal circumstances. The stream had become a torrent, due to the rapid runoff from the nearby mountains. High water raged through a barbed wire fence that crossed the creek; the forceful water swept Clancy solidly up against it. He struggled to swim toward shore, but the more he struggled, the more entangled he became.

When she reached the bridge, Lori saw Clancy impaled against the barbed wire fence, struggling and whimpering in desperation, trying to free himself. Lori took one look at this frightful scene and instantly jumped into the swift flowing stream. Her heavy boots and down jacket immediately began to pull her down into the deep icy water, leaving her gasping for breath. In a matter of seconds she also was impaled on the fence next to a struggling Clancy. She grabbed him and held his head up with one hand and grasped the wire with her other.

She knew they had to get out of the freezing water before hypothermia set in. With the frigid water draining her strength, Lori knew she had to either let go of Clancy or risk both of them drowning. "I can't let go of Clancy, God," she prayed, "But I can't hold on much longer. *Please*, I need your help!"

At that moment, a pickup truck appeared, approaching the bridge.

Lori prayed once more in desperation, "Dear God, please help us!"

The truck neared... then crossed the bridge, causing Lori's heart to drop in despair. Then it stopped and backed up onto the bridge again. Two men emerged from the truck and in seconds they ran down the embankment, yelling, "Hold on there! We'll be right down."

One grabbed the fence and reached out his hand. New strength surged through Lori as she swung Clancy over so the man could reach him. He grabbed him then passed him up the bank to his buddy. Then he reached out once again, this time for Lori. She thrust her free hand and he pulled her out of the water—boots and all.

Crowded in the pickup, on the way back to the ranch, Lori asked the rescuers, "How did you ever see me in the water?"

"I really don't know," one said. "We just decided to take this road instead of our usual route. As we were talking, I happened to glance out my window, and I saw your blond head above the murky water—lucky you."

But Lori knew it wasn't luck that stopped their truck on the deserted road, it was God answering her desperate prayer.

~James A. Nelson
Chicken Soup for the Christian Soul 2

77

Sled Dogs without Snow

One summer day my dogs and I were hiking along, making our way through the Cleveland Metro parks, when we came to a picnic area. Off to our left I saw several Port-O-Lets—those portable toilets shaped like telephone booths—and noticed that one was being used in a very unusual fashion.

Parked next to this particular Port-O-Let was a cart. It looked like some sort of sled-training cart with wheels used when there is no snow, but that was pure speculation on my part. In any case, the cart was not the unusual part. What was truly unusual were the four Siberian husky/Alaskan malamute–type dogs in harnesses, all hooked to one gang line that went directly into the door of the Port-O-Let, making it appear that they were out on a Port-O-Let/sled-riding mission. I can only assume there was no way to anchor the cart and the dogs while taking care of business, so the cart driver got the brilliant idea to just take the gang line into the Port-O-Let and hold on to the dogs while using the facilities.

Perhaps you're thinking the same thing I was thinking when I saw this little setup. I began fishing in my pack for my digital camera to take a picture of the "Port-O-Let-pulling team" when my dogs started yanking on their leashes, almost toppling me over. I looked around to see what in blazes had set them off.

It was a squirrel that had decided to stop in the middle of the wide-open field to my left, pick up a nut and chew on it. The problem was that my three dogs and the four Port-O-Let-anchored sled dogs were hanging out in the very same field. So far the potty chain gang hadn't seen the squirrel, but it was only a matter of time as my dogs were doing the if-we-weren't-on-this-leash-we-would-kick-that-squirrel's-butt dance with increasing intensity.

Sure enough, within seconds, the potty-pullers' heads all snapped in the direction of my dogs, then in the direction of the squirrel. They appeared to have the same idea as my pack, who were still straining vigorously at their leashes. At that point, my dogs saw the sled dogs spot the squirrel, and some sort of dog tribal-hunting, nonverbal communication thing happened: every one of the seven dogs on either end of the field realized that it was a race to see which of the two groups could get to the squirrel first. My dogs redoubled their pulling efforts, and the four-dog sled team reacted as one, barking furiously and lunging full steam for the squirrel.

The dogs' motion caused the Port-O-Let to spin about thirty degrees and rock like the dickens. Luckily it didn't tip over, just teetered back and forth a time or two, then righted itself. But nothing was going to stop the sled team in their pursuit of the squirrel. They gave another huge yank. The Port-O-Let spun yet again, and from inside the green tower of potty privacy came a human screech, finally piercing through the dogs' din. The screech had the immediate effect of slowing the port-o-pullers down, and they settled into a nervous stand.

Unfortunately, at this point, the squirrel realized that my dogs weren't going to get him, and the port-o-pullers couldn't get him, so he started doing some kind of nah-nah-nah-nah-nah-you-can't-get-me dance, once more infuriating the port-o-pullers and driving my dogs crazy.

If you've ever wondered why dogsleds are built long and low to the ground, as opposed to square and tall—like, say, the shape of a Port-O-Let—you needn't wonder any longer whether this is a design flaw. When the pulling and barking started up again, the Port-O-Let did its best to stay upright, rocking heavily back and forth. The dogs, sensing victory, forgot completely about the squirrel and started timing their pulls with the rocking. They gave one last enormous tug and yanked the Port-O-Let over. Toppling the tall green box seemed to give the dog team a sense of satisfaction; they immediately stopped pulling after the Port-O-Let crashed to the ground. The squirrel had finally gone, and with the dogs quiet, I could now hear a series of cusswords coming from the fallen Port-O-Let.

I figured I'd better head over that way and see if I could help. Sadly, the Port-O-Let had landed facedown, meaning the door was now the bottom—against the ground. I tied my dogs to a tree and ventured closer. I asked if the occupant of the tipped Port-O-Let was okay. A woman's voice said yes—actually, she used far more colorful language, but for the purpose of this story, we'll just say she said yes.

The Port-O-Let hadn't fared as well. You could tell it was badly hurt because there was a lot of blue fluid leaking from it. I told the woman that I would have to roll the Port-O-Let on its side so we could try opening the door, and that she should find something to hang on to. A couple of good shoves later, the Port-O-Let rolled 90 degrees, exposing the door. The door opened and out crawled Mama Smurf. The poor woman was covered in the blue "blood" of the dying Port-O-Let.

Her dogs came running over and decided she needed a bath, which did not make her at all happy. At this point, she suddenly realized she had skipped Step 10 in the bathroom process—pull your pants up—and with a yelp, she quickly disappeared back into the Port-O-Let to finish. When she reappeared, she was in absolutely no mood to talk about her ride on the wild side (I didn't blame her), so I told her the short version of what happened outside the Port-O-Let.

I helped her hook her dogs up to the cart, and off she went, glowing blue as she drove down the path and back into the Metro park woods. I had to laugh imagining the reactions of all the other people walking serenely through the park as they were passed by an irate Smurf and her merry band of blue-tongued dogs.

~Dave Wiley
Chicken Soup for the Dog Lover's Soul

78

Let Sleeping Dogs Lie

No day is so bad it can't be fixed with a nap.
~Carrie Snow

One afternoon, I was in the backyard hanging the laundry when an old, tired-looking dog wandered into the yard. I could tell from his collar and well-fed belly that he had a home. But when I walked into the house, he followed me, sauntered down the hall and fell asleep in a corner. An hour later, he went to the door, and I let him out. The next day he was back. He resumed his position in the hallway and slept for an hour.

This continued for several weeks. Curious, I pinned a note to his collar: "Every afternoon your dog comes to my house for a nap."

The next day he arrived with a different note pinned to his collar: "He lives in a home with ten children—he's trying to catch up on his sleep."

~Susan F. Roman
Chicken Soup for the Pet Lover's Soul

79

A Dog's Day in Court

Justice may be blind, but she has very sophisticated listening devices.
~Edgar Argo

When I was growing up, we lived about a quarter mile from a train crossing. Our dog, Lenny, had a very annoying habit — he howled whenever a train whistled for the crossing. It probably stemmed from his very sensitive hearing. It did not matter if he was outside or in the house. He howled and howled until the train went by. On some days, when the wind was right, he would even howl for the crossings farther down the track. We learned to put up with the noisy ruckus, mainly because we loved our pet so much.

Early one morning while we were eating breakfast, we heard the squeal of a train's braking efforts followed by a terrible crash. My brother dashed out of the house, ran to the end of our lane and discovered a mangled mass jammed on the cowcatcher of the massive locomotive. Parts of a car were strewn everywhere. Unfortunately, the driver of the car had died instantly.

Back in the house, we guessed there had been a crash and called the local rescue squad. But we all immediately said to each other, "Lenny didn't howl. The whistle must not have blown!"

At the scene, my brother recognized what was left of the car as that of his buddy's father and knew immediately the sad, sad news that would now have to be conveyed to the family. When the chief of the rescue squad arrived, my brother told him, "The engineer could not have blown the whistle for the crossing, because our dog did not howl. And he always does!"

The story of Lenny's howling circulated rapidly around our small town as everyone shared in the grief of the wife and family. Speculation ran high as to whether the whistle had truly been blown as the engineer claimed. Some folks even came to witness the "howling dog" phenomenon and left convinced the whistle must not have sounded!

Left without the breadwinner, the family of nine was in dire straits. One of the county's best-known and most successful lawyers decided to pursue a claim against the, by now, infamous Soo Line on behalf of the widow and children. (On contingency, of course!) The lawyer hired an investigator and recording technician. For days, at all hours, the two men frequented our yard and our home listening for oncoming trains and faithfully recording Lenny's howl. Lenny never failed to echo with his characteristic, piercing howl the sharp wail of an approaching freight as it neared the crossing at which the tragedy had occurred. They even recorded his howling as a whistle was blown at the neighboring crossings in both directions when the wind was right. The lawyer was convinced.

The taped evidence, presented in court, along with the testimony of my family members, convinced the judge and jury. The settlement awarded to the family secured their home and future. County court records give evidence of the success of a "dog's day in court!"

~Sr. Mary K. Himens, S.S.C.M.
Chicken Soup for the Dog Lover's Soul

Miracles Do Happen

As a shiny new veterinarian in my mid-twenties, I was sure of everything. The world was black and white with very little gray. In my mind, veterinary medicine was precise and structured, with little room for anything but the rules of science. An experience I had just a few years out of school loosened several stones in that wall of inflexibility.

Two of the most pleasant clients in my small, mountain town practice were an older retired couple. Two kinder, more gentle people could not be found. Their devotion to each other and their pets was luminous. Whenever and wherever they were seen in our little town, their dogs were constant companions. It was assumed that these lovable and loyal dogs were the children they never had. And there was a clear but unobtrusive awareness of this couple's very profound religious faith.

One cold winter morning, they arrived at our clinic with their oldest dog, Fritz. Their big old canine friend could not bear the pain of placing any weight on his hind legs. The great old dog avoided movement as much as possible. When he did feel compelled to move, he pulled himself along with his front legs like a seal, his shrunken, atrophied hind legs dragging outstretched behind him. No amount of encouragement or assistance enabled Fritz to stand or walk on his afflicted rear legs. His owners, with the best of intentions, had been attempting a variety of home treatments for most of the winter, but now his condition had deteriorated to this point.

The look in his eyes was of remarkable intelligence and gentleness, but also of great pain.

My partner and I hospitalized the lovable old dog for a few hours so that we could thoroughly examine him, obtain X-rays and complete other tests. Sadly, we concluded that a lifetime of living with hip dysplasia had taken its full toll on Fritz. His advanced age, atrophied muscles and painful, disfigured joints left no hope that any type of medical or surgical treatment could allow the old couple's dog to enjoy a happy, painless life. We concluded that his only salvation from excruciating pain was to be humanely euthanized.

Later that day, as cold winter darkness fell on our little mountain town, the old couple returned to the clinic to hear our verdict about their beloved pet. As I stood before them in the exam room, I felt a chill pass over me as if I were out in that winter evening. Clearly they knew what I was going to say because they were already softly crying before I began talking. With great hesitation, I explained their old friend Fritz's dire condition. Finally, I struggled to tell them that the kindest act would be to "put him to sleep" so he would suffer no more.

Through their tears, they nodded in agreement. Then the husband asked, "Can we wait to decide about putting him to sleep until the morning?" I agreed that would be fine. He said, "We want to go home and pray tonight. The Lord will help us decide." They told their old friend good night and left him to rest at the clinic overnight. As they left, I sympathetically thought to myself that no amount of praying could help their old dog.

The next morning I came in early to treat our hospitalized cases. The elderly couple's big old crippled dog was just as he had been the evening before — a look of pain on his face, unable to stand, but still showing that kind, intelligent expression. Within an hour the old couple came into the clinic. "We have prayed all night. Can we see Fritz? We will know what the Lord wants when we see him."

I led them through the clinic to the ward where Fritz lay. As I opened the door and peered into the ward, I was numbed by the sight of Fritz eagerly standing in his cage, wagging his tail and bearing an obvious expression of enthusiastic joy at the sound of his owners. He bore not one indication of any pain or dysfunction.

The reunion of Fritz and the old couple was a blur of canine and human cries of joy, kisses and tears. Fritz bounded youthfully out to the car as the couple rejoiced. In their wake, they left a bewildered young veterinarian who was beginning to see that life is not black and white, but includes rather a great deal of gray. I realized that day that miracles do happen.

~Paul H. King, D.V.M.
Chicken Soup for the Pet Lover's Soul

81

The Dog Who Loved to Fly

The reason angels can fly is because they take themselves lightly.
~G.K. Chesterton, "Orthodoxy"

Copper's yearning to fly was apparent from puppyhood. You wouldn't expect a dachshund to want to spend his life airborne, but from the day he cleared the rail of the playpen that was supposed to keep him out of trouble while I was at work, to his last valiant effort at leaving the Earth, there was no stopping him.

It was Copper's soaring spirit that made me choose him as my first dog. The rest of the litter was cute in the traditional puppy way. Copper, however, would have nothing to do with touching noses or cuddling up next to me. He managed to drag himself up on top of the sofa, and before anyone could stop him, off he jumped. He landed with a "poof!" as the air escaped from his tiny belly. Seven-week-old dog legs aren't meant to support skydiving. I knew that, but he didn't.

I'm not big on following rules either, so Copper was the obvious choice for me. I whispered in his little ear, "I like you, flying dog. Do you want to come home with me?" He stared at me intently as if to say, Okay, but don't expect me to obey Newton's Law of Gravity!

Copper's pilot training began the moment we arrived home. He surveyed the landscape, identified the highest elevations and spent his days scampering up and flying down from everything he could. For months, every floor in the house was covered with pillows, blankets, towels and anything soft I could find to cushion his landings.

One day when he was about five months old, I came home to find Copper standing in the middle of the dining room table with that look on his face that said, Fasten your seat belts and hang on for the ride! I ran as fast as I could toward him to catch him, but he hit the ground before I could yell, "No flying in the dining room!"

From that day on, I put the dining room chairs upside down on the table every morning before I went to work. When friends and neighbors asked why, I'd just shrug and say it was an old German custom.

I wished Copper could be happy doing regular dachshund stuff—sniffing the carpet, rolling in strange smells, barking at squirrels and learning to be disobedient in two languages, but it just wasn't in him. "What am I going to do with you, flying dog?" I'd ask him every night when I got home from work. I got him a dog tag shaped like an airplane and prayed that he was strong enough not to get hurt in his airborne escapades.

One day when he was five, Copper jumped up on the back of the couch and flew off. When he landed, he hurt his back. I rushed him to the vet, who said he'd blown a disc and would need surgery. My heart was broken. If I had been a good dog-parent, I thought, I'd have found a way to stop him from flying.

Copper pulled through the surgery with a wagging tail and that same rebellious spark in his eyes. And now that he had a reverse Mohawk from the surgery, he looked even more independent. The last words I heard at the vet were, "Don't let him jump off things!"

I tried, really I did. For three weeks, whenever I wasn't with him, I kept Copper in a crate. He gave me a look that said, How can you take away my freedom, my spirit, my reason for living? And he was right; I had grounded not only his body, but his spirit as well. So as he got stronger, I started letting him out of the crate. I gave him a stern warning to behave himself, but he and I both knew he wouldn't.

As the years went by, Copper found it harder to get around. When he got too old to easily clamber onto the sofa with me, I built him a ramp. Of course, the first thing he did was to use it as a springboard to fly from. And he was just as proud of himself as he ever was.

Then at age thirteen, Copper's entire back end became paralyzed; he couldn't jump at all. I don't know who was sadder that Copper's flying days were over, him or me.

The vet couldn't find anything wrong, so I got Copper a K-9 cart, a little wheelchair for dogs. "Now, Copper," I said, "I looked for a little cart with wings, but they just didn't have one. So I guess you'll just have to stay on the floor like a real dog from now on."

A few minutes later, while I was in the kitchen cooking dinner, I heard a noise in the living room. I ran in and saw Copper at the top of the ramp, with that look in his eye. Before anyone could stop him, he turned and wheeled down the ramp at full speed, his ears flying behind him.

Copper could still fly. I should have known better than to doubt his soaring spirit. And once he landed his new "aircraft," he wheeled back up the ramp and took off again, as elated by his accomplishment as the Wright Brothers must have been.

Copper flew up and down that ramp with his wheels spinning behind him for almost three more years before he escaped the bonds of Earth once and for all.

~Leigh Anne Jasheway-Bryant
Chicken Soup for the Dog Lover's Soul

82

Butch

The fishing was good; it was the catching that was bad.
~A.K. Best

As a young woman, I was determined one summer to learn how to fish. After purchasing fishing gear, based on the advice from a sporting goods clerk, my black lab Butch and I headed for the nearby lake.

I pulled over at what appeared to be the local fishing hot spot; several cars were already parked along the roadside. A morning mist still hovered above the water, clearing as the morning warmed. It was a wonderful day to wet my line for the first time. Fishermen were catching spawning crappie by the bucketsful, some probably destined to be buried in the garden for fertilizer rather than landing in a frying pan. Actually, I was hoping for a little more luck—I wanted to catch a bass.

I tied on a lure and added a brightly colored round bobber. I proceeded to cast my line and work my lure with what I thought was a most enticing jigging motion. When I quickly got a bite, I remembered the need to set the hook, so I pulled my pole up with gusto and sent my little fish flying in the air past my head. The poor fish hit the steep bank behind me with a smack. I repeated this several times with the fish usually falling off my hook and flipping back into the water. Butch lay well behind me, wary of my casting backswing after I'd managed to hit him with a soaring fish or two. I scrambled in pursuit of each escaping fish, stepping into the lake water—and a couple of times into underwater critter holes. I kept getting wet, first up to my knees and finally above the waist, much to the amusement of the experienced onlookers.

Apparently my knot-tying skills also needed improvement. I had soon lost all of my lures, with few fish to show for my efforts. The fisherman next to me took pity (or maybe wanted further entertainment) and offered some tie-ups so I could continue fishing. I thanked him and went back to work. His kindness and my persistence paid off. I had a hard strike! My pole bowed down, almost touching the water. My mentor was excited too, shouting, "Bet you hooked a bass! Bring him in easy now. Don't jerk too hard."

Laughing, I landed the fish without it becoming airborne. But it, too, came loose when my line broke just above the bobber, and both the bobber and my fish slipped back into the lake. As the other fishermen groaned, we watched the bright red bobber mark where the fish traveled. The fish towed the bobber round and round the cove, sometimes tantalizingly close to the bank, only for it to disappear underwater for what seemed like a long time and then pop up somewhere else. The fish grew in size, at least in our minds, the longer it stayed under. As the bobber cruised its course past other fisherman, they cast out, trying to snag it without success.

A rowboat was hailed to help. Just about the time they'd get close enough to grab it, the bobber would sink out of sight. "It's over here now!" a spotter would yell. One enterprising fellow climbed a tree, broke off a long branch and joined the rowboat's efforts. They finally gave up and went back to their own fishing.

Discouraged, wet and muddy, I prepared to leave. I called my dog and ruffled his neck. I was seeking consolation. Suddenly I got an idea — one of those lightbulb kind. As the bobber made another pass, I said, "Go get the ball, Butch!"

As everyone watched, Butch wagged his tail, spotted the ball moving across the water and happily fetched it, fish and all. We went home with a nice-sized bass.

A few days later, I returned to the same cove and set up next to another woman. She commented that more women must be taking up fishing, then told my own fish story back to me, as her fisherman husband had related to her. I nodded and giggled in all the right places. The story, being a fish story, was slightly embellished, of course.

"That's quite a fish story," I acknowledged. "I have one, too. I'm that same lady. It was my dog that fetched the fish!"

She wasn't the only one who unknowingly repeated my story to me. On a visit to replenish my lost gear, I shared my experience with the sporting goods clerk.

"That was you and your dog?" he grinned. "A customer was just in here this morning telling me about it!"

For one fishing season, at least, Butch and I became the legends of the lake.

~Dixie Ross
Chicken Soup for the Fisherman's Soul

83

Does God Care About Lost Dogs?

The bitter cold weather had forced the large red dog to curl into a tighter ball, tucking his nose under his big, muddy feet. Old Red lived outside Larry's Barber Shop, sleeping on a small scrap of carpeting. The mongrel dog had panted through a hot summer, watching hopefully as the children came out of the small grocery store that adjoined the barber shop. Many shared their treats with him. On Valentine's Day, someone left a handful of candy hearts on Old Red's carpet.

Old Red once had a buddy—a scrawny black dog. Constant companions, they slept curled together. During a cold spell the smaller dog disappeared. Old Red mourned his friend by keeping his usually wagging tail motionless. As friends stooped to pat him, Old Red wouldn't even look up.

Someone dumped a puppy out one day, and Old Red immediately adopted him. He followed the puppy around like a mother hen. During the cold nights, Old Red shared his carpet with the frisky puppy, letting him sleep against the wall. Old Red slept on the cold outside.

Soon that puppy disappeared too, and the old dog was alone again.

I would have taken him home in a minute. Any homeless dog or cat could win my instant friendship—all it took was one hopeful look. But my husband had explained time and again that we simply could not take in stray animals. I knew he was right, but sometimes my heart forgot. With great determination I tried to steel myself against looking into the eyes of any stray, hungry dog or cat. Old Red never looked hungry, though, so I decided it was all right to form a relationship with him.

One day I found out by accident from the barber's wife that her husband was feeding the dog daily. "He won't even buy cheap food," she laughed. "He buys the most expensive there is."

I stopped by the barber shop to tell Larry how grateful I was that he was feeding the dog. He brushed aside my thanks and insisted the dog meant nothing to him. "I'm thinking of having him taken off," Larry mumbled gruffly.

He didn't fool me a bit.

During a snowstorm Old Red disappeared. I haunted the barber shop. "Larry, where can he be?" I'd ask.

"I'm glad he's gone. He was a bother, and it was getting expensive feeding him." Larry continued to cut a customer's hair, not looking at me.

Later, his wife told me that Larry had driven for miles looking for the dog.

On the third day the dog reappeared. I ran to him and patted his head. The big, dirty tail didn't flop once. He didn't even raise his head. I felt his nose: hot and dry. Bursting into the barber shop, I hollered, "Larry, Old Red's sick!"

Larry continued cutting a customer's hair. "I know. Won't eat."

"Where do you think he's been?"

"I can't prove it, but I think someone at the shopping center complained and he was hauled off. Did you see his feet? Looks like he's been walking for days to get back."

I lowered my voice. "Let him inside, Larry."

The customers seemed to be enjoying our conversation.

"I can't do that. This is a place of business."

I left the shop, and for hours I tried to get someone involved in helping Old Red. The Humane Society said they'd take the dog, but they were an hour's drive across Atlanta, and I had no idea how to get there. Anyway, no one would adopt a sick dog, and they'd put him to sleep. A vet I phoned said right away that he didn't take charity cases. The police, fire department, and manager of the shopping center could offer no help. None of my friends were interested.

I knew I was about to bring Old Red home despite my husband's rules about strays. I hadn't brought an animal home in a long time.

As I fixed supper that night I said very little. My husband finally asked grimly, "Do you want me to go look at that dog with you?" Translated, this meant: "I'll get involved a little bit. But we cannot keep the dog."

I ran to the attic and got a large box and a blanket. Grabbing some aspirin and an antibiotic one of the children had been taking, then warming some milk, I finally announced, "I'm ready." We piled our four children in the car and started for the shopping center. Snow covered the ground. Hold on, Old Red. We're coming.

As we entered the shopping center, all my hopes faded. He was gone. "Oh, he's gone off to die," I moaned. We drove around and looked and called, but the dog didn't come.

The next day I took the boys in for a haircut. Old Red was back! But he looked worse than ever. After feeling his hot nose, I ran into the barber shop. "Larry, the dog is going to die right in front of your shop."

Larry liked to tease me—even about this. He didn't look up. "Think he's already dead. Haven't seen him move all morning."

"Larry," I screamed, "you've got to do something!"

I left the barber shop with a heavy heart. It took all my willpower not to put Old Red in our car. He seemed resigned to his fate. I was almost in tears. One of my twins kept asking me something as we sat in our car. He repeated his question for the third time.

"Does God care about lost dogs, Mama?"

I knew I had to answer Jeremy even though God seemed far away. I felt a little guilty, too, because I never thought about bothering God with this. "Yes, Jeremy, God cares about all his creatures." I was afraid of his next question.

"Then let's ask him to make Old Red well. Can we do that, Mama?"

"Of course, Jeremy," I answered, somewhat exasperated. What else could I say to a five-year-old?

Jeremy bowed his head, folded his hands, shut his eyes and said, "God, I want to ask you to make Old Red well again. And please... send a little boy to love him. Amen."

Jeremy waited patiently for my prayer. I felt like explaining to him that animals were suffering everywhere. But I prayed, "Dear Lord, thank you for caring about all your creatures. Please send someone to care about Old Red. Please hurry."

Jon added his prayer to ours, and I backed out of the parking place. I was crying now, but Jeremy and Jon didn't seem to notice. Jeremy let down the window and called out cheerfully, "Bye, Old Red. You're gonna be okay. Someone's coming to get you."

The tired old dog raised his head slightly as we drove off.

Two days later Larry called. "Guess what?" he said.

I was afraid to ask.

"Your dog's well."

"What... how...."

There was unmistakable excitement in Larry's voice. "Yesterday a vet came in to have his hair cut, and I asked him to take a look at the dog—'cause you were about to drive me crazy. He gave Old Red a shot, and he's all well."

Weeks passed, and Old Red continued to live outside the barber shop. I sometimes wondered if he ever noticed the dogs that came to the stores with families. Dogs often leaned out of car windows and barked at Old Red, or just looked at him. Old Red didn't pay any attention.

Jeremy continued to talk about the someone whom God would send to love Old Red.

One day we rode by the barber shop and Old Red was gone. I went in and asked Larry where he was.

Larry started grinning as soon as I came in. "Strangest thing happened yesterday. This lady brought her little boy in for a haircut. I didn't know them. New in this area. She asked about the dog. Her little boy had a fit over him. When I told her he didn't belong to anyone, she took him home with her."

"Larry, don't tease me."

"I'm not teasing. I'll give you her telephone number. I got it. She was going to take the dog to the vet for shots and a bath. Man, you should have seen Old Red sitting up in the front seat of that Buick. If I didn't know better, I'd say he was grinning. Happiest dog I've ever seen."

I walked out of the barber shop quickly. I didn't want Larry to see me crying.

~Marion Bond West
A 5th Portion of Chicken Soup for the Soul

She Dares to Race the Iditarod

Life is like a dog sled team.
If you ain't the lead dog, the scenery never changes.
~Lewis Grizzard

Tekla lies beside the sled, too tired to go on. I look down at my most experienced lead dog and curse my luck.

A wrong turn in a heavy snowstorm had taken me more than thirty kilometers out of my way. The four hours lost in regaining the trail have put me far behind the front-runners in the world's longest sled-dog race — the Iditarod — which crosses Alaska from Anchorage to Nome. More important, I have lost Tekla for the remainder of the course.

The grueling route, more than 1,600 kilometers long, has in past races taken from twelve to thirty-two days to complete. It approximates one blazed in the early 1900s between the gold-rush towns of Iditarod and Nome, and the ice-free port of Seward. This is the 1982 running of the Iditarod, held annually early in March since 1973.

I was born into a comfortable family life in Cambridge, Massachusetts. During childhood summers at the seashore, I spent every waking hour outdoors. Of many pets, my favorite was my dog.

As I grew older, I yearned for a life that would combine dogs and the outdoors. And deep inside I had a feeling that there was a place where I could breathe more freely and where my own hard work would be the measure of my success.

I came to Alaska in 1975, hoping to find my dream. Today, from my cabin door 225 kilometers northwest of Fairbanks and 6 kilometers from my nearest neighbor, I look at my sled-dog team and know my dream is as real as Mount McKinley far beyond. And as challenging as the Iditarod.

For three years I lived in the wilderness, raising huskies and building and training a team for my first Iditarod in 1978. I finished nineteenth, barely in the money. Only the first twenty into Nome share in some $100,000 in cash prizes. I came in ninth the next year, then fifth in 1980 and '81.

Of the fifty dogs I own, I race only fifteen, but more are always being trained to keep this number at full strength. Good racers must be able to trot at nineteen kilometers an hour, lope at twenty-nine. Mine are Alaskan huskies, descended from Eskimo and Indian dogs, bred for stamina and feet that won't be cut by ice or form snowballs between the pads. The dogs average fifty pounds and have long legs and slim builds. They must have an inherent love of running and a never-say-die attitude.

However, each has a distinct personality. Every evening, after training runs of as much as 100 kilometers, I invite some into the cabin for a treat and a discussion of the day's workout. Copilot voices her opinion with a loud howl when I commend her performance. The others thump their tails as their names are mentioned. When it's time to check paws for possible injuries, Tekla and Daiquiri roll on their backs, feet in the air, begging for immediate attention.

February has arrived, and I must put together 700 kilograms of food and equipment to be stashed at twenty-four checkpoints along the course: seventy-five burlap sacks filled with lamb, beef liver, beaver meat, lard, commercial dog food, fish, booties to protect paws, and extra batteries for the head lamp I will use along the trail. Meat must be cut into chunks for easy feeding en route. Honey balls must be made of ground beef, honey, vegetable oil, and vitamin and mineral supplements.

The dogs and I arrive in Anchorage to join an eventual field of fifty-four mushers and 796 dogs. We hear talk of an icy trail with dangerous turns. This only adds to the severe butterflies I already have. Now there is just one day left before I am out on the trail alone with my dogs and the life I love.

There is so little snow in Anchorage this year that our start has been moved eighty-four kilometers northeast to Settlers Bay. The teams will go off at three-minute intervals; I have drawn the twenty-sixth starting position.

My dogs are so eager to get going that it takes ten people to hold them as the earlier starters move out. My friend Kathy Jones, who helped raise my expense money, tucks herself onto the sled amid the gear that every contestant must carry: snowshoes, ax and sleeping bag. The rules require each musher to carry a passenger for the first thirteen kilometers in case of early trouble.

My countdown begins, then we're off! A kilometer and a half out we go into a slide on an icy hill, hitting a downed tree. Kathy and I feel only a few aches and pains, but the team has suffered. Cracker, Ruff and Screamer are running off-pace. Even so, we pass two teams.

Kathy leaves us at Knik Lake, and I continue on alone. It begins to snow as darkness falls. One by one, I overtake twenty-two teams; only three are ahead of me now.

Cracker, Ruff and Screamer quit pulling and begin to limp. As much as it will slow me, I load them onto the sled to prevent further injury.

Kilometer after kilometer I ride behind them on the runners; I should have seen Skwentna, the third checkpoint, by now. I sense something is wrong. At dawn a musher approaches from the opposite direction and hails me with, "We're at least sixteen kilometers off course."

I turn my team around. All year I have nurtured but one thought: to win. Now my hopes are dashed. With three injured dogs aboard I cannot possibly make up the lost time. Then Tekla starts to limp.

At 6:55 A.M. we straggle into Skwentna, four hours behind schedule. My dogs are played out. I feed them, then take Cracker, Ruff and

Screamer to a drop area where they can be flown home. I massage Tekla's shoulder. I can't afford to lose her this early in the race.

We push on. Seventy-two kilometers farther, at Finger Lake, I know my limping Tekla has reached her limit. Tears roll down my cheeks. She, who led my team all the way in my first three Iditarods, who has saved my life more than once, who can even read my mind, now has to be left behind. Her sorrow seems as great as mine as I leave her to wait for a flight home.

With only eleven weary dogs left, I head out again for Nome, still more than 1,500 kilometers away. After just sixteen kilometers, I know we have to rest. I lie in the snow next to Ali and Copilot, now in the lead. They cuddle up against me, and I massage their shoulders and legs. Other teams flash past me. My resolve is shaken, but I'm not ready to give up yet.

On the move again, I think only of reaching Rohn checkpoint, where I will spend a twenty-four-hour layover that the race committee requires. In these first two days on the trail, I have had only four hours sleep.

As we climb into Rainy Pass to cross the Alaska Range, my mind is not fully focused. I let go of the sled so the team can clamber up a steep bank unencumbered by my weight. I have badly misjudged the energy of my dogs; they shoot away and are out of sight before I reach its top.

For ten kilometers I pursue them. Around one more bend and there they are, the sled on its side but intact. They bark and wag their tails as if to say, "Where the hell have you been?"

I know this close call was the result of my defeatist attitude, and I resolve to have no more of that. We finally arrive at Rohn at 5:01 P.M.

After our twenty-four-hour rest and four hot meals my team is yowling and barking to be off, and my determination to stay in the race is firmer than ever. Even Jimmy is running hard despite sore feet, which I have been treating with medication.

As night falls, the snow grows heavier, wiping out the trail. But I manage to catch up with the leaders, who have lost their way and are waiting for daylight.

Up until this point we have raced as individuals, every musher for himself. But now we must work together, taking turns at trail breaking through the deep, soft snow. As soon as circumstances permit, we'll be off on our own again. We travel in this tedious, time-consuming way for four days and 568 kilometers.

At Ruby, the sky clears, but the temperature drops to minus forty-two degrees as I start out alone down the frozen Yukon River. If I stay too long on the sled, I risk frostbite. Too long jogging behind can impair my lungs. I alternate between running and riding. Jimmy's feet are worse; I'm forced to drop him at Galena. Then a raging storm buries the trail. Those of us in the lead take refuge in a trapper's tent for the night.

Another day's travel brings us to Unalakleet. Only 436 kilometers to Nome! The weather worsens; winds increase to ninety-five kilometers an hour. My eyelashes and those of the dogs freeze shut, and I stop often to clear their eyes and check their feet.

It's midnight. Even with my headlamp, I cannot see the driftwood tripods that mark the trail across this flat, featureless country. Groping from tripod to tripod, I finally reach Shaktoolik with a frostbitten face. Lucy Sockpealuk welcomes us to her home. Even the dogs. It is too cold outside for them to rest easy. And I can't feed them outdoors because their pans blow away. By morning, winds are gusting up to 130 kilometers an hour, piling up nine-meter drifts.

I wait fifty-two hours in the village. When the storm lets up, all the mushers resume the race with new spirit. Only 372 kilometers to go, but the going is tough. We push through the continuing storm, seven lead teams traveling close together.

Then Taboo, worn out from punching too long through heavy snow, must drop out, leaving me with nine dogs of my original fifteen. Emmitt Peters is now running ten, Rick Swenson twelve and Jerry Austin fourteen. Even so, I feel this is still a wide-open race. Thoughts of winning again consume my mind.

Sixty-five kilometers from the finish line, we run into winds as strong as those at Shaktoolik. By the time they have died away, Ali, my best command leader, is tired of taking orders. So I put Copilot up front with Stripe. Both dogs drive hard, and the team picks up its pace.

I am now in fifth place, only a short distance behind Rick, Jerry, Emmitt and Ernie Baumgartner. The final push is on; fifty kilometers to go. My adrenaline is pumping.

I pass Ernie and pull away. I pass Emmitt, but he stays right on my tail. Through the last checkpoint we dash; only thirty-five kilometers now. Someone yells that Rick and Jerry are just two minutes ahead of me. Emmitt remains close behind.

Stripe falters. The change is quick, only forty seconds to switch Ali and Stripe. Emmitt is halfway by me when I holler at Ali and Copilot:

"Go! Go! Go!" The instant I feel my dogs diving forward, I know I've done the trick. I soon outdistance Emmitt.

Ali has raced with me to Nome before and senses he's into the homestretch. He knows his job and gives it his full measure. The other dogs respond to his leadership. I chase hard for thirteen kilometers to pass Jerry. But there's still Rick, barely visible in the distance.

My dogs and I try with all the energy we can muster to overtake him, but he still beats us into Nome by three minutes, forty-three seconds, in a race that has lasted sixteen days. Cheers ring out around me. I gratefully accept $16,000 second-prize money. The last musher will not cross the finish line until ten days later.

The wilderness is my life now, and the Iditarod its ultimate experience. I have only one dream to go. To be number one.

~Susan Butcher
Chicken Soup for the Sports Fan's Soul

[*Editors' Note*: Susan Butcher went on to win the Iditarod in 1986, the first of four wins in the next five years.]

85

More than Chocolate

I arrived at Ground Zero as part of the Emergency Animal Rescue Services (EARS) team on September 19, a week and a day after the terrorist attacks. Although there were plenty of agencies providing food and drink to the rescue personnel, everyone was still mostly running on adrenaline. There was so much to do, so much chaos and wreckage—so much energy tied up in helping in any way it was possible.

The devastation at the WTC area was unimaginable. Over three hundred search-and-rescue canine teams had come from all over to help find survivors, and when it became obvious that there were precious few of those, the teams looked for bodies. Many of the human/dog teams weren't strictly search-and-rescue; if someone had a drug-or bomb-sniffing dog, they came, too. Everyone wanted to do something.

EARS helped at a triage area for the dogs working at the site. When a team came off a shift, they brought the dogs to us for cleaning and decontamination. There was a lot of asbestos in the omnipresent dust that covered the animals' fur. Plus the dogs had to trample through pools of foul and unsanitary water that collected as a result of the rain and the hose jets directed at the rubble to keep the dust out of the air.

After the dogs were clean, veterinarians did exams, paying particular attention to the dogs' eyes, noses and feet. Many of the dogs needed eye flushes because of the abrasive nature of the dust. Others had minor cuts on their feet that in that environment could have become easily infected.

One man, a police officer from Canada, had heard the news and decided to drive down immediately. He and his large German Shepherd, Ranger, had arrived on the 12th and, within hours, had begun that amazing duet called search-and-rescue work: the dog's instinct and intense concentration combined with the handler's keen attention and response to the dog's cues. Back and forth, over and over, the pair scoured the surface of enormous piles of broken concrete, twisted metal and shattered glass.

When the police officer's days off from his job at home were finished, he didn't want to leave what he felt was such important work in New York. He called his police station up in Canada and requested to take his vacation time. They refused his request.

"Then I quit," he told them and hung up.

When the people in his community heard about this situation, they immediately took up a collection to show their support of this man. The police station received so much flak over their unfortunate decision that they called the man and told him to stay as long as he liked; his job would be waiting.

It was late in the afternoon on the day I arrived in New York when Ranger and his handler came to our triage area. We scrubbed Ranger down and passed him over to the veterinary team. I noticed Ranger's handler sitting in a chair close by, staring straight ahead. He was a large man and looked like a combination of Arnold Schwarzenegger and Rambo—bald head and camouflage fatigues. The adrenaline had finally run out and the reality of the disaster around him was finally catching up with him. He had that look on his face I recognized from the over fifty disasters I've witnessed—a look that said, "I don't think I can do this much longer."

It was probably the first time the man had sat down in a very long time, and he didn't look at anyone or talk except to answer questions the veterinarians asked about his dog.

The doctor asked, "When was the last time your dog ate?"

The man answered, "Last night," in a voice as blank as his face.

Someone put some food in a bowl and placed it at Ranger's head. The big dog was lying on the pavement and, although he sniffed at the food once or twice, it seemed he was just too exhausted to eat.

I found a dog biscuit, squatted down near the dog, scooped up some of the gravy from the dog food in the bowl and offered it to Ranger. He lifted his head and slowly licked the liquid from the biscuit, so I dunked the biscuit in the bowl again, bringing up a little of the food with the gravy this time. Once more, he licked the food and gravy from the biscuit. I continued "spoon-feeding" Ranger while the triage workers and veterinarians looked on.

While I was feeding Ranger, I had the thought that someone should probably ask Ranger's handler the same question. After all, we were here to help people, too. When I finished, I turned to ask the man when he had eaten last, but before I could open my mouth, he looked directly at me and said, "Do you know how I get through this?"

I shook my head.

He reached his massive hand into his pocket and pulled out a small plastic baggy with two chocolate kisses, two dog biscuits and a note inside.

I recognized it as one of the "care packages" children at the local school had made for the handlers and their dogs. What could be inside that had sustained the large and powerful man in front of me through this tremendously draining and demanding work? I knew from experience that it would take a lot more than chocolate.

He handed it to me, his eyes bright with tears. "Read it."

I took out the note, and unfolded it. There, written in a child's handwriting, were the words, "Thank you for helping to find people. I know Lassie would be so proud of you."

~Terri Crisp as told to Carol Kline
Chicken Soup for the Soul of America

Loving Our Dogs

Canine Matchmakers

*Nobody can fully understand the meaning of love unless
he's owned a dog. A dog can show you more honest affection
with a flick of his tail than a man can gather
through a lifetime of handshakes.*

~Gene Hill

86

Lucy

Love stretches your heart and makes you big inside.
~Margaret Abigail Walker

The honeymoon was definitely over. Although Larry and I had been married less than a year, we were headed for disaster. My expectations of marriage were high—probably too high. My parents' relationship had been happy, loving, full of laughter and mutual respect. Larry didn't come to the marriage with the same kind of dreams, and he felt pressured by my needs. Our home was not a happy one, with tensions, resentment and hurt feelings seething just below the surface. We just couldn't communicate.

During this rocky time, I had the idea to get a dog. Larry and I talked about it, and he said a dog would be fine, as long as it wasn't a "yappy little thing." He had grown up with German shepherds and liked them. I called the local pound and asked if they had a German shepherd who needed a home. It just so happened that they had a white German shepherd mix, so I went right over to see the dog.

At the pound, I made my way to the white dog's cage. She was part shepherd all right, but the other part must have been Mexican jumping bean. She moved like she had springs on the bottoms of her four paws, continuously jumping five feet in the air and barking enthusiastically—just the way a kid waves his arms and yells, "Pick me! Pick me! Me! Me! Me!" when captains are choosing their teams. I took her out of the run and she tore around the room, stopping only to jump up on me and try to lick my face as she streaked by. I was impressed by her vibrant personality.

I brought Larry to see her a few hours later, and he liked her well enough for us to walk out with her. She strained on her leash, obviously eager to leave the pound behind.

We named her Lucy, and she and I became best friends. I loved getting up in the early morning and walking her when the streets were quiet. A long walk in the park every afternoon became another wonderful part of our daily routine. She liked to be wherever I was, watching me or snoozing in the sun as I went about my housework and gardening. I took her in the car when I went into town to do errands, and she sat in the backseat, her nose stuck out of the window to sniff the wind. I found her company entertaining and comforting. Larry seemed to like her, too.

As the weeks went by, I felt happier and more settled. I have to admit that I talked to Lucy when we were alone together during the day. I even made up silly songs and sang them to her when we were out driving. She seemed to like the sound of my voice, and she wagged her tail and always looked right at me when I told her things. I relished my position at the center of her universe.

One evening, I was showing Larry a silly game that Lucy and I played—I would stand in front of Lucy and poke her with my right hand a few times, then when she was expecting a poke from the right, I'd poke her from the left. Then a poke from the top, and then from the bottom. She seemed to love trying to figure out where my hand would come from next. We were playing this game when Larry came up behind me and started playing, too. I leaned back into the warm bulk of Larry's chest, and his arms closed around me. We stood like that for a moment, before I turned around and held him tight. We hadn't done that for a long time.

Things began to fall into place after that. All that canine companionship had enabled me to stop demanding love and attention from Larry—and as I felt happier, I was able to be more loving and certainly more fun to be around. Our wounds began to heal, and our marriage blossomed.

We've been married for over ten years now. When people ask me the secret of our happy partnership, I always tell them, "It's simple. If you want dog-like devotion... get a dog!"

~Carol Kline
Chicken Soup for the Dog Lover's Soul

Boris in New York

When you come to the end of your rope, tie a knot and hang on.
~Franklin D. Roosevelt

It was nearly midnight on a rainy Christmas Eve. Barbara Listenik walked the cold dark streets of Queens, New York, alone. "Excuse me," she said to a stranger in front of an all-night market. Showing the man a photograph, she asked, "Have you seen my lost dog?"

Only hours ago, Barbara had been on her way to La Guardia Airport to pick up her four-year-old boxer-mix dog, Boris. Barbara had moved to New York one week previously, hoping to further her art career, while Boris stayed behind with a friend in Florida. New York was such a big place; Barbara found it overwhelming and sometimes lonely. And now that she was settled into her new apartment in Brooklyn, Barbara couldn't wait to see her best four-legged buddy. It's the perfect Christmas gift to myself, she thought as she waited in line at the airline baggage counter.

But then an airline employee took Barbara aside to tell her there'd been an accident. During offloading, Boris's carrier had opened, and he had escaped. Several baggage handlers and airport police had chased the frightened dog across busy runways and through a terminal jam-packed with holiday travelers. But Boris had eluded them all, and now he was running loose somewhere in neighboring Queens.

For several hours Barbara and the baggage handlers and police canvassed nearby neighborhoods searching for Boris. Then Barbara returned to her apartment for a photo of him. She then spent Christmas Eve showing the photo to strangers and calling Boris's name until her voice grew hoarse and she felt nearly frozen from the icy rain.

Christmas morning, Barbara resumed her search. Thinking of how frightened her dog must be, she found herself crying as she ventured into yet another bleak alleyway. Boris had never known cold weather or the big city with all its unfamiliar smells and loud noises. And there were so many cars and trucks to avoid. What was worse, Boris had no collar or ID tags on. For safety reasons, the airline insisted that animals not wear their collars during transport. It seemed hopeless—she was just one person trying to find one small dog in an enormous city. She trudged through the streets, calling the dog's name over and over, until she was exhausted.

Bright and early the next morning, Barbara began telephoning area shelters. Boris wasn't in any of them. But he had not been reported dead, either, which Barbara considered a good sign.

Soon Barbara was back in Queens posting fliers to utility poles and inside markets and laundromats. She asked everyone she met if they'd seen Boris. No one had. But then toward evening one man told her, "An off-duty transit cop was just here asking about that same dog."

Barbara was surprised and touched. Well, Boris, there's at least one person in this big, cold city who cares if we're reunited.

What Barbara didn't realize was that there were many others who cared. Many hundreds of others, as it turned out. For as word of Boris's plight spread, people began telephoning Barbara with messages of support and more than three thousand dollars were contributed to a reward fund established by a local newspaper. Well-wishers from as far away as New Jersey turned up in droves to join the search.

Meanwhile, an animal welfare society began organizing search parties. Every weekend more than one hundred volunteers fanned out through the neighborhoods bordering the airport. Barbara marveled at this show of support as she thanked her new friends for their help and their words of encouragement.

But after seven weeks Barbara began to lose hope. Maybe it's time for me to get on with the rest of my life, she considered as she traveled home to Brooklyn late one night.

There, Barbara discovered fifteen messages on her machine. Only she was too depressed to listen to them. She was afraid they would be more false leads. So far Barbara had looked at over one hundred strays that turned out not to be Boris. Each time she'd felt a little bit of herself dying deep inside.

When the telephone abruptly rang, Barbara picked it up without thinking. It was one of the volunteers searching for Boris. "I think we found him!" the woman said.

A young college student named Johnny had been on his way to a family function when he spotted one of Barbara's fliers at a cab stand. "This looks like the dog we've been feeding behind the empty barber shop next door," he told his wife. Johnny telephoned one of the volunteers, who traveled to Queens to see for herself. She'd been trying all night to reach Barbara with the good news.

Barbara suspected it would turn out to be another dead end, but she hurried anyway to the address that was only two miles from the airport. Sure enough, her heart sank when she was escorted into the tiny house to see the dog. This stray was bone thin, and his coat was solid gray.

"Boris is fawn and white," she murmured, crestfallen. "I'm sorry—that's not my dog."

Tentatively, the pup approached Barbara. He sniffed once, then began wagging his tail. Their eyes met.

"Boris? Is that you?" Barbara gasped. He had lost fifteen pounds, and grime and road tar had turned his coat completely gray. But there was no mistaking those loving brown eyes.

"Boris! It is you!" Barbara exclaimed. An instant later her knees gave out, and she collapsed onto the floor. "Oh Boris," she said, laughing and crying as her faithful companion began licking the tears from her cheeks.

Before they left, Boris padded over to Johnny and offered up his paw. "If he wasn't your dog, I was planning to keep him for myself, he's so sweet," Johnny said as he took the proffered paw.

At home Barbara gave Boris a much-needed bath. Now that they were together once again, she finally lit the holiday lights and celebrated Christmas. She then stayed up all night feeding him dog biscuits and gourmet pet food. She was too excited to sleep; she kept trying to absorb the fact that Boris was really there with her.

These days Barbara and Boris enjoy spending time with the many kind people Barbara met while Boris was M.I.A. Flying Boris to New York had been her big Christmas present to herself, but Boris's present to her had been even bigger. He'd given her a whole city of friends.

~Bill Holton
Chicken Soup for the Cat and Dog Lover's Soul

88

Lucky in Love

Dogs are not our whole life, but they make our lives whole.
~Roger Caras

I wanted a puppy, but the timing couldn't have been worse. My three-year marriage was crumbling and the last thing I needed was a new responsibility. Trying to escape the inevitable, my husband and I decided to go on a vacation to Big Sur on the California coast. The last day of our trip, we had stopped for lunch at a restaurant. As we returned to the car, we noticed a cage by a staircase at the edge of the parking lot. I moved closer to investigate and saw a little, irresistible black ball of fluff gazing longingly out of the bars, begging me to let her out. Someone had simply left her there and put a sign on top of the cage: "Puppy for Free. Name is Lucky. Take her."

I looked at my husband, and he shook his head no, but I persisted. I needed someone to love. I took the puppy from the cage, and happy to be free, she dove into our car. We started to drive the windy Pacific Coast Highway home. A wide, grassy meadow came into view, and we stopped so she could run. As we lay on our blanket on the grass, she trampled field daisies, sniffed for gophers and jumped in circles. Her joy at liberation was my elixir.

We renamed her Bosco, and she turned out to be a Belgian sheepdog. My loyal friend, she stayed by my side through a difficult divorce and was my guardian angel through the many years of single life that followed.

One morning, when she was nine years old, I awoke to find her panting heavily, her black curls damp and matted. With trembling fingers, I grabbed for the phone to call my veterinarian. Bosco tiredly snuggled on my lap, her labored breathing ragged on my chest, and I kissed the top of her head over and over again, waiting for the receptionist to answer.

"I'm sorry, Jennifer. The doctor's out of town." My right hand kept stroking the side of Bosco's long, smooth nose, the left hand gripping the receiver even more fiercely as I held back tears. She directed me to another veterinary clinic. How could I trust someone else with my baby? But I had no choice.

I tenderly placed my limp dog on the passenger seat of the car. With one hand I turned the key in the ignition, and with the other I gently stroked the quiet body underneath the faded green and blue stadium blanket that I used for picnics—the one I'd used the day we found Bosco.

I pulled into the clinic parking lot. I took a deep breath, said a prayer and slowly took my bundle through the doors. A matronly receptionist recognized my name and immediately summoned the doctor on call. As I waited for this unknown person to take my dog's life in his hands, I looked around the cozy, wood-paneled waiting room. A pit bull sat meekly at the feet of the woman next to me; Bosco didn't even seem to notice. A man called out my name.

Dr. Summers wore an air of urgency, his blue eyes filled with compassion and concern. As I followed him to the exam room, I noticed broad, strong shoulders and a confident stride. I laid Bosco softly on the narrow steel table and then slowly took her blanket off, clutching it in my arms. Her sweet smell still lingered on the wool. Dr. Summers listened intently as I explained the symptoms, his gentle hands resting on Bosco's side. He thought it was gastroenteritis and wanted to keep her in the clinic for observation. But he stressed that I was welcome to come by and visit. I kissed Bosco's nose and whispered goodbye. Dr. Summers smiled. "Go home. Get some rest. I promise I'll take care of her." And somehow I knew that he would, that there was no better place to leave my best friend than in his arms.

The next day, after work, I went directly to the clinic to see Bosco. The receptionist waved me into the back, and I made a beeline for the cages, trying not to run. I sat on the cold, cement floor and put my hand through the cage, stroking Bosco's fur, watching her tail give me a faint wag. When Dr. Summers discovered I was there, he came back and opened Bosco's cage. I held her tightly on my lap, happy to feel her warmth. Dr. Summers knelt on the floor near us. Talking softly so Bosco could sleep, we shared stories about our families, our careers, our dreams, our lives.

During the next few weeks, I came in every day to see Bosco and my new friend, Dr. Summers. A biopsy later confirmed bad news: lymphocytic plasmacytic enteritis (LPE). I couldn't pronounce it, let alone understand the nature of the disease. Because of the vomiting and diarrhea associated with LPE, Dr. Summers kept her in the clinic on an IV for fluids. Then, on top of LPE, Bosco developed pancreatitis, which complicated treatment.

The day came when the medicines were failing, Bosco wasn't getting any better—and I had to make a decision. Dr. Summers encouraged me to take her home, to be with her for a couple of days. He knew I needed to say goodbye. I wrapped her in her blanket and drove her home.

We snuggled on the couch, and I told her how much I had loved her, how grateful I was that a puppy named Lucky had come into my life to be my best friend. She listened, her weary brown eyes looking beyond me for peace. It was time for her to go.

Two weeks after I placed her in Dr. Summers's arms for the last time, I made a call to the clinic. I wanted to talk to someone who understood—Dr. Summers, now my friend, had been the person who had helped me close the last door. He took me to lunch and we showed each other pictures of our families. We shared memories of Bosco and he gently wiped the tears off my cheek as tears welled in his own eyes. That day opened a new door for us and we moved through it.

On April 3, two years to the day Bosco passed away, I married Dr. Summers, the man who had so tenderly cared for her—and for me. My father gave a speech during the ceremony, pausing to look up to the heavens. He smiled and said, "I know Bosco is here with us today, blessing this marriage." I smiled, too, through happy tears. Bosco had always, even in her passing, brought love into my life.

~Jennifer Gay Summers
Chicken Soup for the Dog Lover's Soul

89

Woman's Best Friend

At age thirty-two, I had just about given up on ever getting married. Over the years, I'd had numerous relationships. Some were wonderful—and some were real disasters. About the only thing they had in common was that they all ended.

The entire relationship and dating scene was wearing me down. I was tired of relationships with no potential. I was weary of putting my heart out there and getting it smashed. Getting married was starting to look like it wasn't in the stars for me.

Giving up on marriage was one thing. But I wouldn't, and couldn't, give up on my heart. I wanted to love and be loved. I needed to nourish my heart in a way that even my best-intentioned friends and family members hadn't done for me.

I needed a dog.

Soon, on an afternoon in early May, I found myself peering into a pen on a friend's farm, studying a litter of eight black and white puppies who were playing on and around their mother, a champion Border collie. The puppies were six weeks old and as cute as only puppies can be. I slid through the door and sat down. The puppies, wiggling with excitement and apprehension, quickly jitterbugged over to the safety of their mother's side. All except one.

The littlest one, an almost all-black ball of downy fur with two white front paws and a white breast, came sidling over to me and crawled into my lap. I lifted her up and looked into her puppy-hazy brown eyes. It was instant love.

"Just remember, Puppy, you chose me, okay?" I whispered. That was the beginning of the longest successful relationship I've ever had.

I named my puppy Miso. The next weeks of a glorious early spring were spent basking in the glow of literal puppy love while housebreaking, training and establishing new routines. When I look back, that whole spring and summer was spent incorporating her into my life and me into hers.

Miso's Border collie heritage dictated lots of time outdoors, preferably running. I'd been eager to have company while I ran my almost-daily three to five miles in predawn darkness, and now I had a running buddy. Miso and I were out in all kinds of weather, rarely missing a day.

Weekends and evenings were spent in quiet, loving solitude with Miso. At my writing desk or art table, Miso would lie relaxed at my side and sigh with contentment. Anywhere I went, Miso came too: camping, swimming at a local lake on weekends, long car rides to my parents' home in the summer. If an activity precluded taking a dog along, I wasn't much interested in it anyway. We were a happy couple... inseparable and self-sufficient. My heart was nourished, and I felt content and full. We spent two years this way.

Looking back, it's remarkable that I met my husband-to-be at all. I certainly wasn't looking for Mr. Right anymore, not when I was so happy being a "single mom" to Miso. Bob just kind of popped into my life, or rather, our lives, because Miso was definitely impacted by Bob's appearance on the scene.

At first, Bob accepted Miso as part of the "package." Our dating consisted of lots of outdoor activities where Miso accompanied us easily. But as fall and winter approached, and Miso needed to be indoors more due to cold and wet weather, trouble brewed. Bob wasn't enthusiastic about dog hair or mud on the furniture and insisted that Miso stay outside when we spent time at his house.

Since the amount of time spent there was increasing, it bothered both Miso and me that she was required to stay outdoors. This was an uncomfortable blip on the radar screen of an otherwise growing and loving relationship with Bob.

A crisis point was reached one particularly cold January night. Bob insisted that Miso bunk out on the enclosed porch for the night, a location Miso and I felt was unacceptable considering the temperature. I argued that anything less than Miso's admittance to the basement was cruel and inhumane treatment. He argued that I was being unreasonable, and he felt I should respect his "house rules."

We went back and forth like two lawyers arguing a Supreme Court case. Things got heated. Tempers flared. We reached an impasse and stood, staring steely-eyed at each other.

The next thing I knew I heard my own voice, thick with emotion, declare, "Don't make me choose between you and Miso, because you may be in for an unpleasant surprise!"

Bob looked shocked, and in the face of my determination, wisely backed off.

Miso was admitted to the warm basement for the night. The entire indoor/outdoor Miso arrangement was renegotiated over the next couple days and we reached a satisfactory compromise for all three of us.

That crisis was a turning point. I realized I had issued my ultimatum in all seriousness. Bob realized that I did not solely depend on him for love and affection—I had loyalties beyond him. And Miso found her new place in my life, no longer my one-and-only, but as a beloved member of a family.

For that's what we became. Bob and I married, and soon our threesome became a foursome with the birth of our daughter.

Eleven years later, Miso is over fourteen years old. Partially blind and deaf, she suffers the infirmities of old age now, enduring diabetes and arthritis with dignity and grace. The relationship between Bob and Miso has undergone an amazing transformation.

Now I watch Bob tenderly guide Miso to find me when she has "misplaced me" in our house, and lovingly help her up the front steps on a rainy night. I believe Bob has grown to respect the debt he owes Miso. For Miso held a place ready in my life for Bob. She gave love a foothold.

There was never any need to choose between Bob and Miso—both had already laid claim to my heart.

Sometimes now I look into Miso's eyes, which see only shadows, and speak in her ear, though I know she no longer hears, and tell her once again: "Remember, you chose me."

~Holly Manon Moore
Chicken Soup for the Cat and Dog Lover's Soul

90

The Way Home

Unless someone like you cares a whole awful lot,
nothing is going to get better. It's not.
~Dr. Seuss

I'd spent the night rushing to the window every time I heard a branch fall. Now, looking out into the early morning light, the devastation was obvious. Not one tree in our rural neighbourhood in Kingston, Ontario, had been left untouched. Jagged branches lay everywhere. The Great Ice Storm of January 1998 was upon us.

The house had an eerie silence: no hum from the furnace, no buzz from the refrigerator, no morning news blasting from the TV. All the clocks were frozen at 10:49 P.M.

Alex and I were fumbling around in the basement with a shared flashlight, trying to find our camping stove. We needed coffee — some sense of our morning ritual to start the day. I heard the screen door open, then a timid knock. Doris Lee, our closest neighbour, had somehow managed to make her way through the maze of ice, wood and downed power lines, to arrive at our door. She looked anxious.

"Have you seen Harold and Prince?"

Our property backs onto a wooded area, and every morning we would watch Doris's husband Harold with Prince, his golden Lab, ramble off down the trail. Prince trotted quietly on the lead and always brought Harold home safely. Harold had been diagnosed with Alzheimer's disease the previous summer. Doris had been adamant about maintaining their life together and trying to keep things as normal as possible. However, she hadn't reckoned on an ice storm.

"I was upstairs, looking for batteries for the radio, when I heard the door close. Harold is so used to his routine, I just couldn't stop him from taking Prince out."

Alex rushed to pull on his coat as he asked, "How long have they been gone?" Doris hesitated. "About half an hour. I didn't want to bother you, and Prince is usually so good about finding his way home."

Alex looked at me. I turned to Doris and said, "You go home. I'll be right over. I'm going to find our camping stove. I'll bring it over, and we'll make some coffee while Alex finds Harold. They'll want a warm drink when they get home."

Doris turned and headed back to her house while Alex sprinted across the yard toward the woods. I finally found the stove, and, making my way across the icy war zone, I arrived safely at Doris's home.

She and I waited in her kitchen. I made the coffee, but Doris didn't even notice. She stood by the sink staring out into the yard, her cup untouched. I sat at her table, reading all the carefully printed notes she had placed around the kitchen — beside the stove, the light switch, the electric kettle — to remind Harold to turn off or unplug things. There were also notes on the refrigerator door, mapping out a daily routine for Harold: walk the dog, eat breakfast, wash. Doris had done everything possible to make life easier for Harold. Now she turned from the sink and walked over to the table.

"Prince always brings him home, you know," she said softly.

I wanted to say something to comfort her but I felt unqualified. I was just beginning to understand the burden Doris dealt with on a daily basis. Instead, we simply waited together quietly. An eternity seemed to pass before I finally saw Alex coming across our yard. He was carrying Harold's beloved golden Lab in his arms. Harold was walking behind him, tears streaming down his cheeks.

"Prince was hit by a falling branch," Alex explained. "Get some towels or blankets. He's alive but he must be in shock. He's been bleeding from that cut over his eye."

We covered Prince with blankets, and Doris coaxed Harold into dry clothes while Alex told us his story. At first he had called for Prince, thinking it would be the easiest way to find the pair. He was almost ready to turn back and get more help when he heard Harold's voice.

"Harold was sitting on the ground comforting Prince. He'd taken off his coat and put it over the dog. It was all I could do to convince Harold to put his jacket back on."

We sat around the kitchen table, four silent people, unable to pull our thoughts away from the dog in the corner. Prince was more than just a faithful companion. He helped care for Harold. Without him, Harold would lose his independence. We anxiously watched the pile of blankets covering the injured dog, fearing the worst. Suddenly, there was a small movement.

Alex put his hand on Harold's shoulder. "Look, Harold, he's waking up."

A doggie nose popped out from under the pile of blankets. We watched Prince wiggle out and come across to the table. Harold put a trembling hand on his dog's head. Prince gazed at him with his soft brown eyes and gave a halfhearted wag of his tail. Doris whispered a private thank you. I looked at Alex, and the ice storm and power outage were forgotten. Until that day we hadn't appreciated how isolated Doris and Harold were, and what a struggle they had just coping day-to-day. In that moment we decided we were going to change all that. Starting then, Prince and Doris were getting two new assistants.

~Susan Owen
Chicken Soup for the Canadian Soul

Chapter 11

Loving Our Dogs

Letting Go

The dog is a gentleman; I hope to go to his heaven, not man's.
~Mark Twain, letter to W.D. Howells, 2 April 1899

91

Saying Goodbye

To live in hearts we leave behind is not to die.
~Clyde Campbell

What troubled me most was the recurring thought: I didn't get to say goodbye.

I was away from home for the weekend. The door was left open and my two white shepherd-mix dogs, Lucy and Hannah, had gotten out. My husband called me on Saturday night to tell me that Lucy had been hit by a car. She was alive, but her back legs were severely injured. The vets were observing her and would decide what to do on Monday. He told me not to come home since there was nothing I could do.

I started driving home on Monday morning, calling every few hours en route to get a progress report. With my first call I learned they had decided to amputate one of her hind legs. Many anxious calls later, the vet's office told me the operation had gone smoothly and Lucy was resting comfortably. I knew I wouldn't arrive home in time to see her that day, but they told me I could come as soon as they opened on Tuesday.

Tuesday morning, I was getting ready to leave when the phone rang. It was the vet.

"I'm sorry, but we lost her during the night," he told me. "Last night, I went to the clinic for an emergency call around two in the morning, and I went in to check on your dog. She was laboring for breath, so I gave her some medicine. Then I sat with her—I was holding her when she died."

My breath wouldn't come and I felt hollow inside. I hung up the phone and my husband took me in his arms. While he tried to comfort me, I thought: Oh, Lucy, I'm glad you didn't die alone. Did you think I'd abandoned you? Now you're gone and I'll never see you again. What I also thought was: Not again.

Only two weeks earlier, one of my best friends, Sandie, had been killed in a car accident. I received an equally shocking phone call and then, grief. She was gone and I'd never see her again. Too much for me to take in, it hadn't seemed real. And now, neither did Lucy's sudden but permanent absence from my life.

My other dog, Hannah, had seen Lucy get hit. She still seemed confused and upset, searching frantically for Lucy whenever she went outside. I decided that we both needed a strong dose of reality. I called the vet back and asked him not to do anything with Lucy's body—I was coming over and I wanted to see her.

While I felt it was the right thing to do, I still felt apprehensive. I had never seen a dead body in my life—much less the dead body of anyone I had known and loved. Could I handle it?

Hannah and I drove to the vet's office. I had Hannah on a leash as we walked into the room where Lucy lay. I don't know what I was expecting, but the still white form lying on the table was devastatingly beautiful to me. Hannah, distracted by all the interesting smells of the vet's office, had her large nose to the ground and wasn't aware of Lucy until I gently pulled her over to the little waist-high table where Lucy lay. Lucy's tail, her three remaining paws and the tip of her nose stuck out over the table's edge. The instant Hannah's nose scented Lucy's tail, her eyes actually widened. She walked slowly around the table, sniffing every inch of Lucy that she could reach. When she was done, she lay down at my feet, rested her head on her paws and sighed loudly.

I stroked Lucy and felt the texture of her upright ears, her soft fur and the denseness of her muscular body. She looked the same but she felt different, cold and somehow more solid. It was certainly her body, but Lucy was gone. I startled myself by leaning over and kissing Lucy on the head. There were tears running down my face as Hannah and I left.

Hannah was subdued for the rest of the day, her agitation completely gone. For the next few weeks we babied her, taking her for more walks, giving her extra treats and letting her sleep on the couch—a previously forbidden zone. She seemed to be adjusting and perhaps even enjoying her new "only-dog" status.

For me, losing Sandie and then, so immediately, Lucy had been hard. Yet it was actually seeing Lucy's body that finally made the concept of death real. After that, the way I experienced my losses—Lucy, Sandie, even my father, who'd died twenty years earlier—shifted, and as time passed, I could feel that I was steadily healing and moving beyond the pain. It helped to have Hannah to comfort and be comforted by, and I was moved by the unwavering support and love my husband and close friends offered me.

It has been three years since Sandie and Lucy died. I am amazed at how often I still think of them. But now it is always with wistful fondness and a smile, the pain long gone. I am glad that I had the courage to go and see Lucy one last time. For she taught me how to say goodbye.

~Carol Kline
Chicken Soup for the Pet Lover's Soul

92

The Haunted Bowl

Leftovers in their less visible form are called memories.
Stored in the refrigerator of the mind and the cupboard of the heart.
~Thomas Fuller

It's not much to look at. Just a big old cream-colored bowl. You know, one of those old-fashioned crock bowls with a shiny glaze except on the bottom and around the rim. It's thick and heavy with short vertical sides. For almost thirty years that old bowl has occupied a place on my kitchen floor. It came from Jackson's Hay and Feed, one of those tin-roofed feed stores, the kind with a dusty wooden floor, the pungent aromas of alfalfa and bags of feed, and the sounds of cheep-cheeping fuzzy yellow chicks in an incubator. At $4.95 it represented a major investment for a college student drawing $90 a month on the GI Bill.

Today, it came out of the cupboard where it was stored after Cheddar, my dear old yellow Lab, had to be put down. It had just seemed too big to feed the puppy—until now. The puppy, another yellow girl I named Chamois, is growing fast. Now, at almost eighteen weeks of age, she's ready for the bowl. She'll be the third Lab to eat from it.

Swamp was the first. For thirteen years, Swamp ate her meals from the bowl. Now as I look at it sitting on my kitchen floor, I can see Swamp as clearly as if she were here. She liked to lie on the floor with the bowl between her front legs when she ate. Her last meal came from that bowl; a special food for dogs with failing kidneys. She'd been on it since September. The vet told me she had about four months left so I started looking for a puppy.

Swamp rode with me out to a farm on a windy Kansas prairie. The farmer had about ten kennel runs. On one side were Labs and on the other were pointers. He said, "I don't usually sell 'em to people who don't hunt." I confessed I was not a hunter, but Swamp worked her magic on him and soon we were driving home with a precocious yellow puppy we named Cheddar.

The bowl got Cheddar into trouble. She tried to eat from it when Swamp was holding it between her paws. A quick growl and a snap of Swamp's powerful jaws and we were racing to the vet's for a couple of stitches on her nose. I hadn't thought of that for years. Now with the bowl sitting here on the kitchen floor, it seems like yesterday. And, as if it were yesterday, I again experienced the sharp pangs of grief felt so many years ago when we drove Swamp to the same clinic and said goodbye. That night Cheddar ate her first meal from the bowl, and for the next fifteen years it was filled for her every morning.

Cheddar's technique was different from Swamp's. She'd walk up to the bowl, get a chunk or two in her mouth and walk away as she crunched the kibble. Then she'd circle back for another bite. She always ate half the food in the morning and the other half just before bedtime. It was a pattern that never varied.

That old $4.95 bowl is probably the only thing I still own that was mine thirty years ago. It has served us well, and tonight Chamois will eat her first meal from it. I wonder if she knows how valuable it is and what it means to me. I wonder if she knows it's Halloween and that her meal tonight will be served in a haunted bowl: a big old cream-colored bowl haunted by the ghosts of Swamp and Cheddar—and a thousand poignant memories. Will she know as she eats that a black ghost will lie down and wrap her front legs around the bowl and that a yellow ghost will grab a bite and then circle back for more? Will she see the tears in my eyes before I turn away and stare into the past? Or will she just devour the food, lick her chops and wag her busy tail?

~John Arrington
Chicken Soup for the Dog Lover's Soul

Soul to Soul

I work at the Colorado State University Veterinary Teaching Hospital as a counselor in The Changes Program. We help people deal with the experience of losing a pet, whether through illness, accident or euthanasia.

One time, I had a client named Bonnie, a woman in her midfifties. Bonnie had driven an hour and a half from Laramie, Wyoming, to see if the doctors at the hospital could do anything to help her fourteen-year-old black standard poodle, Cassandra, affectionately called Cassie. The dog had been lethargic for a week or so and seemed to be confused at times. The local veterinarian had not been able to diagnose any underlying medical problem, so Bonnie had decided to head to CSU for a second opinion.

Unfortunately, Bonnie hadn't gotten the answer she had hoped for. She had been told earlier that morning by neurologist Dr. Jane Bush that Cassie had a brain tumor that could take Cassie's life at any time.

Bonnie was devastated to learn that her companion animal was so ill. She had been given detailed information about all the treatment options that were available to her. They all would only buy Cassie a few weeks. There was, they emphasized, no hope for a cure.

That was when Bonnie was introduced to me. The Changes Program often helps people while they wrestle with the difficult decision of whether to euthanize a pet or let nature take its course.

Bonnie had graying, light-brown wavy hair that she pulled back into a large barrette. The day I met her she was wearing jeans, tennis shoes and a white blouse with pink stripes. She had sparkling light blue eyes that immediately drew my attention, and there was a calmness about her that told me she was a person who thought things through, a woman who did not make hasty decisions. She seemed familiar and down to earth, like the kind of people I grew up with in Nebraska.

I began by telling her I realized how tough it was to be in her situation. Then I explained that the doctor had asked me to become involved in her case because there were many difficult decisions she needed to make. When I finished, she commented quite matter-of-factly, "I know about grief and I know that sometimes we need help to get through it."

For twenty years, Bonnie had been married to a man who mistreated her. He was abusive and neglectful in all ways possible. He was an alcoholic, so it was often impossible to predict what would happen from one day to the next. Bonnie had tried many, many times to leave him, but she just couldn't do it. Finally, when she turned forty-five years old, she found the courage to walk away. She and Cassie, who was four years old at the time, moved to Laramie, Wyoming, to heal the old hurts and begin a new life. Cassie loved her and needed her and, for Bonnie, the feeling was mutual. There were many rough times ahead, but Bonnie and Cassie got through them together.

Six years later, Bonnie met Hank, a man who loved her in a way that she had never been loved. They met through her church and soon learned they had a great deal in common. They were married one year later. Their marriage was ripe with discussion, affection, simple routines and happiness. Bonnie was living the life for which she had always hoped.

One morning, Hank was preparing to leave for work at his tree-trimming service. As always, he and Bonnie embraced one another in the doorway of their home and acknowledged out loud how blessed they were to have each other. It was not unusual for them to say these things. They both were very aware of the "specialness" of the other.

Bonnie worked at home that day rather than going into her

office, where she held a position as an office assistant. Late in the afternoon, her phone rang. When she picked it up, she heard the voice of the team leader who headed the search-and-rescue service for which Bonnie was a volunteer. Bonnie was often one of the first volunteers called when someone was in trouble.

That day, Margie told her a man had been electrocuted on a power line just two blocks from Bonnie's house. Bonnie dropped everything, flew out of her house and jumped into her truck.

When Bonnie arrived at the house, she saw an image that would be engraved in her mind for the rest of her life. Her beloved Hank hung lifelessly from the branches of a tall cottonwood tree.

All of the training that Bonnie had received about safely helping someone who has been electrocuted left her. She wasn't concerned about her own safety. She had to do everything she could to save Hank. She just had to get him down. She grabbed the ladder stowed in her truck, threw it up against the house and began climbing. Bonnie crawled onto the top of the roof and pulled Hank's body out of the tree toward her. Miraculously, even though she touched his body, which was touching the power line, she was not electrocuted herself. She pulled Hank onto the brown shingles of the roof and cradled his head in the crook of her arm. She wailed as she looked at his ashen face. His eyes stared out into the bright blue Wyoming sky. He was dead. Gone. He could not be brought back to life. She knew to the core of her being that the life they shared was over.

In the four years that followed Hank's death, Bonnie tried to put her life back together. She was up and down, but mostly down. She learned a lot about grief—the accompanying depression, anger, sense of betrayal and the endless questions about why Hank had been taken from her in such a violent and unpredictable way. She lived with the frustration of not having said goodbye, of not having the opportunity to say all of the things she wanted to say, of not being able to comfort him, soothe him, help him leave this life and move into the next. She wasn't prepared for this kind of ending. It was not the way she wanted her best friend, her lover, her partner to die.

When Bonnie finished talking, we both sat in silence for a while.

Finally I said, "Would you like Cassie's death to be different from Hank's? By that, I mean would you like to plan and prepare for her death? That way, you won't have any surprises, and although you may shorten her life by a few days, you will ensure that you are with her to the very end. I'm talking now, Bonnie, about euthanasia. With euthanasia, you won't have to worry about coming home from work and finding Cassie dead, and you can ensure that she won't die in pain. If we help Cassie die by euthanasia, you can be with her, hold her, talk to her and comfort her. You can peacefully send her on to the next life. The choice is up to you."

Bonnie's eyes opened wide. Her shoulders relaxed and her face softened in relief.

"I just need control this time," she said. "I want this death to be different from Hank's — for my girl."

The decision was made to euthanize Cassie that afternoon. I left the two of them alone, and Bonnie and Cassie spent the next few hours lying outside under the maple tree. Bonnie talked to Cassie, stroked her curly black fur and helped her get comfortable when she seemed unable to do so on her own. A soft breeze moved through the trees, adding a gentle rustling to the peaceful scene.

When it was time, Bonnie brought Cassie into the client comfort room, an area that those of us associated with The Changes Program had adapted to be more conducive to humane animal death and client grief. I encouraged Bonnie to tell me if there was anything she wanted to do for Cassie before she died. She laughed and said, "She likes to eat Kleenex. I'd like to give her some."

I laughed, too. "In this business we have plenty of that on hand," I said.

The dog was lying down by Bonnie, who was on the floor on a soft pad. Bonnie began to pet and talk to her. "There you are, girl. You're right here by Mom. Everything is okay."

Over the next half-hour, Bonnie and Cassie "talked" to one another and "finished business." Everything that needed to be said was said.

The time for euthanasia arrived and Cassie was sleeping peacefully, her head resting on Bonnie's stomach. She looked comfortable, very much at ease. Dr. Bush whispered, "May we begin the procedure?" and Bonnie nodded in affirmation.

"But first," she said softly, "I would like to say a prayer."

She reached out to take our hands and we all reached out our hands to one another. Within this sacred circle, Bonnie softly prayed, "Dear Lord, thank you for giving me this beautiful dog for the past fourteen years. I know she was a gift from you. Today, as painful as it is, I know it is time to give her back. And, dear Lord, thank you for bringing these women to me. They have helped me beyond measure. I attribute their presence to you. Amen."

Through our tears, we whispered our own "amens," all squeezing one another's hands in support of the rightfulness of the moment.

And then, while Cassie continued to sleep peacefully on her caretaker's belly, the doctor gave the dog the final injection. Cassie did not wake up. Through it all, she did not move. She just slipped out of this life into the next. It was quick, peaceful and painless, just as we had predicted. Immediately following Cassie's passing, I made a clay impression of her front paw. I handed the paw print to Bonnie and she held it tenderly against her cheek. We all sat quietly until Bonnie broke the silence, saying, "If my husband had to die, I wish he could have died this way."

So do I, Bonnie, I thought. So do I.

Six weeks later, I received a letter from Bonnie. She had scattered Cassie's remains on the same mountain where Hank's were scattered. Now her two best friends were together again. She said somehow Cassie's death, and especially the way in which she had died, had helped her resolve the death of her husband.

"Cassie's death was a bridge to Hank for me," she wrote. "Through her death, I let him know that if I had had the choice when he died, I would have had the courage and the dedication necessary to be with him when he died, too. I needed him to know that and I hadn't been able to find a way. Cassie provided the way. I think that is the reason for and the meaning of her death. Somehow, she knew she could reconnect us, soul to soul."

Eight months later, Bonnie traveled once again from Wyoming to the Veterinary Teaching Hospital. This time, she brought her new, healthy puppy Clyde—a nine-month-old Lab mix, full of life and love. Bonnie was beginning again.

~Carolyn Butler with Laurel Lagoni
Chicken Soup for the Pet Lover's Soul

Pumpkin

At first she wouldn't let me close, wouldn't let me see her tag. Every day she sat near me on the beach, her shiny buff coat blending in with the sand.

She used to be the neighbor's dog, until she was abandoned and left to fend for herself. And then, from her spot on the sand, she discovered me and my kayak.

Each day I would get into my boat and paddle off. The clear water goes from pale blue to deep bottle green, and I can see the kelp moving like a hula girl, waving through schools of small silver fish, reaching up to the reflection of clouds dancing on the glassy surface.

As I paddled above rocks covered with mussels and starfish, looking for dolphins, I would see her: an aging Golden Lab following me along the shoreline. Her huge webbed feet made it awkward for her on the sand.

Often, when I tired in the kayak, I would stretch out in the boat on my back. This day I bobbed around in the ocean just beyond the surf break, watching pelicans as they hovered above.

It was peaceful out there, listening to the water lap and the seagulls fight over a morsel on a rock. I was completely relaxed, drowsy from the sun and the lull of the waves, when I heard a distinct labored breathing.

Something bumped the boat, something heavy in the water next to me. Disorientated and suddenly fearing the worst in the form of a shark, I bolted upright, setting the boat rocking, looking for the oncoming fin.

It was Pumpkin.

She was just as wild-eyed until she saw me. I realized that she had come to find me. When I'd lain back in the boat, I disappeared from her view, and she came to the rescue, a wet, blond Lassie. The clumsy gait that had made her so ungainly on shore was gone as she fluidly swam around the kayak, a serene look in her big brown eyes. From that moment on, she was my dog.

Years went by, and Pumpkin's health failed her on every level but one: She could still swim. It was heartbreaking to watch her navigate the stairs and sand, but I let her do it, knowing the freedom that the water brought to her.

One Saturday, Pumpkin was having a hard day, and I locked her behind the gate so she wouldn't overdo it. I headed out in the kayak, slicing through small green waves and bubbles of white foam, and came across a pod of dolphins relaxing just beyond the break.

I lay back in the boat as they drifted nearby, their delicate puffs of air meshing with the tranquil sounds of the beach.

Then I heard another creature's breath and the familiar bump on my yellow kayak. Pumpkin. She had broken through the gate and dragged herself across the sand the moment I reclined in my kayak.

She still watched over me, swimming out to the friend she had chosen. The dolphins didn't seem to mind. Like a beautiful surreal dream, three species gently floated together on top of another world.

Pumpkin died later that year. I sprinkled half of her ashes on the sand where we met, and then I paddled out, releasing the rest into the ocean that set her free.

~Jewel Palovak
Chicken Soup for the Nature Lover's Soul

With These Hands

To ease another's heartache is to forget one's own.
~Abraham Lincoln

With my bare hands, I finished mounding the dirt over Pepsi's grave. Then I sat back, reflecting on the past and absorbing all that had happened.

As I stared at my dirt-stained hands, tears instantly welled in my eyes. These were the same hands that, as a veterinarian, had pulled Pepsi, a little miniature schnauzer, wiggling from his mother. Born the runt and only half-alive, I had literally breathed life into the dog that was destined to become my father's closest friend on earth. I didn't know then just how close.

Pepsi was my gift to Dad. My father always had big dogs on our farm in southern Idaho, but instantly, Pepsi and Dad formed an inseparable bond. For ten years, they shared the same food, the same chair, the same bed, the same everything. Wherever Dad was, Pepsi was. In town, on the farm or on the run... they were always side-by-side. My mom accepted that Dad and the little dog had a marriage of sorts.

Now Pepsi was gone. And less than three months earlier, we had buried my dad.

Dad had been depressed for a number of years. And one afternoon, just days after his eightieth birthday, Dad decided to take his own life in the basement of our old farmhouse. We were all shocked and devastated.

Family and friends gathered at the house that evening to comfort my mother and me. Later, after the police and all the others had left, I finally noticed Pepsi's frantic barking and let him into the house. I realized then that the little dog had been barking for hours. He had been the only one home that day when Dad decided to end his life. Like a lightning bolt, Pepsi immediately ran down to the basement.

Earlier that evening, I had promised myself that I would never go back into that basement again. It was just too painful. But now, filled with fear and dread, I found myself heading down the basement stairs in hot pursuit of Pepsi.

When I got to the bottom of the stairs, I found Pepsi standing rigid as a statue, staring at the spot where Dad had lain dying just hours before. He was trembling and agitated. I picked him up gently and started back up the stairs. Once we reached the top, Pepsi went from rigid to limp in my arms and emitted an anguished moan. I placed him tenderly in Dad's bed, and he immediately closed his eyes and went to sleep.

When I told my mom what had happened, she was amazed. In the ten years Pepsi had lived in that house, the little dog had never once been in the basement. Mom reminded me that Pepsi was scared to death of stairs and always had to be carried up even the lowest and broadest of steps.

Why, then, had Pepsi charged down those narrow, steep basement steps? Had Dad cried out for help earlier that day? Had he called goodbye to his beloved companion? Or had Pepsi simply sensed that Dad was in trouble? What had called out to him so strongly that Pepsi was compelled to go down to the basement, despite his fears?

The next morning when Pepsi awoke, he searched for my father. Distraught, the little dog continued looking for Dad for weeks.

Pepsi never recovered from my father's death. He became withdrawn and progressively weaker. Dozens of tests and a second opinion confirmed the diagnosis I knew to be true—Pepsi was dying of a broken heart. Now, despite my years of training, I felt helpless to prevent the death of my father's cherished dog.

Sitting by Pepsi's freshly mounded grave, suddenly things became clear. Over the years, I'd marveled at the acute senses dogs possess. Their hearing, sight and smell are all superior to humans. Sadly, their life span is short in comparison, and I had counseled and comforted thousands of people grieving over the loss of their adored pets.

Never before, though, had I considered how it was for pets to say goodbye to their human companions. Having watched Pepsi's unflagging devotion to Dad and the dog's rapid decline after Dad's death, I realized that our pets' sense of loss was at least equal to our own.

I am grateful for the love Pepsi lavished on my father. And for his gift to me—a deeper compassion and understanding of pets, which has made me a better veterinarian. Pepsi's search for Dad is over now; together again, my father and his loyal little dog have finally found peace.

~Marty Becker, D.V.M.
Chicken Soup for the Pet Lover's Soul

Missy and Me

I sold my bike to a friend in my sixth-grade class when we moved from Oklahoma. I planned to buy a new one in California when we got settled, but that never happened. The house we bought in San Diego was near a busy highway, outside town, and I wasn't allowed to ride there, even if I had wanted to.

Instead I spent my bike money on Missy, a cuddly, brown-eyed cocker spaniel puppy. It was love at first sight. The other puppies at the kennel hopped all over each other, but Missy walked straight up to me and gently licked my hand with her pink tongue. When I picked her up, she looked at me with those big, sad eyes, and I was hooked.

I missed my friends in Oklahoma. I wrote to all of them every week. The kids in my new school made fun of my Southern accent. One red-haired girl named Melissa mimicked me every time I spoke. She showed off by arguing with the school bus driver and using swear words. When I heard him call her "missy," I felt like changing my puppy's name.

In those days, my only friend was my dog. Every day, I spent hours training her and brushing her blond, wavy coat. Within a few weeks, she was house trained. At night, she slept curled up in my bed. In the morning, she licked my face to let me know she was awake and wanted to go outside.

One morning when she was six months old, I was dressing for school when I heard screeching brakes and a yelp. I ran down our driveway to see a huge truck pulled over to the side of the highway and the limp body of Missy lying in the ditch. "You hit my dog!" I screamed at the driver. I jumped into the ditch and picked up Missy's lifeless body. "Wake up, wake up!" I yelled at her.

My parents thanked the man for stopping. "The dog ran out right in front of me," he said. "I tried to stop." I knew he meant it, but all I could do was cry.

I carried Missy into the house and wrapped her in her favorite blanket. I rocked her and cried, hoping she would wake up, but she never did.

Before my dad went to work, we dug a little grave and buried her. The three of us held hands, and my dad thanked God for giving us Missy. Then he prayed to God, asking for him to send me new friends here in California. My dad ended his prayer by thanking God for the joy Missy had brought to my life. But I didn't feel thankful. The thoughts just went around and around in my head. Why hadn't God protected her? Why hadn't he kept her from running out on the highway? He knew how lonely I was. Why had he taken my only friend away?

For weeks, I cried myself to sleep. I woke up every morning to the bad dream that was my reality—Missy was gone. Classes, teachers, homework and weekends all blurred together through my tears. I tried to concentrate on my schoolwork, but all I could think about was Missy. My parents offered to buy me another dog, but I didn't want just any dog. I wanted Missy. Nothing else mattered anymore.

One day, my gym teacher gave me a hall pass and told me to go to see the vice principal. I must be in trouble if I'm being sent to Mrs. Stevens's office, I thought.

Mrs. Stevens asked me to sit down. In a gentle voice, she said, "You must be wondering why I called you in. Your teachers are concerned about you. They have seen you crying in class. Do you want to talk about it?"

I began sobbing so violently that I couldn't speak. She handed me a box of tissues. Finally I choked out, "My dog got run over." We talked for the whole gym period. When the bell rang, Mrs. Stevens gave me a little notebook.

"Sometimes it helps when you write down your feelings," she said. "Be honest. You don't have to ever show it to anyone—it's just for you. It may help you decide what you are learning about life and death." She smiled and led me to the door with her arm around my shoulder.

For the next week, I did what she said, spilling out all my sadness and anger. I wrote to God about letting Missy die. I wrote about my parents moving to this awful place. I wrote about Melissa and the kids who hurt my feelings. I even wrote to Missy: "I loved you so much. Why were you so stupid? I taught you not to go near the highway! Now you are gone forever. Forever. Things will never be the same. Never."

When I couldn't write any more, I finally closed my notebook and wept. I cried and cried. I cried because things never would be the same, because Missy wasn't coming back and because I knew we weren't going to move back to Oklahoma. When I was finished crying, there was nothing else to do. I decided I would just have to make the best of it.

As difficult as it was, Missy and her death helped me to grow up that year. God answered my dad's prayer and gave me new friends to fill my loneliness. I finally stopped missing all my old friends. My time was filled with school and activities instead of just memories. I was surprised that these friends became just as special as the ones that I had left behind in Oklahoma. My heart was starting to heal.

Even though I still believe that no other dog could ever take Missy's place in my heart, maybe one of these days I'll let my parents buy me another dog. Maybe.

~Glenda Palmer
Chicken Soup for the Kid's Soul

Pepper's Place

I have a simple philosophy: Fill what's empty. Empty what's full. Scratch where it itches.
~Alice Roosevelt Longworth

As we turned the key to open our little pet shop for the day, we heard the persistent ring of the telephone. I ran for the phone while my husband acknowledged the excited greetings from the cockatiels, canaries and puppies. It wasn't uncommon to receive an early morning phone call, but the voice of this caller seemed different. The voice was raspy, and I detected an air of sadness. The elderly caller did not have a question, but rather a story to tell.

"You see," the gentleman explained, "my wife and I were just sitting down to breakfast alone. We used to have a schnauzer whose name was Pepper." The man went on to share how Pepper had been with them every morning for the past sixteen years as they ate breakfast, drank their coffee and read the morning paper. "He was a member of the family," the man said. Pepper had been with them when their last child left home. He was there when the man's wife became ill and was hospitalized. Pepper had always been there—until this morning.

He went on, "Time passes more quickly than we realize, and time isn't always kind." It happened that Pepper had developed a severe case of arthritis. They waited out the winter, they waited for spring, they waited until yesterday. Pepper was in constant pain, needed to be helped outside, and the man and his wife couldn't watch his suffering any longer. So together, he and his wife, Ruth, and their veterinarian made the decision to "let Pepper go."

His voice cracking, he said, "He was the best dog, and today is our first day alone, and we're having a hard time of it." They didn't want another dog. No other dog could begin to replace Pepper, but they were just curious. "Do you carry schnauzer puppies? Male puppies? Salt-and-pepper male schnauzer puppies?"

I said that we did, in fact, have two male salt-and-pepper schnauzer puppies on hand. "You do?" the aged voice asked incredulously. Not that they would ever or could ever replace Pepper, and besides, "Ruth has an appointment so we won't be coming this morning." We said goodbye and hung up.

The shop filled with people, and soon thoughts of Pepper and his loving family were replaced with the hectic activity of attending to the customers and the attention-seeking residents of the pet shop.

We were still bustling about at mid-morning when two elderly gentlemen came in the door. I knew the one man instantly. His face, weathered and sad, mirrored the voice I heard that morning on the phone.

He introduced himself. "My name is Bill," he said. "Ruth went to an appointment." He explained that he and his neighbor had decided to go for a ride (thirty-five miles) and "just happened over this way." They wondered if they could just take a quick look at a schnauzer puppy while they were here.

I brought out both of the puppies. They wagged their tails and wiggled their roly-poly bodies as they chased each other and tumbled over our feet. They put on their best "take-me-home" faces when Bill's neighbor, picking them up, wondered out loud, "Bill, how could you ever pick just one?" He put them back on the floor, and we continued watching their puppy antics.

Bill seemed reluctant to pick up either of them. He finally yielded to the little one that had contentedly sprawled across his feet, chewing on his shoelaces. He picked him up with the tenderness and wonderment of a young father picking up his first child, and he cradled the puppy against his chest.

"Well," he explained to the puppy, "I can't take you home. Ruth would probably throw us both out." But once in his arms, Bill couldn't put the puppy down. We talked about the weather, his children, our children, and finally, as polite conversation does, it began to wane. There was nothing left to say, no more postponing the inevitable. Bill concentrated on the pups, saying, "Ruth isn't going to like this. Ruth isn't going to like this at all."

We watched as Bill looked from puppy to puppy. At last, shaking his head, he asked with a grin, "If I take this guy home and Ruth kicks us out, would you have a doghouse for us tonight?" With his decision made, I helped Bill to the counter with his puppy, while his brother was returned to his cage to wait for another chance to be adopted.

The brother puppy had never been alone before, and he made us all painfully aware that he did not enjoy his new only-child status. Bill, standing at the counter, watching the remaining puppy expressing its displeasure, remarked, "It's no good to be alone."

Bill paid for his purchase, and then he and the neighbor left with the puppy affectionately secured in Bill's arms. Smiles and back-slapping congratulations accompanied them out the door. With a warm feeling, we returned to our day's chores, as visions of the elderly couple enjoying the new puppy danced through our minds.

Within minutes the door opened again. It was Bill, shaking his head. "We started up the road, and I just couldn't do it...." His voice trailed off. "It's no good to be alone. Ruth's going to be boiling mad at me, and I'm going to need that doghouse tonight for sure. But I'm going home with the brother pup, too. It's just no good to be alone!"

The day ended as it had started, with a ringing phone. It was Bill and Ruth. They were just calling to let us know that Bill wouldn't be needing the doghouse after all. "Well," he said, "Ruth loves the boys and taking them both home was the best decision I've ever made — on my own, anyway."

We heard from Bill and the "boys" just last month. Bill's voice had an uplifted lilt and a smile in it. "The boys are great and are even picking up a taste for toast and eggs. You see," he explained, "Pepper left some pretty big shoes to fill. That's why it takes two."

~Dawn Uittenbogaard
Chicken Soup for the Pet Lover's Soul

98

Maddy

Death leaves a heartache no one can heal,
love leaves a memory no one can steal.
~ From a headstone in Ireland

As I opened the front door of my house, I heard a dog bark. My older sister, Amanda, was holding up a chew toy, as a furry, brown and white puppy tried to bite it. "Molly!" my sister cried, as soon as she saw my face. "Guess what!" I didn't have an interest in dogs at the time and I didn't understand what was so great about them. I didn't answer Amanda.

"Where's Mom?" I asked. Amanda said that she was upstairs, so I rushed up. "Mommy?"

"Hi, Honey," Mom said, excitedly. "Did you see her? We have a new puppy."

I immediately grabbed the neck of my mom's dog, Emily, and squeezed it. Emily growled. Emily had never liked me. "Why does Amanda get to have a dog?" I grumbled.

Mom sighed, and sat me down on her lap. "You can have your own dog when you're older," Mom started, "But right now you are too young to take care of a dog."

"Ugh!" I cried. "I'm going to call Sam." Samantha was my friend. My mother had known her mother for a long time. Later that evening, Sam and her mom, Alexis, came over to see our new dog. I wouldn't go downstairs. I stayed in my mom's room, watching a movie. Later,

Sam came upstairs, grinning. "Your puppy's name is Maddy," she said. "Your mom and dad and sister all agreed on it."

"Maddy!" I cried. "I don't want to own a dog named Maddy!"

"Come downstairs, Mol. Maddy's cute!" Sam said. I was stubborn, though, and refused.

That night, while I was in bed, I felt something furry cuddle up next to me. "Maddy?" I said. Maddy looked up at me. I looked down at her. From that moment on, I realized that I loved her.

Maddy and I did a lot of things together. My mom let me take her for walks, and sometimes Maddy and I would gang up on our old dog, Emily. Maddy gave me love, love that no human can give. The kind of love that they can't tell you, they just show it—and you just feel that love when they do.

A few years later, my parents separated. Then they got a divorce. Maddy stuck by my side through the whole thing. My dad moved to an apartment downtown. Amanda and I would be with my dad on Saturdays.

On one Saturday, Amanda suggested that we bring Maddy along with us to Dad's. When we got to Dad's apartment we decided to take her for a walk. We were all hungry, so Dad tied Maddy to a large pole outside of a restaurant. When we finished eating, it was dark, and we started to walk home. While walking down the sidewalk, I stroked Maddy's fur. Her soft, warm fur. Suddenly, Maddy spotted another dog on the other side of the street. Breaking free from Amanda's grip, Maddy ran across the street. Because it was late at night, and the drivers in the cars couldn't see Maddy, she almost got hit by a blue Jeep, but she got away. As she was about to reach the other side of the street, a car hit Maddy.

"Maddy!" my sister cried and dodged into the street with my dad. I just stood there, alone on the sidewalk, crying, replaying the scene over and over in my head. My love for Maddy was unbearable; I didn't know what to do. About fifteen minutes later, Amanda came back, tears streaming down her face.

"We couldn't find her," she sobbed. "But I think she'll be okay." I didn't believe her because she was crying, but I nodded my head.

"I'm s-scared," I stuttered. I didn't know what to think anymore. Was Maddy dead or was she going to be okay? We had raised Maddy since she was a puppy, and I couldn't imagine all of the awful possibilities that could happen. My dad came back, looking very sad and discouraged. "Come on," he said. "We're going to find her. She couldn't have gone far, if she is hurt."

He called the police, asking about reports. Finally, after over an hour of searching, my dad got a phone call, saying that they got an injured sheltie. We zoomed to the pound. There was Maddy, inside a cage, covered in a blanket. I couldn't look at her. I was too scared and frightened. My sister and dad thanked the people at the pound, and the people who brought her in, and Amanda carefully sat in the back seat of the car, Maddy on her lap. I crawled into the front, crying and moaning. Maddy was bleeding badly, and she was suffering.

When we got to the vet, my sister charged out with Maddy in her hands, and handed her to my dad. I still refused to look. I sat down in a waiting room chair, and after my dad had given Maddy to the vet, he came and sat with me. He dialed my home phone number. My mom answered sleepily, and my dad explained the whole thing to her.

My dad told me that this was too much for me, and that my mom was coming to pick me up. When Mom got to the vet's, I burst into her arms. "Molly, come on—let's go home. She'll be okay." And then my mom started crying, too.

The car ride was silent. When I got home, I felt too afraid and lonely to sleep alone. So, I climbed into bed with my mom, as she prayed a million times for Maddy. The next morning, I woke up and climbed into my own bed. About an hour after I was awake, my mom came into my room, sobbing. "I'm so sorry!" she wailed. "Oh Molly—I'm so sorry! She's gone!" And she wouldn't stop hugging me.

I didn't cry. I couldn't. I felt like I needed to, but it just wouldn't come out. More than anything else, I felt anger. But, I was sort of glad for Maddy. She wasn't suffering anymore.

About four weeks later, we got a new dog, and I named her

Baylee. She was very shy at first, but once she got used to the house, she was very happy. At first, I didn't want another dog. I wanted Maddy. I finally learned to love Baylee—but nothing can replace how much I loved Maddy. It's always hard to lose someone you love. I realize that if I hadn't gotten Baylee, I probably would have kept feeling angry and mad. Everyone dies sometime—and it was just Maddy's turn to die. She may not be with me physically, but she will always be with me in my heart... and in my soul.

~Molly Miller, ten
Chicken Soup for the Preteen Soul 2

99

Forever Rocky

One gray morning I took the day off from work, knowing that today was the day it had to be done. Our dog, Rocky, had to be put to sleep. Sickness had ravaged his once-strong body, and despite every effort to heal our beloved boxer, his illness was intensifying.

I remember calling him into the car... how he loved car rides! But he seemed to sense that this time was going to be different. I drove around for hours, looking for any errand or excuse not to go to the vet's office, but I could no longer put off the inevitable. As I wrote the check to the vet for Rocky to be "put down," my eyes welled with tears and stained the check so it was almost unreadable.

We had gotten Rocky four years earlier, just before my first son, Robert, was born. We all loved him dearly, especially little Robert.

My heart ached as I drove home. I already missed Rocky. Robert greeted me as I got out of the car. When he asked me where our dog was, I explained that Rocky was in heaven now. I told him Rocky had been so sick, but now he would be happy and be able to run and play all the time. My little four-year-old paused, then looking at me with his clear blue eyes and an innocent smile on his face, he pointed to the sky and said, "He's up there, right, Dad?" I managed to nod yes, and walked into the house. My wife took one look at my face and started weeping softly herself. Then she asked me where Robert was, and I went back out to the yard to find him.

In the yard, Robert was running back and forth, tossing a large stick into the air, waiting for it to return to the ground and then picking it up and throwing it higher and higher each time. When I asked what he was doing, he simply turned and smiled.

"I'm playing with Rocky, Dad...."

~S. C. Edwards
Chicken Soup for the Pet Lover's Soul

Saying Goodbye to Bubba

Dogs' lives are too short. Their only fault, really.
~Agnes Sligh Turnbull

Parents can appreciate the anticipation and excitement of their children's first words. Some parents even work hard every day to ensure they are the first to be summoned and to encourage those long-awaited sounds: "Da Da" or "Ma Ma."

The day came for Derek's first word. We heard it and were thrilled that all our efforts, coaching and hours of repetition had finally produced the desired results. Even the dog was excited to hear a recognizable word and ran to share a wet kiss! As we laughed and carefully noted this milestone in his baby book, I have to admit my husband and I were a little heartbroken. We knew there was no way to contort the word into "Ma Ma" or "Da Da" as our baby sat on the floor calling "Ubba." Yes, he was definitely calling for Bubba, our beloved family dog. It had been love at first sight for the two of them. As any friend would, Bubba was teaching Derek many things: love, caring and responsibility, and along with a nightly ritual of feeding Bubba dog bones, Derek was learning to count.

Derek was now twenty months old and I lay in the hospital awaiting the arrival of our second son. I began to get a little concerned because my husband and mother had not made it to the hospital yet. Finally, they arrived and I saw it in their faces. They didn't want to tell me but I knew something had happened, and a feeling of sadness in my heart told me it was Bubba. It was true, they had found him dead that morning and buried him before Derek woke up. The next few months were very hard. Bubba had been with me for many years and the bond between a little boy and his dog was broken. I now had the responsibility to somehow explain to Derek in a way he could understand that Bubba was gone, forever.

For weeks Derek faithfully continued his nightly feeding rituals. He would search the house and stand at the door calling for Bubba. We struggled with ways to help his young mind understand.

A few months later we had flown to my hometown for a visit, and on our return flight Derek scrambled across the seats and into my lap. Always looking for a learning experience in everything we do, I began talking about the clouds and how we were on top of them and would soon be flying through them and then would be underneath them. Derek pressed his face against the window, shook his head and exclaimed, "No, Mommy!" Then I heard him softly calling, "Bubba." As my heart broke and eyes filled with tears, my baby looked at me for help in finding his lost friend amongst all the clouds. I prayed, "God, help me know the right things to say and please help his little heart mend." Derek was now pointing out the window and saying, "God-Heaven-Clouds-Stars-Bubba." At that moment, I realized in his own little way he understood.

The flight captain came on and announced our final descent. As I worked to get us both buckled in, Derek again pressed his face to the window, called for Bubba and patiently waited. As the last cloud passed our window, he lovingly looked upward, waved and said, "Bye-bye, God! Bye-bye, Bubba!"

We landed that afternoon with pieces of our hearts left drifting in the clouds. Derek never searched or called for Bubba again.

~Shelly D. Dunford
Chicken Soup for the Christian Soul 2

Rites of Passage

Every child comes with the message that God is not yet discouraged of man.
~Rabindranath Tagore

Some of the most poignant moments I spend as a veterinarian are those spent with my clients assisting the transition of my animal patients from this world to the next. When living becomes a burden, whether from pain or loss of normal functions, I can help a family by ensuring that their beloved pet has an easy passing. Making this final decision is painful, and I have often felt powerless to comfort the grieving owners.

That was before I met Shane.

I had been called to examine a ten-year-old blue heeler named Belker who had developed a serious health problem. The dog's owners—Ron, his wife, Lisa, and their little boy, Shane—were all very attached to Belker and they were hoping for a miracle. I examined Belker and found he was dying of cancer.

I told the family there were no miracles left for Belker, and offered to perform the euthanasia procedure for the old dog in their home. As we made the arrangements, Ron and Lisa told me they thought it would be good for the four-year-old Shane to observe the procedure. They felt Shane could learn something from the experience.

The next day, I felt the familiar catch in my throat as Belker's family surrounded him. Shane seemed so calm, petting the old dog for the last time, that I wondered if he understood what was going on.

Within a few minutes, Belker slipped peacefully away. The little boy seemed to accept Belker's transition without any difficulty or confusion. We sat together for a while after Belker's death, wondering aloud about the sad fact that animal lives are shorter than human lives.

Shane, who had been listening quietly, piped up, "I know why."

Startled, we all turned to him. What came out of his mouth next stunned me — I'd never heard a more comforting explanation.

He said, "Everybody is born so they can learn how to live a good life — like loving everybody and being nice, right?" The four-year-old continued, "Well, animals already know how to do that, so they don't have to stay as long."

~Robin Downing, D.V.M.
Chicken Soup for the Pet Lover's Soul

Chicken Soup for the Soul

Share with Us

We would like to know how these stories affected you and which ones were your favorite. Please write to us and let us know.

We also would like to share your stories with future readers. You may be able to help another reader, and become a published author at the same time. Please send us your own stories and poems for our future books. Some of our past contributors have launched writing and speaking careers from the publication of their stories in our books!

The best way to submit your stories is through our web site, at

www.chickensoup.com

If you do not have access to the Internet, you may submit your stories by mail or by facsimile.

Chicken Soup for the Soul
P.O. Box 700
Cos Cob, CT 06807-0700
Fax 1-203-861-7194

We're crazy about our mysterious cats. Sometimes they are our best friends; sometimes they are aloof. They are fun to watch and often surprise us. And they are always well loved members of our families.

This new book from Chicken Soup for the Soul contains the 101 best cat stories from the company's extensive library. Readers will revel in the heartwarming, amusing, inspirational, and occasionally tearful stories about our best friends and faithful companions—our cats.

These true stories will make readers appreciate their own cats and see them with a new eye. They will read of cats that healed people or other pets, saved lives, rejuvenated friendships, gave new meaning to lives, and saved family relationships.

978-1-935096-08-5

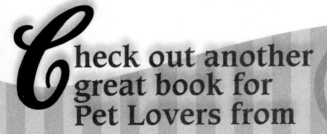

Chicken Soup for the Dog Lover's Soul
0-7573-0331-5

Chicken Soup for the Pet Lover's Soul
1-55874-571-8

Chicken Soup for the Cat and Dog Lover's Soul
1-55874-710-9

Chicken Soup for the Cat Lover's Soul
0-7573-0332-3

Chicken Soup for the Horse Lover's Soul
0-7573-0098-7

Chicken Soup for the Horse Lover's Soul II
0-7573-0402-8

Chicken Soup for the Soul®

Enjoy these other fine books about our beloved pets!

Chicken Soup for the Soul

Who Is
Jack Canfield?

J ack Canfield is the co-creator and editor of the Chicken Soup for the Soul series, which *Time* magazine has called "the publishing phenomenon of the decade." Jack is also the co-author of eight other bestselling books including The Success Principles™: How to Get from Where You Are to Where You Want to Be, Dare to Win, The Aladdin Factor, You've Got to Read This Book, and On Mutual Love and Admiration of Focus: How to Hit Your Business and Personal and Financial Targets with Absolute Certainty.

Jack has recently developed a telephone coaching program and an online coaching program based on his most recent book The Success Principles. He also offers a seven-day Breakthrough to Success seminar every summer, which attracts 400 people from fifteen countries around the world.

Jack is the CEO of the Canfield Training Group in Santa Barbara, California, and founder of the Foundation for Self-Esteem in Culver City, California. He has conducted intensive personal and professional development seminars on the principles of success for over a million people in twenty-three countries. Jack is a dynamic keynote speaker and he has spoken to hundreds of thousands of others at more than 1,000 corporations, universities, professional conferences and conventions, and has been seen by millions more on national television shows such as The Today Show, Fox and Friends, Inside Edition, Hard Copy, CNN's Talk Back Live, 20/20, Eye to Eye, and the NBC Nightly News and the CBS Evening News.

Jack is the recipient of many awards and honors, including three honorary doctorates and a Guinness World Records Certificate for having seven books from the Chicken Soup for the Soul series appearing on the *New York Times* bestseller list on May 24, 1998.

To write to Jack or for inquiries about Jack as a speaker, his coaching programs, trainings or seminars, use the following contact information:

Jack Canfield
The Canfield Companies
P.O. Box 30880 • Santa Barbara, CA 93130
phone: 805-563-2935 • fax: 805-563-2945
E-mail: info@jackcanfield.com
www.jackcanfield.com

Who Is
Mark Victor Hansen?

Mark Victor Hansen is the co-founder of Chicken Soup for the Soul, along with Jack Canfield. He is also a sought-after keynote speaker, bestselling author, and marketing maven. For more than thirty years, Mark has focused solely on helping people from all walks of life reshape their personal vision of what's possible. His powerful messages of possibility, opportunity, and action have created powerful change in thousands of organizations and millions of individuals worldwide.

Mark's credentials include a lifetime of entrepreneurial success. He is a prolific writer with many bestselling books, such as The One Minute Millionaire, Cracking the Millionaire Code, How to Make the Rest of Your Life the Best of Your Life, On Mutual Love and Admiration of Focus, The Aladdin Factor, and Dare to Win, in addition to the Chicken Soup for the Soul series. Mark has had a profound influence in the field of human potential through his library of audios, videos, and articles in the areas of big thinking, sales achievement, wealth building, publishing success, and personal and professional development.

Mark is the founder of the MEGA Seminar Series. MEGA Book Marketing University and Building Your MEGA Speaking Empire are annual conferences where Mark coaches and teaches new and aspiring authors, speakers, and experts on building lucrative publishing and speaking careers. Other MEGA events include MEGA Info-Marketing and My MEGA Life.

He has appeared on Oprah, CNN, and The Today Show. He has been quoted in Time, U.S. News & World Report, USA Today, New York Times, and Entrepreneur and has had countless radio interviews, assuring our planet's people that "You can easily create the life you deserve."

As a philanthropist and humanitarian, Mark works tirelessly for organizations such as Habitat for Humanity, American Red Cross, March of Dimes, Childhelp USA, and many others. He is the recipient of numerous awards that honor his entrepreneurial spirit, philanthropic heart, and business acumen. He is a lifetime member of the Horatio Alger Association of Distinguished Americans, an organization that honored Mark with the prestigious Horatio Alger Award for his extraordinary life achievements.

Mark Victor Hansen is an enthusiastic crusader of what's possible and is driven to make the world a better place.

Mark Victor Hansen & Associates, Inc.
P.O. Box 7665 • Newport Beach, CA 92658
phone: 949-764-2640 • fax: 949-722-6912
www.markvictorhansen.com

Who Is
Amy Newmark?

A my Newmark was recently named publisher of Chicken Soup for the Soul, after a thirty-year career as a writer, speaker, financial analyst, and business executive in the worlds of finance and telecommunications.

Amy is a graduate of Harvard College, where she majored in Portuguese, minored in French, and traveled extensively. She is also the mother of two children in college and has two grown stepchildren.

After a long career writing books on telecommunications, voluminous financial reports, business plans, and corporate press releases, Chicken Soup for the Soul is a breath of fresh air for Amy. She has fallen in love with Chicken Soup for the Soul and its life-changing books, and found it a true pleasure to conceptualize, compile, and edit the "101 Best Stories" books for our readers.

The best way to contact Chicken Soup for the Soul is through our web site, at www.chickensoup.com. This will always get the fastest attention.

If you do not have access to the Internet, please contact us by mail or by facsimile.

Chicken Soup for the Soul
P.O. Box 700
Cos Cob, CT 06807-0700
Fax 1-203-861-7194

Chicken Soup for the Soul

Thank You!

We would like to thank the entire staff of Chicken Soup for the Soul for their help on this project and the 101 Best series in general. Among our California staff, we would especially like to single out D'ette Corona, who is the heart and soul of the Chicken Soup publishing operation, and who put together the first draft of this manuscript, Barbara LoMonaco for invaluable assistance in obtaining the fabulous quotations that add depth and meaning to this book, Patty Hansen for her extra special help with the permissions for these fabulous stories and for her amazing knowledge of the Chicken Soup library, and Patti Clement for her help with permissions and other organizational matters. In our Connecticut office, we would like to thank our able editorial assistants, Valerie Howlett and Madeline Clapps, for their assistance in setting up our new offices, editing, and helping us put together the best possible books. We would also like to thank our master of design, Creative Director and book producer Brian Taylor at Pneuma Books, for his brilliant vision for our covers and interiors. Finally, none of this would be possible without the business and creative leadership of our CEO, Bill Rouhana, and our president, Bob Jacobs.